Walking Weekends
Lake District

Mark Reid

24 circular walks from 12 villages
throughout the Lake District,
with two walks of varying lengths
from each village – ideal for a weekend break.

(IWP)

Walking Weekends
Lake District

© Mark Reid 2009
First Edition October 2009

A catalogue record for this book is available from the British Library.
British Library Cataloguing in Publication Data.

All maps within this publication are based upon Ordnance Survey mapping reproduced by permission of Ordnance Survey on behalf of HMSO © Crown Copyright 2005.
Ordnance Survey Licence Number: 100011978

The contents of this publication are believed correct at time of copyright. Nevertheless the author can not accept responsibility for errors and omissions, or for changes in details given. The information contained within this publication is intended only as a general guide.

Publisher's Note
Many of the walks within this publication head across high, mountainous terrain. In places, the walks follow steep, rocky paths over mountain passes or summits and there are stretches of fell-walking across remote terrain with few landmarks. The weather is a particular hazard with mist and cloud often making navigation difficult across the high fells. Winter walking brings with it additional challenges and hazards, including limited daylight, snow and ice. Walking and outdoor activities can be strenuous and individuals must ensure that they have suitable clothing, footwear, equipment, provisions, maps and are suitably fit before starting a walk; inexperienced walkers should be supervised.

You are responsible for your own safety and for others in your care, so be prepared for the unexpected - make sure you are fully equipped for the hills and mountains. Preparation is essential, including a detailed weather forecast. All of the walks contained in this publication should only be attempted with the relevant OS Explorer maps (1:25000) as well as a compass/GPS.

'The Inn Way' is a Registered Trademark of Mark Reid.

Published by:
INNWAY PUBLICATIONS
102 LEEDS ROAD
HARROGATE
HG2 8HB
www.innway.co.uk
ISBN: 978-1-902001-13-5

CONTENTS

For my daughter, Isla

Thou who hast given me eyes to see,
And love this sight so fair,
Give me a heart to find out Thee,
And read Thee everywhere.

(J. Keble)

Thank you to Gordon Dixon, Pat and Ron Kassell, Nick Ranns, Pete Harris and Graeme Tiffany for accompanying me on many of the walks.

Cover photographs: 'Buttermere reflections'
© Mike Kipling **www.mikekipling.com**

4-page colour insert photographs © Mark Reid 2009

Illustrations © John A. Ives, Dringhouses, York. **www.johnaives.co.uk**

Typeset, printed and bound by Spectrum Print, Cleethorpes.

This guidebook was researched, written, typeset, printed and bound in England.

THE
LAKE DISTRICT

BASSENTHWAITE LAKE

BRAITHWAITE

● KESWICK

LOWESWATER

DERWENTWATER

ULLSWATER

CRUMMOCK
WATER

GLENRIDDING

●BUTTERMERE

PATTERDALE

ENNERDALE
WATER

ROSTHWAITE

THIRLMERE

HAWESWATER

● WASDALE HEAD

● GRASMERE

GREAT LANGLANGDALE●

RYDAL WATER

WAST WATER

GRASMERE

● AMBLESIDE

ELTER WATER

● BOOT

ESTHWAITE
WATER

CONISTON ●

WINDERMERE

CONISTON
WATER

INTRODUCTION

I arrived late in the evening, driving through the dark along narrow, twisting lanes hemmed in on either side by drystone walls; I felt like a mouse that had been swallowed by a giant, sinuous snake. All I could see was the road in front of me illuminated by my headlights, a bubble of fast-moving light travelling through the night heading deeper into the heart of Lakeland. I eventually arrived at Rosthwaite, a lovely village with whitewashed cottages lining an amazingly narrow main street. The vernacular architecture said Lakeland, but I was otherwise unaware of my surroundings.

After a sound night's sleep, I woke early and jumped out of bed to check the Lakeland weather forecast - I opened my curtains and looked out of the window. A gentle autumnal mist filled the valley floor where Herdwicks grazed on the cold, damp pastures around the village. Above the misty bottoms, the valley slopes soared skywards, a near-vertical patchwork of bracken, copse, crag and grass brushed with an autumnal palette of red, gold, bronze and deep green with the upper slopes bathed in golden morning sunshine. The fell tops were clear, and above was only blue sky. Fantastic! A full day's fell-walking lay ahead. Dressed, I went downstairs, with maps under my arm, to plan my day over breakfast.

A day spent walking amongst the fells and valleys of the Lake District breathes new life into your mind, body and soul. You re-connect with the natural environment, as you immerse yourself in the magnificent Lakeland landscape. But it is much more than visual, for this stimulation is multi-sensory as you become enveloped by the elements, feel the texture of the mountains and smell the scents of the outdoors. It is these memories that you take with you from your day amongst the fells; the sight of a valley far below through a break in the clouds, the caw of a raven soaring above a crag, the soft touch of moss on a drystone wall, the smell of wood smoke as you walk back into the village at dusk and the taste of your first pint of Cumberland Ale after a day on the fells.

Mark Reid
October 2009

ROUTE DESCRIPTIONS & MAPS

ROUTE DESCRIPTIONS

The following abbreviations have been used throughout the route descriptions:

SP   Signpost   FB   Footbridge

Glossary of terms

Arête:	Narrow ridge between two valleys or corries
Beck:	Stream
Cairn:	Pile of stones alongside paths or marking a summit
Col, saddle:	Depression along a mountain ridge
Combe, comb, cove or corrie:	An upland hollow
Fell:	Mountain or hill
Force:	Waterfall
Gill:	Steep-sided ravine
Hause:	Depression along a mountain ridge, usually a mountain pass
Scree:	Small, loose rocks on a steep slope
Tarn:	Small lake
Trig Point:	Ordnance Survey Triangulation Point

The detailed route descriptions and hand-drawn maps should guide you safely around the routes featured in this book. However, always take Ordnance Survey Explorer maps (scale 1:25,000) with you on your walks, as well as a compass or GPS. The countryside is slowly evolving and changing; stiles may become bridle-gates, gates may disappear, paths may be re-surfaced, pubs or shops may close. Occasionally, Rights of Way may be altered or diverted. Any changes will be clearly signposted and must be followed, and are usually marked on the most up-to-date Ordnance Survey maps. Feedback concerning these changes is always welcome, as this book is updated at each reprint.

Footpaths and bridleways throughout the Lake District National Park are generally well maintained with good waymarking, especially in the valleys. The signposts are often colour-coded as follows: yellow for footpaths, blue for bridleways and red for byways. However, waymarkers and signposts are virtually non-existent on the high fells and mountains, where there are also few landmarks. The Lake District is one of England's most popular walking areas, which means that many upland paths are now wide, eroded scars. These blazed upland paths are generally easy to follow; however, they must be approached with caution as the visible path often disappears across rocky terrain, there are sometimes 'alternative' unofficial paths and the lack of waymarkers at upland path junctions or on mountain summits can be confusing, especially in mist.

An average walking speed is 4 km/hr (2.5 mph) over the course of a day, plus 10 additional minutes per 100 metres of climbing. Poor weather, rough terrain and tiredness can all reduce walking speed. The distances quoted within this book are 'map miles' estimated from OS maps.

Grid References
Grid References have been given within the Route Descriptions to assist route finding; for example the Grid Reference for Grasmere Church is NY 337 074 and for Burnthwaite Farm at Wasdale Head is NY 193 091.

MAPS

The following Ordnance Survey Explorer maps (1:25,000) cover the walks featured in this book.

OL4   *'The English Lake District, North-western area'*. This map covers Braithwaite, Buttermere, Keswick and Rosthwaite.

OL5   *'The English Lake District, North-eastern area'*. This map covers Glenridding and Patterdale.

OL6   *'The English Lake District, South-western area'*. This map covers Boot, Coniston, Wasdale Head and Great Langdale.

OL7   *'The English Lake District, South-eastern area'*. This map covers Ambleside and Grasmere.

Always take Ordnance Survey Explorer maps with you on your walk, as well as a compass or GPS.

MOUNTAIN / FELL SAFETY

Never underestimate the strenuous nature of walking particularly when this is combined with high ground and the elements. Do not attempt to complete a walk that is beyond your skill, experience or level of fitness. *Know your ability and limits; the mountains will always be there tomorrow.*

Weather - obtain a detailed weather forecast before you set out on your walk, as well as sunset times. If the weather turns bad then turn back the way you have walked. Conditions can change for the worse within minutes reducing visibility and making walking hazardous with cloud, mist, strong winds and rain all year round. Expect snow on the mountains anytime between autumn and early summer. Conditions on the mountains and fells will vary significantly from sheltered valleys. On average, air temperature drops by 1 degree C for every 100 metres of ascent.

Winter conditions - never head up onto the fells or mountains in winter conditions unless fully equipped with full winter clothing, 4-season boots, ice axe and crampons - and the knowledge of how to use them. The combination of steep ground and snow/ice may prove fatal if you are not equipped for the conditions.

Maps - take Ordnance Survey maps (1:25,000) as well as a compass.

Boots - your boots are important; make sure that they are waterproof, comfortable and have good ankle support and sturdy soles.

Clothing - it is important to wear a 'layering system' of clothing as follows: base layer to wick moisture away (T-shirt), insulating mid layer (fleece) and a waterproof and breathable outer shell (waterproof coat and over-trousers), plus walking trousers and a suitable hat and pair of gloves. Wear clothing that is made from synthetic fibres, which are quick drying and help 'wick' moisture away from your skin. Do NOT wear cotton as cotton soaks up moisture. Always carry a spare fleece.

Food - eat food regularly to keep energy levels up. Always take lunch with you as well as high energy snack foods.

Water - Drink plenty of fluids (not alcohol) throughout the day. Take at least 1 litre of water with you (2 litres or more in summer).

Essential kit - In addition to the above, carry a basic first aid kit, blister plasters, sun cream and sunglasses (spring to autumn), whistle, torch and spare batteries, watch, 'survival' bag and mobile 'phone. Line your rucksack with a large plastic bag to keep the contents dry.

Navigation - regularly check your location against the map and route description. Always look for at least three landmarks to confirm your location. If you become misplaced (or lost), re-trace your steps back to your last known location.

Safety - always walk in a group unless you are very experienced. Leave details of your intended route with a responsible person and report your safe arrival. If you are delayed but safe then make sure you let someone know so that the Mountain Rescue Team is not called out. Do not rely on a mobile phone or GPS to get you out of difficulty.

Take care when crossing rivers or roads and walk in single file when walking along country lanes (make yourself visible to traffic). Do not explore old mine or quarry workings. Never attempt to cross flooded land or a stream/river that is in flood.

Emergency - in an emergency in a remote location call the Mountain Rescue Team by 'phoning 999 and asking for Mountain Rescue (via the Police), giving details of the incident and location. If you do not have a mobile 'phone then summon help with six blasts of your whistle or flashes of your torch. *NB: Mountain Rescue is an Emergency Service.*

Animals - keep dogs under close control at all times, preferably on a lead. Dogs and livestock can be dangerous, particularly cows with calves. If you come across cows with their calves whilst walking your dog, do not walk between them but walk around them giving them a wide berth. If a situation appears to be developing, look for a way of leaving the enclosure safely. If you feel threatened let the dog go as it can run faster than a cow, and this will make you less of a threat.

When walking through moorland or bracken keep a watchful eye for adders, Britain's only poisonous snake. If bitten, seek medical help.

REMEMBER: "An experienced walker knows when to turn back"

COUNTRYSIDE CODE

Consider other people
Showing consideration and respect for other people makes the countryside a pleasant environment for everyone - at home, at work and at leisure.

Enjoy the countryside and respect its life and work
We have a responsibility to protect our countryside now and for future generations. Tread gently - discover the beauty of the natural environment and take care not to damage, destroy or remove features such as rocks, plants and trees. Do not touch crops, machinery or livestock.

Leave gates and property as you find them
Please respect the working life of the countryside, as our actions can affect people's livelihoods, our heritage, and the safety and welfare of animals and ourselves. Use stiles and gates to cross fences and walls and close gates behind you.

Keep to public Rights of Way or Open Access areas
Footpaths are for walkers; bridleways are for cyclists, horse-riders and walkers. Motorbikes and cars should keep to roads.

Do not make excessive noise
The hills and valleys should be quiet places.

Take care on country roads
Face oncoming traffic and walk in single file.

Safeguard water supplies
Streams are used by livestock and often feed reservoirs for drinking supplies.

Guard against risk of fire
Uncontrolled fires can devastate grassy hillsides or moorland.

Keep dogs under control
A loose dog can be catastrophic for ground nesting birds, sheep and sometimes the dog itself. By law, farmers are entitled to destroy a dog that injures or worries their animals.

Take litter home
Litter is dangerous and unsightly.

Safety
Weather can change quickly; are you fully equipped for the hills?

AMBLESIDE

Ambleside lies at the northern tip of Windermere and is the gateway to Lakeland's mountains. The Romans recognised the strategic importance of this site and built a fort (Galava) in AD79 near the confluence of the rivers Brathay and Rothay to protect the trade routes of High Street to the north and the Wrynose and Hardknott passes which led to the Roman port of Ravenglass to the southwest. However, it was the Norse farmers who first settled in 'Amelsate', which means 'pastures by the river sandbanks', and began to farm the rich meadowland along the banks of the Rothay. During the 17th Century Ambleside began to develop into the town we see today after gaining a market charter in 1650. During this period the first of several water-powered mills were built alongside Stock Beck to process commodities such as corn, cotton, paper and wool from the local Herdwick sheep. The mills were still in use well into the 20th Century. Possibly the most famous house in Lakeland is the 17th Century Bridge House, which was built as both a bridge across Stock Beck and summerhouse and apple store for the long-demolished Ambleside Hall. Arguably England's smallest house, during the 19th Century a chair repairer, his wife and six children lived in it! The discovery of the scenic charms of the Lake District by the Victorians and arrival of the railway at Windermere heralded the main growth period for Ambleside when numerous large villas and hotels were built using local slate. Ambleside has more literary associations than anywhere else in Lakeland. William Wordsworth once had an office in the town while he held the post of Distributor of Stamps for Westmorland. The writer Harriet Martineau lived just outside Ambleside until her death in 1876. Charlotte Brontë and George Eliot visited her and many other literary figures stayed in the area including Ruskin, Coleridge, Keats and Southey.

THE TOWN

Ambleside is a thriving town and offers several pubs, hotels, B&Bs, Youth Hostel, cafés, restaurants, fish and chip shops, small supermarket, general stores, newsagents, bookshops, craft and gift shops, art galleries, outdoor shops, Post Office, chemist, cinema, garage, various high street banks, bus services, public conveniences, large car parks, police station, health centre and tourist information centre.

ACCOMMODATION

Tourist Information Centre, Ambleside: 015394 32582

AMBLESIDE PUBS

There are several pubs in Ambleside. These are my three favourites:

Golden Rule, Ambleside   **015394 32257**
Traditional pub in the heart of 'old' Ambleside frequented by locals, climbers and walkers who come to enjoy its convivial atmosphere in one of several small rooms warmed by open fires. No music, no machines – just good beer and conversation. But what is the 'golden rule'?

Royal Oak, Ambleside   **01539 433382**
This traditional pub retains much of its character with low beams, open fires and a separate small, cosy bar. Outside, there is a patio area where you can watch the world go by.

Unicorn Inn, Ambleside   **015394 33216**
Situated on what was once the main road north to Keswick and the Kirkstone Pass, this traditional coaching inn has plenty of character with open fires and exposed beams. Regular folk nights.

PUBS ALONG THE WALKS

Mortal Man, Troutbeck   015394 33193
Queen's Head Hotel, Troutbeck   015394 32174

Ambleside Walking Weekend
- Saturday Walk -
Ambleside, Heron Pike, Fairfield, Dove Crag
& High Sweden Bridge

WALK INFORMATION

Highlights: A picturesque garden, Wordsworth's home, Lakeland's most famous horseshoe walk, the summit of Fairfield, gravity-defying walls and an ancient packhorse bridge.

Distance: 11.25 miles (18 km)   Time: Allow 6 - 7 hours

Map: OS Explorer maps OL5 & OL7 – *always take a map on your walk.*

Refreshments: Pubs, cafés and shops at Ambleside. Cafe at Rydal Hall. No other facilities en route – take plenty of provisions with you.

Terrain: Mountainous terrain almost all the way, although there are tracks and lanes across fields at the start and end of the walk. This walk follows well-worn paths, however, it heads across high and exposed mountain ridges with no shelter from the elements and few navigational features. There is steep, rocky ground as well as steep drops to the side of the path in places.

Highest point: Fairfield – 873 metres above sea level.

Total ascent: 970 metres

Escape Route: Before the summit, simply re-trace your steps; after the summit, continue along the walk. In bad weather, the quickest and safest way from the summit is to re-trace your steps back across Great Rigg and Heron Pike to Rydal.

Caution: **Mountain Walk.** This is a strenuous walk to the summit of Fairfield across high and exposed ridges, with steep ground and mountainous terrain for most of the way as well as steep drops to the side of the path in places. The summit of Fairfield is confusing in mist, and there are sheer cliffs on its north and eastern faces. Map and compass essential. Do not attempt this walk in bad weather.

Ambleside

The Fairfield Horseshoe is perhaps Lakeland's most famous mountain horseshoe walk. This challenging yet rewarding walk follows the crest of a broad ridge that encircles the valley of Rydal Beck connecting the summits of Heron Pike, Great Rigg, Fairfield, Hart Crag, Dove Crag and High Pike.

Rydal Hall dates back to the late 16th Century, although much modified during the 19th Century. It was built by the influential Fleming family, who had acquired the manor of Rydal back in 1409 when Sir Thomas Fleming married Isobel de Lancaster who held the feudal lordship of the manor. It was during the late Georgian and early Victorian period that the fortunes of the family and hall flourished. It became one of the first country estates in England to embrace the idea of 'picturesque nature' in its gardens, a sort of 'tamed wilderness' that could be viewed and enjoyed by visitors and travellers who came to marvel at the natural landscape. This dramatic natural environment was enhanced with trees and walkways where viewpoints were opened up to take in the surrounding lakes and mountains. By the late 19th Century Rydal Hall had become a well-known destination for romantic writers and artists, with a more formal Edwardian garden laid out in 1910 by Thomas Mawson to reflect the changing styles and tastes of the era. The hall remained in the Fleming family until 1970 when it became a conference centre and retreat for the Diocese of Carlisle. The house still retains its park-like gardens through which the boisterous Rydal Beck cascades over waterfalls, an attractive scene that inspired Constable to sketch it.

The village of Rydal has many literary connections, most notably William Wordsworth who lived at Rydal Mount from 1813 until his death in 1850. During his lifetime Wordsworth's outlook, and to an extent his work, developed from the radical and unconventional to the staid and conservative. It has been said by many critics that Wordsworth had produced his best work by the time he moved into Rydal Mount; however, he continued to write poetry, often gaining inspiration from the beautiful gardens he designed that surround the house. Wordsworth moved to Rydal Mount to escape from the unhappy memories of Grasmere following the death of two of his children. He shared the house with his wife Mary as well as his sister-in-law Sara Hutchinson and his sister Dorothy, an acclaimed writer in her own right. His position as Distributor of Stamps eased the cost of living in such a grand house, as the income from his writings alone could not have afforded such luxury! Many learned people, literary figures and tourists visited Rydal Mount during Wordsworth's lifetime as he had become something of a tourist attraction. The house dates back to the 16th Century and takes its name from the knoll, or mount, in front of the house that was originally used as an observation or beacon site. It is still owned by the Wordsworth family and is open to the public. Close by is Nab Cottage, which was the home of Thomas De Quincey, who was one of the renowned Lakes Poet along with Samuel Taylor Coleridge, Robert Southey and Wordsworth.

From Rydal, the long climb to the summit of Fairfield begins, with a steep climb up onto Nab Scar, from where there are superlative views across Rydal Water, one of the smallest yet most beautiful of all the lakes. There are sixteen lakes in the Lake District, although only one has the distinction of being named a lake – Bassenthwaite Lake. The remaining lakes have either water or mere in their name. All of the other small sheets of water in the Lake District are tarns. From Nab Scar, our route heads up to the first 'summit' of Heron Pike, a small, grassy rise of land that marks the start of the broad ridge known as Rydal Fell that forms a barrier between the deep valleys of Greenhead Gill to your left and Rydal Beck to your right (east). This ridge extends northwards for about two kilometres before rising up onto the rounded bulk of Great Rigg that towers above the head of Greenhead Gill. The views from this ridge are superb with the Langdale Pikes and Scafell Pike clearly visible. From Great Rigg, the ridge continues down into a fairly narrow col above Calf Cove before climbing steadily up onto the broad summit plateau of Fairfield, some 873 metres above sea level.

From the summit plateau there is a wonderful panorama north and eastwards across mountains and plunging valleys, with precipitous crags and gullies falling away into Cawk Cove at the head of Deepdale. Of particular note is the view to the north across Dollywaggon Pike towards Helvellyn, whilst to the north-east a narrow ridge leads across the small 'peak' of Cofa Pike towards St Sunday Crag that separates Grisedale and Deepdale. The different topography between the southern and northern approaches to Fairfield is striking, for the southern aspects are dominated by steep grassy slopes and rounded fells, but to the north lies a dramatic mountain landscape of crags and corries. This is due to more significant glacial erosion many thousands of years ago on the north and east facing slopes. The summit can be confusing in mist and care must be taken to pick up the correct path towards Hart Crag – the route off the summit does not take in any steep ground.

The descent from Fairfield is long and steady following the high ridge of land that encloses the valley of Rydal Beck that sweeps away to the south. This ridge is punctuated by rocky 'summits' including Hart Crag, Dove Crag and High Pike. Link Hause is a narrow saddle of land between Fairfield and Hart Crag, with magnificent views down into the hanging valley of Link Cove that feeds into Deepdale. The summit of Hart Crag is rough and rocky, with valleys falling steeply away on three sides. A stone wall traces the crest of this ridge all the way down from Hart Crag to Low Sweden Bridge via Dove Crag and High Pike, an amazing feat of construction that skilfully tackles some very steep ground. As you approach High Pike, views open out across the deep valley of Scandale to the east, with Windermere in the distance. From below Low Pike, our route turns down to reach High Sweden Bridge, a simple stone structure that spans Scandale Beck. This is a fine example of a centuries-old packhorse bridge, built without parapets to allow laden horses to cross unhindered. The bridge formed part of the old packhorse trail between Ambleside and Patterdale via Scandale Pass, and has a wonderful setting amidst waterfalls and scattered trees.

AMBLESIDE SATURDAY WALK

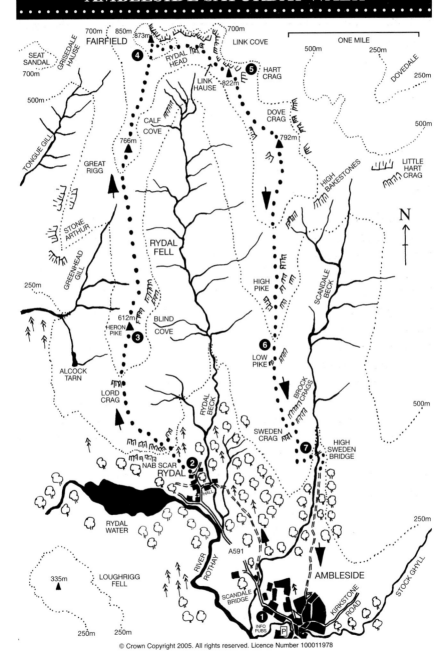

19

THE WALK

1. Leave Ambleside along the main road (A591) towards 'Grasmere, Keswick' and follow this road (Rydal Road) passing Bridge House on your left and then the main car park and continue along the road out of Ambleside. You soon come to Scandale Bridge (road bridge) across Scandale Beck, immediately after which turn right through gates (beside a gatehouse) along a stony driveway (SP 'Rydal Hall'). Follow this enclosed track straight on with Scandale Beck on your right at first then across wooded pastures to reach a gate across the track after 1.25 km that leads into woodland (Rydal Park). Head through this gate and follow the stony track straight on through the woods then bear left after a short distance to reach a junction of tracks (just before a bridge across Rydal Beck). At this track junction, bear up to the right (SP 'Rydal Mount, Coffin Route, Nab Scar') to reach a group of buildings (outbuildings of Rydal Hall) where you head left along the lane through the yard, over a bridge across Rydal Beck then bear up to the right passing above Rydal Hall. Follow the lane straight on passing Rydal Hall on your left then on to reach the road through the hamlet of Rydal (at the entrance to Rydal Hall). Turn right uphill (SP 'Coffin Route, Nab Scar') to quickly reach a fork in the road at the entrance to Rydal Mount, where you continue straight on along the lane climbing up to reach a gate across the lane at the top of the hamlet. Head through the gate and follow the concrete track bearing up to the left passing a converted barn on your left then, where this concrete track bends sharp left into the yard of the house, head straight up along the path to quickly reach a bridle-gate beside a gate (NY 364 065).

2. Head through the gate and follow the stony path climbing uphill alongside a wall on your left then, after 150 metres, follow the pitched-stone path bearing up to the right away from the wall (waymarker) climbing quite steeply up – the path winds up and becomes enclosed by walls on either side, which funnel the path up to a ladder stile over a wall across your path. Cross the stile and follow the path straight on rising steadily up, with the crags of Nab

Scar ahead. The enclosing walls soon open out and you continue up along the stone-pitched path alongside the wall on your left for 75 metres then follow the path to the right (away from the wall) zig-zagging up at first then slanting up across the hillside skirting below the crags of Nab Scar (lower eastern slopes). As you reach some crags, the path bends sharply round to the left then round to the right climbing steeply up across the hillside before bending left again and levelling out (wooden handrail). Follow this path straight on across the flanks of Nab Scar – the path soon bends up to the right across rough and rocky ground (views down to Rydal Water) climbing up above the crags of Nab Scar *(caution – steep drops to your left)*. As you reach the top of the crags of Nab Scar, the path bears slightly away from the edge of the crags and levels out for about 100 metres before climbing up again across rocky/grassy hillside onto the top of the fellside above Nab Scar to join a wall just to your left which you follow straight on to soon reach a ladder stile over a wall across your path (NY 356 072). Cross this ladder stile and follow the undulating path straight on for 400 metres across the top of the broad rocky/grassy ridge alongside an old tumbledown wall on your left to reach the foot of a steep slope just below the conspicuous outcrop of Lord Crag to your left (old wall leads up to this crag). Carry straight on climbing steadily up across the middle of the broad ridge for a further 0.75 km onto the small summit of Heron Pike (NY 356 083) *Caution: steep slopes on its eastern face.*

3. From Heron Pike, head straight on along the path dropping down into a slight col (with Blind Cove falling away to your right into the valley of Rydal Beck) then continue straight on along the ridge-top path rising up to soon reach the top of an unnamed rocky rise (above Erne Crag just to the east). At the top of this rocky rise, follow the path bearing very slightly left then straight on along the crest of the broad ridge of Rydal Fell (views down towards Rydal Beck to your right) for a further 1km before the path climbs steeply up onto the rocky summit of Great Rigg (cairn), which towers above the head of Greenhead Gill *(take care – steep drops to side of path)*. From the summit of Great Rigg, continue straight on along the ridge-top path dropping slightly down into a col and a narrow section of ridge (with

Calf Cove falling steeply away to your right into Rydal Head), before climbing steadily up along the crest of the broad ridge (keep to right-hand side of ridge), with steep drops to your right down into Rydal Head, up onto the broad summit of Fairfield. As you approach the domed summit plateau, follow the path (cairns) as it bears very slightly to the left (away from the steep slopes down to Rydal Head) up across the summit plateau to reach a stone windbreak on Fairfield's summit (NY 358 117). *NB: There are two stone windbreaks and a pile of stones in close proximity on the rocky summit plateau. Our route navigates to and from the first windbreak you reach – ignore the windbreak just ahead above the cliffs of Fairfield's north-eastern face above Deepdale. In poor visibility, do NOT walk beyond this first windbreak.*

4. As you reach the (first) windbreak on the summit of Fairfield, turn sharp right heading back on yourself slightly following a path marked by a series of cairns across the middle of the broad summit plateau in a south-easterly direction *(compass bearing from the windbreak: 144 degrees)*. Follow this cairned path across the summit plateau for 150 metres to reach the top of a steep gully to your left (NY 359 116) where you follow the cairned path bending round to the left heading across the top of the summit plateau's south-eastern arm *(now heading in an easterly direction / compass bearing: 82 degrees)*. Follow this clear path straight on (cairns) heading very gently down away from the summit across the top of this broad ridge of land, with Rydal Head sweeping away to your right. This broad ridge levels out for a short distance (superb views to your right) and you then come to an area of low outcrops, just beyond which the path gently curves round to the right (skirting above Rydal Head) before dropping quite steeply down across outcrops into Link Hause (narrow col) between Fairfield and Hart Crag (Link Cove to your left, Rydal Head to your right). From Link Hause, carry straight on climbing quite steeply up across rocky ground to reach the cairn on the rocky summit of Hart Crag (NY 368 113).

5. From Hart Crag's summit cairn, follow the rocky path straight on *(compass bearing from cairn: 164 degrees)* heading quite steeply down

across outcrops to soon join the start of a wall on your right along the top of the broad ridge *(this wall accompanies you all the way down off the fells into Scandale)*. Head straight on alongside this wall on your right heading along the top of the broad ridge, which soon gently rises up onto the broad summit of Dove Crag, marked by a cairn *(the actual crags of Dove Crag are some distance away to the north east)*. From Dove Crag, continue alongside the wall on your right heading steadily down for 1.75 km along the top of the broad ridge, which gradually narrows, then up a gentle rise onto the 'summit' of High Pike, with fine views down into Scandale to your left. From High Pike, continue along the path alongside the wall on your right heading quite steeply down some rocky sections at first *(take care – steep drops to your left)*, at the bottom of which the gradient eases and the path leads straight on along the top of the narrow ridge (wall still on your right) to reach a ladder stile over a wall across your path, with Low Pike just ahead (NY 374 081).

6. Cross the ladder stile and head straight on then, as you reach the outcrops of Low Pike, follow the path straight on skirting to the left below these outcrops, beyond which the path leads down (wall just across to your right) to reach a tumbledown wall across your path. Cross over this wall and follow the path straight on, with the wall on your right, heading gradually down across the tail-end of the ridge for 400 metres to reach another wall across your path. Head through the wall-gap and follow the path straight on for 75 metres then bear slightly left away from the wall *(do not continue along the wall - difficult rock step ahead)*. The path soon curves round to the right back towards the wall then, after a short distance, turns sharp left alongside High Brock Crags on your left. The path soon bends to the right then leads gradually down across the hillside to reach an old wall across your path, beside the outcrops of Low Brock Crags on your right. Cross this wall and carry straight on, with Scandale Beck down to your left, for 400 metres to reach a junction of paths just before a wall across your path (marker-post). Turn left at this path junction heading down into Scandale to soon reach a ladder stile over a wall, after which carry straight on down alongside the wall on your left to reach High Sweden Bridge across Scandale Beck (NY 379 067).

7. Cross the bridge and follow the path to the right alongside the stream to quickly join a stony track. Follow this straight on (to the right) alongside Scandale Beck on your right to soon reach a gate in a wall across the track. Head through this gate and follow the track straight on down through the wooded valley (Scandale Beck to your right) for 0.75 km to reach another gate across the track, after which follow the enclosed track straight on leaving the woodland and Scandale Beck behind meandering across pastures heading gradually down to reach a gate on the edge of Ambleside. Head through this gate and follow the enclosed metalled lane (Sweden Bridge Lane) down through the outskirts of Ambleside to reach its junction with Kirkstone Road. Turn right down along this road back into Ambleside.

Ambleside Walking Weekend
- Sunday Walk -
Ambleside, Wansfell Pike, Troutbeck
& Jenkin Crag

WALK INFORMATION

Highlights:	The beautiful waterfalls of Stockghyll, a superb viewpoint, the valley of the Romans, a village that thinks it's a town and Lakeland's most romantic spot.
Distance:	6.5 miles (10.5 km) Time: Allow 3 - 4 hours
Map:	OS Explorer map OL7 – *always take a map on your walk.*
Refreshments:	Pubs, cafés and shops at Ambleside and Troutbeck.
Terrain:	A lane leads up out of Ambleside before a path cuts off through woodland to reach Stockghyll Force (waterfalls). A path then climbs steeply up (pitched stone path all the way) to the 'summit' of Wansfell Pike. A stony path then heads down across the open moorland of Wansfell before joining the grassy/stony track of Nanny Lane that leads down to Troutbeck. From Troutbeck, a clear track leads all the way back to Ambleside across pastureland and through woodland.
Highest point:	Wansfell Pike – 482 metres above sea level.
Total ascent:	500 metres
Caution:	The climb up to Wansfell Pike is steep in places, whilst the summit is rocky underfoot and exposed to the elements. There is rough terrain in places. Take care when visiting Jenkin Crag as there are sheer drops.

POINTS OF INTEREST

Ambleside lies at the head of Windermere, England's largest lake, and is surrounded by some of Lakeland's highest fells. Stockghyll Force waterfall can be found a short walk from Ambleside where Stock Beck cascades down through a ravine with moss-covered rocks and overhanging trees. Beyond, a path leads up to the rocky summit of Wansfell Pike. Despite its modest height, this is one of Lakeland's finest viewpoints with unrivalled views across Windermere towards the rugged peaks of Lakeland. The descent follows a meandering path across rocky moorland to join the enclosed track of Nanny Lane, which leads down to join the road through Troutbeck, a classic example of a linear settlement with houses clustered around wells that once provided villagers with their drinking water. Troutbeck perhaps has pretensions of grandeur with Town Head and Town End at each end of the mile-long straggle of houses, and it even has its own mayor! The village boasts some of the finest vernacular architecture in Lakeland with slate houses and farm buildings dating back many centuries. Townend is a superb example of an early 17th Century yeoman farmer's house with cylindrical chimneys, mullion windows and exquisitely carved oak furniture. It was the home of the Browne family for over four centuries until acquired by The National Trust in the 1940s. Also of note are Troutbeck's two hostelries; the Queen's Head, a 17th Century coaching inn, and the Mortal Man that is famed for its poetic pub sign.

The Troutbeck Valley carves a slender cleft of greenery into the heart of some of Lakeland's highest fells. On its western side, the busy Kirkstone Pass road climbs steadily up over the hills to Patterdale. This was also the way the Romans came nearly 2,000 years ago; however, they chose a slightly different route across the fells to link up their forts at Ambleside and Brougham via the high-level ridge of High Street at 828 metres above sea level. The 'return leg' of this walk follows Robin Lane across the lower slopes of Wansfell and then through Skelghyll Wood with Jenkin Crag offering lovely views across Windermere. In 2007, this crag was voted Cumbria's most romantic spot for celebrating Valentine's Day.

AMBLESIDE SUNDAY WALK

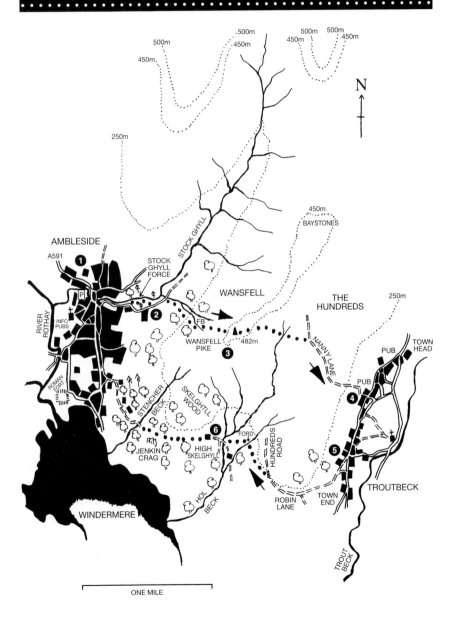

ONE MILE

THE WALK

1. From the stepped market cross in the centre of Ambleside (with your back to the Salutation Hotel) turn left along the main road then, where it bends down to the right after a short distance, take the lane to the left (off this bend) passing between Barclay's Bank and the old Market Hall. Follow this lane for a short distance then, where it forks, head left towards 'Stockghyll & Wansfell Pike' (SP 'To the Waterfalls') and follow this up out of Ambleside. You soon leave Ambleside behind – continue up along the tree-shaded lane with Stock Ghyll (stream) down to your left then, just after you have passed the turning of Stock Ghyll Brow, take the path off to the left through a gate that leads into woodland (signpost 'This Way to the Waterfalls'). Follow the waymarked path through woodland, with Stock Ghyll to your left, to reach Stockghyll Force (waterfalls). As you reach the viewing area (iron railings) and a picnic bench turn right along a clear path (sign 'revolving gate exit') through woodland (away from the waterfalls) to soon reach the large revolving gate that leads back onto the lane.

2. Turn left along the lane and follow this up to reach a cattle grid at the top of the woodland, after which continue up along the unenclosed lane for 200 metres then, just before the road crosses a stream, take the path to the right up some stone steps (SP 'Troutbeck via Wansfell'). After the stile, follow the stony path climbing steadily up, with the stream on your left, to reach a kissing gate in a wall across your path, after which continue straight on climbing steeply up along a stone-pitched path (stream still to your left) heading straight up the hillside then, as you reach the top of the trees on your left, follow the path to the left over a small wooden FB across the stream. After the FB, follow the stone-pitched path climbing steeply up across the hillside to reach a gap in a wall. Head through this gap and continue up along the stone-pitched path winding steeply up to reach the rocky outcrops on the summit of Wansfell Pike (NY 394 042).

3. Cross the ladder stile over the fence that runs along the top of the ridge just beyond the 'summit' crags, after which follow the clear path straight on bearing slightly to the left dropping down off the ridge across the undulating moorland for 0.75 km to reach a kissing gate in a wall across your path. Head through this kissing gate and follow the path straight on to soon reach a gate that leads onto the walled track of Nanny Lane. Turn right along this track and follow it heading steadily down for 1.25 km to reach the road through Troutbeck at Lane Foot Farm (NY 410 034). *Pubs short detour to your left along the road.*

4. Turn right along the road through the scattered village of Troutbeck and follow this road for 0.75 km to reach the cluster of houses in the High Fold and Low Fold areas of Troutbeck where you carry straight on along the road passing a road turning down to your left (small 'green' with a bench in the middle of the junction) just beyond which you reach the Post Office. Just after the Post Office and shop take the lane up to the right, marked by an old signpost on the wall of the Post Office 'Footpath via Skelgill & Jenkin Crag to Ambleside' (SP 'Robin Lane').

5. Follow this metalled lane rising up out of Troutbeck passing some cottages on your right beyond which the lane becomes a stony enclosed track (Robin Lane). Continue straight on along this track gently rising up (ignore tracks off this main track) following the hillside as it gradually curves round to the right *(Windermere comes into view)* to reach a gate across the track after 1km (where Robin Lane becomes Hundreds Road) and a path branches off to the left through a kissing-gate beside another gate (NY 398 024). Head left through the kissing-gate (SP 'Skelghyll & Jenkin Crag') and follow this stony path dropping down alongside a wall on your left (leaving the enclosed track of Hundreds Road behind) to reach a ford across a stream after 0.5km. After the ford, follow the path to the left then across pastures before curving down to the left to reach a metalled lane beside a bridge across Hol Beck. Turn right along the lane (SP 'Ambleside') and follow this up to reach High Skelghyll Farm.

6. Head straight on through the farmyard and through a gate immediately to the left of the whitewashed farmhouse then almost

immediately through another gate, after which follow the wide stony path straight on across the hillside to soon reach another gate in a wall across the wide path that leads into Skelghyll Wood. After the gate, follow the broad path straight on across the wooded hillside very gradually dropping down through the woods alongside a wall on your left for 0.5 km to reach a path to the left that quickly leads to the viewpoint of Jenkin Crag (National Trust sign 'Jenkyn Crag'). After visiting Jenkin Crag, return to the broad path and continue down along this path through woodland alongside the wall on your left. The broad path soon heads more steeply down *(where the path forks, choose either route as they both lead to the same place)* to reach a bridge across Stencher Beck. After the bridge, follow the broad stony path curving down to the left (wooded stream down to your left) then, after a short distance, follow the broad path curving round to the right (away from the stream) heading through woodland to join a clear track beside the entrance to a house. Continue straight on along this track down to join a metalled lane which you follow straight on winding quite steeply down to join Old Lake Road at the bottom of the hill on the edge of Ambleside. Turn right along this quiet road (which runs parallel with the busier A591) and follow it to join the A591 in the centre of Ambleside. Turn right along this main road back to the Salutation Hotel.

BOOT

Boot is the 'capital' of the sparsely populated upper reaches of Eskdale and is little more than a handful of old miners' cottages along a quiet country lane. Boot's unusual name is derived from an old English word meaning 'bend in the valley' as the village actually lies in the heart of Eskdale some seven miles from the source of the River Esk, which rises in the boulder-strewn wilderness in the shadow of Scafell Pike. Eskdale differs from the other main Lakeland valleys because it does not have a lake and also its underlying rocks are formed from granite. This igneous rock sparkles in sunlight and varies in colour from grey to pink. Take a look at the stone walls that divide Eskdale's pastures as they are constructed from large granite boulders instead of the more usual flat slates. Beside the ancient packhorse bridge that spans Whillan Beck in the heart of Boot stands a 16th Century corn mill, although there has probably been a mill on this site since the 13th Century. The mill retains much of its late 18th Century machinery including two waterwheels and was in constant use grinding cereals from 1578 until commercial milling ended in the 1930s. The waterwheel was then adapted to supply electricity to the houses of Eskdale, as the mains supply did not reach the valley until the 1950s. The historic mill machinery was left untouched, gathering dust, until the mill was bought by Cumbria County Council in the 1970s. They restored this historic mill and opened it to the public. In 2006 the Eskdale Mill and Heritage Trust bought the mill from the County Council to secure its future. Eskdale Mill is Lakeland's last working mill and one of the oldest water-powered corn mills in England.

THE VILLAGE

Boot offers bed and breakfast accommodation, campsites, youth hostel, self catering accommodation, three pubs, shop, arts and craft gallery, cafe, gift shop, car park, public toilets and steam trains along the Ravenglass and Eskdale Railway.

ACCOMMODATION

Tourist Information Centre, Egremont   01946 820693

BOOT PUBS

Boot Inn, Boot   **01946 723224**
Hidden away in the heart of Boot this traditional Lakeland pub was known as the Masons Arms in the 19th Century and, more recently, the Burnmoor Inn. It dates back 400 years and maintains the relaxed atmosphere of a country pub. The opened up interior retains a snug area, games room and lounge warmed by an open fire, whilst outside is a large beer garden.

Brook House Inn, Boot   **019467 23288**
Interesting and unusual bric-a-brac adorns the walls of the Poachers Bar of this comfortable pub/hotel, with a distinct hunting theme. The pub is renowned for its wide range of local hand-pulled ales as well as an impressive selection of whiskies. Good reputation for food.

Woolpack Inn, Boot   **019467 23230**
A remote inn that once served travellers on the many packhorse routes that came this way, in particular the Hardknott Pass. A pub of considerable age with several small rooms as well as its own micro-brewery, the Hardknott Brewery.

PUBS ALONG THE WALKS

King George IV, Eskdale Green   019467 23262

Boot Walking Weekend
- Saturday Walk -
Boot, Penny Hill Farm, Harter Fell, Hardknott Pass
& Jubilee Bridge

WALK INFORMATION

Highlights: The church of the White Ship, old packhorse and peat roads, Lakeland's perfect mountain, England's most notorious road and a Roman fort with a dramatic setting.

Distance: 9.25 miles (14.75 km)   Time: Allow 5 - 6 hours

Map: OS Explorer map OL6 - *always take a map on your walk.*

Refreshments: Pubs, cafe and shop at Boot. No facilities en route.

Terrain: Quiet lanes and a riverside path lead to Penny Hill Farm, from where a grassy track and then a rough path climbs up to the rocky summit of Harter Fell, with rough ground in places, several stream crossings and steep sections. From Harter Fell, a grassy path leads down to join Hardknott Pass (road); the path is indistinct in places with wet ground and a number of stream crossings. This unenclosed road winds steeply down to Jubilee Bridge, from where a grassy path/track leads back to Penny Hill Farm. *Please note:* Hardknott Forest is being transformed into a broadleaved woodland, therefore its appearance may change.

Highest point: Harter Fell - 653 metres above sea level.

Total ascent: 600 metres

Escape Route: As you join the Eskdale to Duddon Valley bridleway just beyond Spothow Gill, turn left and follow this bridleway down to Jubilee Bridge. Follow the route description from Point 6.

Open Access The section from Spothow Gill to Harter Fell then down to Hardknott Pass heads across Open Access land **www.openaccess.gov.uk**

Caution **Mountain Walk.** This is a strenuous walk up to the summit of Harter Fell. There is rough and rocky ground in places with some steep sections. The path to and from the summit of Harter Fell is indistinct in places across open moorland; navigation may be difficult in mist. There are numerous steam crossings as well as boggy ground in places. OS map and compass essential. Do not attempt this walk in bad weather.

St Catherine's Church has a beautiful setting beside the River Esk, and is constructed from pink granite that sparkles in the sunlight. The present building dates predominantly from the restoration of 1881, although there has been a place of worship in this area for 800 years. The church has been linked to the loss of the White Ship in 1120 on St Catherine's Day when the son of Henry I and the nephew of Ranulph le Meschines, the Earl of Chester, drowned. The le Meschines family founded St Bees Priory in 1125 and established four chapels in western Lakeland with one at Eskdale. The first reference to a church on this site was in the 15th Century when the Abbot of Calder Abbey agreed to upgrade the chapel into a church. A medieval bell, dedicated to St Catherine, has survived from when the chapel was upgraded, whilst the font dates from 1330. Above the track that leads to Doctor Bridge is St Catherine's Well, thought to be the site of the ancient chapel.

Almost half of Eskdale is free from traffic as the narrow road that winds through the valley forsakes the wild upper reaches of Eskdale for Hardknott Pass, one of the most difficult roads in the country with 1-in-3 hairpin bends. The River Esk is born on Esk Hause which, at 759 metres, is the highest pass (walking boots only) in Lakeland and the wettest uninhabited place in England. The infant Esk tumbles through the barren land at the head of the dale known as Great Moss, with towering mountains all around. The farm of Brotherilkeld marks the end of the wild upper reaches and the start of the road and civilisation. The name Brotherilkeld conjures up images of times past as this was already an established Norse sheep farm when Furness Abbey gained control of most of the land in the upper dale in 1242. The valley has numerous old packhorse routes that are now 'green lanes', a good example is the track that runs along the south bank of the Esk from Whahouse Bridge to Eskdale Green and on to Ravenglass. This track passes Penny Hill Farm, which once served as an inn along this route. Just down from this farm stands Doctor Bridge, named after Dr Edward Tyson who widened the old packhorse bridge in 1734. Penny Hill Farm also marks the start of the climb up onto Harter Fell by way of an old peat road. Many farms in Eskdale had well engineered tracks that climbed up to the open fell where peat was cut and stored to dry in stone huts, some of which can still be seen today.

Harter Fell is a conical mountain described by many as perfect in terms of shape, rocks, position and views. It separates the valleys of the Esk and Duddon but is not the source of these rivers. The summit, with its rock towers, affords wonderful views of the mountains that encircle the upper reaches of Eskdale including Scafell Pike and Bow Fell as well as a bird's eye view of Hardknott Roman Fort. To the west are views towards the Irish Sea with, on a clear day, the Isle of Man visible on the horizon. The southern and eastern flanks of Harter Fell were planted extensively by the Forestry Commission in the decades that followed the 1930s. Back in 1935 the proposed plantations sparked outrage amongst conservationists, most notably H.H. Symonds, who objected to the proposed afforestation of 7,000 acres in the Duddon Valley and Eskdale. Their protestations were heeded and the Forestry Commission decided against planting in Eskdale's upper reaches and carried out more sensitive planting in the Duddon Valley. Hardknott Forest on the eastern flanks of Harter Fell is currently being felled and transformed into broadleaved woodland that will benefit wildlife.

High on the fells beside the tortuous bends of Hardknott Pass stand the remains of one of England's most impressive Roman forts. Built in 120AD during Emperor Hadrian's reign this fort protected the trade route from the Roman port of Ravenglass to Ambleside and on to Hadrian's Wall. They chose their site well as cliffs fall steeply away to the north and west with views across Eskdale. It is at this point that the valley curves westwards towards the Irish Sea leaving the mountains behind, indeed the Roman name of the fort is believed to be 'Mediobogdum' which means 'fort in the middle of the bend'. It was garrisoned by 500 soldiers from the Fourth Cohort of Dalmatians who originally came from the Adriatic coast; however, it was abandoned in 197AD for reasons unknown. The impressive ruins still stand over six feet high and five feet thick. Just outside the walls are the remains of the bath house and a flat parade ground.

BOOT SATURDAY WALK

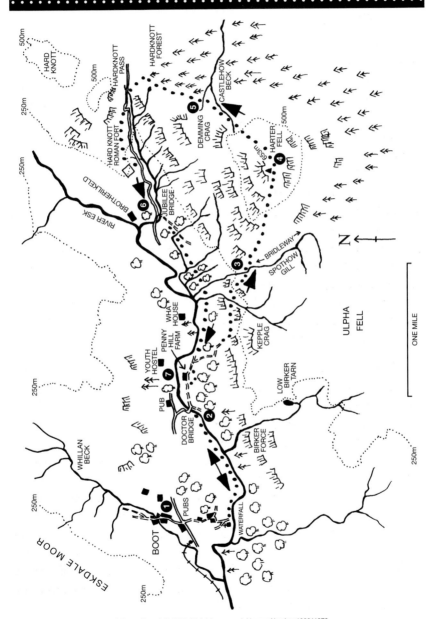

THE WALK

1. From the road junction beside Brook House Inn at Boot, take the enclosed lane opposite the pub (SP 'St Catherine's Eskdale Parish Church') and follow this lane for 400 metres then, where it forks in front of Esk View House, follow the right-hand lane winding round to reach St Catherine's Church beside the River Esk. Walk past the church to quickly reach the riverbank where you follow the riverside path to the left (SP 'Doctor Bridge'). Follow this path straight on, with the Esk on your right, to soon reach a gate in a fence across your path. After the gate, head to the right and follow the slightly higher of the two paths (walking parallel with the lower stony path). Follow this grassy path straight on, with the river just down to your right, then rising gently up through gorse bushes and curving to the left (leaving the stony path and river behind) with walls on either side funnelling the path to reach a gate in the corner of the field. Head through the gate and follow the path straight on to soon join the banks of the river again where you carry straight on (following the river) for 1.25 km to reach Doctor Bridge across the River Esk (NY 189 007).

2. Turn right over Doctor Bridge immediately after which head straight on (SP 'Penny Hill') along the lane to reach Penny Hill Farm. Pass in front of the farmhouse then bear to the right along the walled track to soon reach a gate (walled track ends). *Permissive footpath that avoids Penny Hill farmyard - just before you reach the farm, follow the permissive path to the right that skirts around the enclosure in front of the farmhouse to re-join the track just beyond the farm (with the gate at the end of the walled track leading from the farmyard just down to your left).* After the gate (walled track ends), continue up along the rough track and through another gate in the top left corner of the field, shortly after which the track forks where you follow the grassy track up to the right heading up across the hillside to reach a gate in a fence across the track. After the gate, continue up along the grassy track over a small stream (just beyond this gate) then climbing straight up the hillside for 150 metres

before bending round to the left then rising up across the hillside to join a wall on your left. Follow the grassy path bending to the right up alongside this wall on your left to quickly reach a choice of two gates in a wall. Head through the right-hand gate and follow the path climbing quite steeply up alongside the wall on your left (SP 'Harter Fell' - *ignore path winding up the hillside to the right*) for about 100 metres then follow this wall as it turns sharp left and levels out. Head straight on across the hillside alongside the wall on your left then, after about 200 metres, the path very gradually rises up (wall still on your left) then drops down over a stream set in a small ravine (with a couple of trees - NY 203 003). After the stream, follow the narrow path straight on for 75 metres then follow the grassy path turning up to the right (small waymarker post) heading steeply up through a 'nick' in the crags up to your right. Above this 'nick' in the crags the ground levels out - carry straight on along the grassy path (with Spothow Gill across to your left) to soon reach the end of a tumbledown wall on your left. Follow the path to the left alongside this old wall then, where this wall bends away after a short distance, carry straight on to soon reach Spothow Gill. Cross the stream and through the wall just beyond, after which turn right alongside this wall to quickly reach a stile over a fence immediately after which you join the Eskdale to Duddon Valley bridleway (NY 207 000). *NB: The path we followed over Spothow Gill joins this bridleway some 200 metres to the north of where the Right of Way is shown as joining the bridleway on the OS map.*

3. After the stile, head straight on along the grassy path towards the steep rocky crags of Harter Fell (in front of you) for 150 metres to reach some low outcrops (as the ground begins to rise up), where you follow the path bearing up to the right for another 150 metres then, as you approach the foot of the steep crags, the path turns distinctly to the right and all but levels out. Follow this path gently rising up for 25 metres before turning left climbing quite steeply up across the rocky/heather-covered hillside towards the steep crags (cairns) then, as you reach the foot of the steep crags, you come to an indistinct fork in the path where you follow the left-hand path winding steeply up (series of small cairns) across the rocky fellside passing to the

right-hand side of the imposing crags. The path winds steeply up at first then bears very slightly right climbing up across the boulder-strewn/heather-covered hillside (crags to your left). As you climb higher the gradient eases and the path becomes grassy underfoot as you head up across the rocky fellside to reach the summit outcrops of Harter Fell just to your left. As you approach these summit outcrops (to your left), follow the grassy path straight on rising up passing through a 'gap' immediately to the right-hand (southern) side of the summit outcrops (heading east). *Detour to the left (easy scramble) up to reach the Trig Point on the summit outcrops (SD 218 997).*

4. Carry straight on along the grassy path that passes through the 'gap' in the outcrops immediately to the right (south) of the summit outcrops (Trig Point just up to your left) heading eastwards to quickly reach the 'other side' of the summit where the ground begins to drop down and you almost immediately reach a fork in the grassy path *(Seathwaite Tarn, with its small dam, ahead of you)*. Follow the left-hand path heading in a north-easterly direction down from the summit *(aiming towards the left-hand side of the upper reaches of the Duddon Valley in the distance, with its green fields and couple of farms)*. Follow this grassy path heading down from the summit crags *(still heading in a north-easterly direction)* then, after about 150 metres, follow the path as it bears very slightly left then straight down the grassy hillside for a further 600 metres *(heading towards the left-hand side (top edge) of the forest ahead of you)* down passing to the right-hand side of Demming Crag (about 200 metres to the right of this domed shaped crag) to reach a small stream set in a gully (Castlehow Beck) just after you have passed Demming Crag. Cross over the stream/gully then continue down the hillside alongside this stream on your right, crossing then re-crossing the stream after which continue straight on along the grassy path down across wet/boggy hillside, leaving the stream to bear away to the right, to reach a stile over a fence across your path where it adjoins another fence on your right (felled forest to your right - NY 227 005).

5. Cross the stile and a small stream just beyond then walk straight on alongside the fence on your right (felled forest on right) and follow this across undulating terrain for 600 metres (boggy in places) to reach a stile over a fence across your path, after which continue alongside the fence on your right (and forest) to soon reach an old wall across your path (forest ends on right). Head over this wall then turn immediately left and follow the grassy path with the wall to your left then, where this wall turns across your path, carry straight on over this wall and down to soon reach the top of Hardknott Pass (NY 228 015). Turn left along the unfenced road and follow it down for 350 metres then, at the first hair-pin bend, take the footpath that leads straight on off this bend (SP) and follow this grassy path straight on across rough, boggy ground (road across to your left) down to reach Hardknott Roman Fort. After exploring the fort, head back to re-join the road which you follow winding steeply down to reach a cattle grid across the road at the foot of Hardknott Pass (with Hardknott Gill to your left). Immediately before this cattle grid turn left (SP 'Dunnerdale') down over the diminutive stone-built Jubilee Bridge across Hardknott Gill (NY 213 011).

6. After the bridge, follow the stony path up to quickly reach two kissing-gates in quick succession, after which forsake the clear grassy bridleway rising up ahead but walk alongside the wall on your right heading across the bottom of the field walking parallel with this ascending bridleway. Head alongside this wall on your right then, as you approach the end of the field, head gently up to reach a kissing-gate in a wall across your path. After this kissing-gate, follow the path straight on across the hillside to reach Dodknott Gill and a kissing-gate that leads into woodland. Follow the path straight on through the woods to reach a bridlegate at the end of the woods, just beyond which cross a FB over Spothow Gill. After the FB, follow the path to the left upstream for a short distance then bending to the right away from the stream heading across the hillside (do not head up the hillside) to join a wall on your right (ignore path to the right that leads to Whahouse Bridge). Carry straight on (SP 'Penny Hill') alongside this wall on your right to quickly reach a ford across a

stream and a gate just beyond. After the gate, carry straight on alongside the wall on your right and follow this clear grassy path/track all the way back to Penny Hill Farm.

7. Follow the track through Penny Hill farmyard passing in front of the farmhouse *(follow the permissive path that skirts around the enclosure in front of the farmhouse to re-join the track just beyond the farm)* then follow the track straight on back to reach Doctor Bridge over the River Esk. Immediately after the bridge, turn left (SP 'St Catherine's Church') and re-trace your steps back along the riverside path (River Esk on your left) to reach St Catherine's Church where you re-trace your steps along the enclosed lane into Boot.

Boot

Boot Walking Weekend
- Sunday Walk -
Boot, Stanley Ghyll Force, Eskdale Green & Blea Tarn

WALK INFORMATION

Highlights: A waterfall with three names, wonderful woodland walks, La'al Ratty, the blue teardrop and a spectacular descent with views towards Harter Fell.

Distance: 6 miles (9.75 km)   *Short Route 5.75 km/3.5 miles*

Time: Allow 3 hours

Map: OS Explorer map OL6 - *always take a map on your walk.*

Refreshments: Pubs, cafe and shop at Boot. Pub at Eskdale Green.

Terrain: Quiet lanes, woodland tracks and riverside paths lead to Forge Bridge. The detour to Stanley Ghyll Force follows a clear streamside path up through a wooded gorge; the final section to the waterfall is rough and narrow with steep drops to the side of the path. After some road walking from Forge Bridge to Eskdale Green, a broad path leads up onto Fell End, from where an indistinct path heads across rough and boggy ground (Eskdale Common) to reach Blea Tarn. From Blea Tarn, a path winds steeply down to Beckfoot, with a stretch of road walking to finish.

Highest point: Blea Tarn - 220 metres above sea level.

Total ascent: 300 metres

Short Route:	Catch a train from Eskdale Green Station back to Dalegarth Station using the Ravenglass and Eskdale Railway.
Open Access:	The section from Fell End to Blea Tarn heads across Open Access land **www.openaccess.gov.uk**
Caution:	Take care walking along the roads around Boot, Eskdale Green and Beckfoot. The path up to Stanley Ghyll Force is narrow with steep drops to side of path. There is a maze of paths amongst the rocky outcrops of Eskdale Common (around Blea Tarn); navigation may be difficult in poor weather. OS map and compass required. Descent from Blea Tarn to Beckfoot is steep.

POINTS OF INTEREST

Stanley Ghyll Force lies hidden in a wooded ravine on the flanks of Birker Fell, a pleasant stroll from Dalegarth Station with an exciting finale along a narrow path through the gorge to view the falls. This waterfall has the distinction of being referred to by three names - Stanley Force, Stanley Ghyll Force and Dalegarth Force - and was a 'must' on the itinerary of Victorian tourists. Many people regard this to be Lakeland's most beautiful waterfall and it is easy to see why as the sparkling waters cascade 60 feet (18m) over pink granite rocks. The falls are named after the Stanley family who once lived at nearby Dalegarth Hall, a 16th Century building with distinctive cylindrical chimneys.

During the 19th Century iron and copper deposits were discovered in the hills around Boot. A railway was constructed in 1875 to transport the ore from the mines at Nab Scar to the mainline and port at Ravenglass. Originally built with a three foot gauge track, the railway also carried passengers. The line closed in 1913 following the closure of the mines. In 1915 Mr Bassett Lowke, the famous model engineer, took over the line and converted it into a 15-inch narrow gauge railway as he wanted somewhere to test his model steam engines. The granite quarries at Beckfoot provided extra revenue for the line in the early 20th Century and it continued to carry passengers; however, the closure of the quarries in 1953 put a question mark over the line. The future looked bleak but in 1960 the Ravenglass and Eskdale Railway Preservation Society took control. The railway is known as 'La'al Ratty' after one of the original contractors who surname was Ratcliffe. There are seven stations along the scenic seven miles from Ravenglass to Dalegarth (Boot) with steam engines carrying passengers throughout the summer months.

From Eskdale Green, an old 'peat road' leads up onto Fell End and Eskdale Common, where there are several old peat huts. These were used to store cut peat from the surrounding moors and date back to the 18th Century. Peat was used as domestic fuel throughout Eskdale until the mid 20th Century. Blea Tarn lies hidden on this moorland, its name derived from the Old Norse words 'blea' meaning dark blue and 'tjorn' meaning teardrop or small lake.

45

BOOT SUNDAY WALK

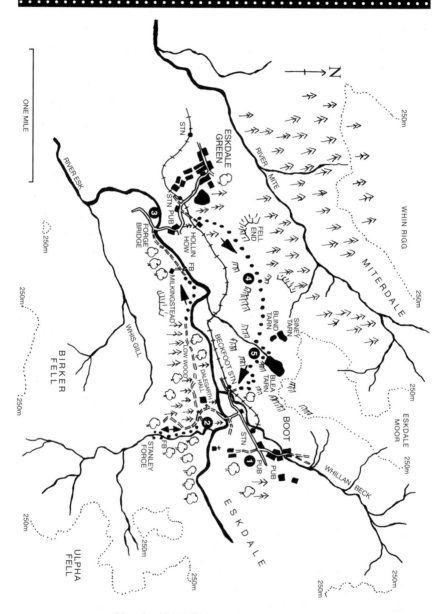

THE WALK

1. From the road junction beside the Brook House Inn (with your back to the pub) turn right along the main valley road for 500 metres (passing Dalegarth Station) then take the first turning to the left opposite the old schoolhouse (Eskdale Centre), with the War Memorial on the corner (SP 'Stanley Ghyll waterfall'). Follow this metalled lane straight on to reach Trough House Bridge across the River Esk. Cross the bridge and carry straight on along the lane passing Trough House Bridge car park on your left, after which the lane becomes a track which you follow straight on for 150 metres to reach a fork in the track. Bear left (SP 'Stanley Ghyll waterfall') along the enclosed track *(Dalegarth Hall with it cylindrical chimneys across to your right)* to soon reach a gate across the track, after which follow the track bearing to the left to soon reach a 'crossroads' of tracks/bridleways where you turn right through a gate in a fence (SP 'Forge Bridge' - NY 172 001).

   Detour to Stanley Ghyll waterfall: From this 'crossroads' of tracks/bridleways, head straight on along the track then, where this bends up to the right after 125 metres, take the footpath to the left through a gate in the wall that leads into woodland (sign 'Stanley Ghyll'). Head straight on through the woods to quickly reach the banks of the stream. Turn right and follow the streamside path up through the wooded gorge, crossing and re-crossing three footbridges to reach Stanley Ghyll waterfall (Caution: the path beyond the third footbridge is rough with steep drops). Re-trace your steps back down along the streamside path then through woodland back to the crossroads of tracks/bridleways near Dalegarth Hall.

2. Head through the gate (SP 'Forge Bridge') and follow the rutted track straight on across the field to soon reach a gate that leads into Low Wood *(Dalegarth Hall just to your right)*. Follow the track straight on through the woods then gently curving left down over a small stream, after which carry straight on *(ignore track off to the left)* along the clear track gently meandering through Low Wood for 900 metres (keep to the clear track all the way) to reach a gate in a wall across your path. Head through the gate (track now becomes a wide,

stony path) and follow the path straight on down to join the banks of the River Esk. Follow this riverside path straight on for 300 metres to reach a ruinous farm building beside the path, where you carry straight on along the enclosed path to quickly reach a gate that leads out onto a field (river bends away to your right). Head through the gate and walk across the field alongside the wall on your right to reach a gate in the field corner that leads back onto the riverside. Follow the riverside track straight on for 250 metres to reach a FB across the river (by a corrugated metal barn). Do not cross this FB but carry straight on along the riverside track with the river on your right (passing Milkingstead Farm across to your left) all the way to join the road beside Forge Bridge across the Esk (SD 149 995).

3. Turn right over Forge Bridge and follow the road to reach a junction beside the King George IV pub at Eskdale Green. Follow the road straight on towards 'Holmrook, Whitehaven, Ravenglass' *(take care)* then bending left then round to the right up through woodland then, as you emerge from the woodland (about 100 metres before the bridge across the Ravenglass & Eskdale Railway at Eskdale Green Station), turn right along a track towards Hollin How (SP 'Blea Tarn, Eskdale Common). Follow this track straight on, over a bridge across the railway and on to reach Hollin How (house) at the end of the track. Just as you reach the gate into the yard of the house, turn left up along an enclosed path that quickly leads to a kissing-gate in a wall, after which follow the grassy path climbing up the hillside for a short distance then curving round to the right alongside a fence on your right *(heading towards the outcrops of Fell End ahead of you)*. Follow this grassy path gently rising up across the hillside with this fence on your right (passing above a small tarn down to your right) then, where this fence ends, carry straight on along the grassy path rising up across the hillside to soon reach a gate in a wall across your path. After the gate the path forks - follow the left-hand path straight on rising steadily up across the rough hillside (towards the outcrops of Fell End ahead) all the way up to the top of the hillside where you reach a ruinous barn. The path now levels out and leads straight on across the hillside (Eskdale falling away down to your right) to soon reach a gate/kissing-gate in a fence

across your path, near where this fence joins a wall to your right and with forest across to your left (NY 155 008).

4. After the gate, follow the path rising up alongside the wall on your right (ignore ladder stile over this wall). The path soon levels out - carry straight on alongside this wall on your right passing a slight 'curve' in the wall (where another wall joins it) then continue straight on alongside the wall across a flat area of boggy ground (wall becomes a fence across this section), beyond which follow the wall gently rising up onto the rocky hillside (Eskdale Common). The path soon levels out then almost immediately begins to drop down then, after 25 metres just as the wall begins to bend away to the right, you reach a fork in the path. Follow the left-hand path heading straight on down the hillside (leaving the wall to bend away to the right), over a tumbledown wall across your path and down to reach a small stream at the bottom of the 'dip' (issuing stream from Blea Tarn). Just as you reach this stream, follow the grassy path to the left heading up to join the tumbledown wall (which you just crossed) and follow this old wall up to reach Blea Tarn. Just as you reach Blea Tarn you join a clear path which you follow to the right, back across the tumbledown wall down to reach the stream issuing from Blea Tarn, with the tarn on your left (NY 164 009).

5. Cross over the stream issuing from Blea Tarn and follow the path straight on (tarn on your left) to soon reach some low outcrops in front of you (just before the end of the tarn) where you turn right along a grassy path then, where these outcrops end on your left after a short distance, follow the path bending to the left (skirting around these low outcrops) to soon reach a ruinous stone building (old peat-store), just beyond which a wonderful view unfolds across Eskdale at the start of the steep descent back down into the valley. Follow the path winding steeply down all the way to reach a gate at the bottom of the hillside that leads across the railway line to join the road beside Beckfoot Station. Turn left along the road *(take care)* and follow this back into Boot.

BRAITHWAITE

Braithwaite is a traditional Cumberland village with narrow winding streets, old cottages, farms, a proper village shop that sells everything and a village green known as Braithwaite Common, which is in the care of The National Trust. Braithwaite Church is only around 100 years old, although is dedicated to St Herbert who lived over 1,300 years ago. St Herbert brought Christianity to the North West of England in the 7th Century and lived in a simple cell on an island in Derwent Water. The village is situated at the foot of Whinlatter Pass beside its junction with the busy A66; amazingly, Whinlatter Pass was once the main route between Keswick and Cockermouth. It also lies at the foot of Grisedale Pike, a magnificent mountain with a distinctive peak that rises steeply up above the village. Grisedale Pike is the first (or last) of several mountains that form the famous Coledale Horseshoe walk, including Sand Hill, Crag Hill (also known as Eel Crag) and Causey Pike, that arc around the head of the valley of Coledale. These mountains offer some of the finest fell-walking in the Lake District. Coledale Beck is born on the high mountain pass known as Coledale Hause before flowing down through this perfect U-shaped valley to reach Braithwaite at the mouth of Coledale. The waters then swell Newlands Beck which flows into Bassenthwaite Lake, the only lake in the Lake District to be called a lake!

THE VILLAGE

Braithwaite provides easy access to the beautiful Newlands Valley and north-western fells. It is a quiet village where you will find several B&Bs and hotels, restaurant, self catering accommodation, a large campsite, general shop, bus service and three pubs.

ACCOMMODATION

Tourist Information Centre, Keswick: 017687 72645

BRAITHWAITE PUBS

Royal Oak, Braithwaite: **017687 78533.**
This traditional village pub boasts a lovely open fireplace as well as a part-flagged bar area, beams and old photographs of the local area on the walls. Good range of Jennings' beers on the bar.

Coledale Inn, Braithwaite: **017687 78282**
Enjoying an elevated position above the village this inn was built in 1824 originally as a woollen mill, later becoming a pencil factory and then a pub. There are two separate bars one of which has an elaborately carved bar counter. The beer garden affords wonderful views of Skiddaw.

Middle Ruddings Country Inn, Braithwaite: 017687 78436
Comfortable lounge bar in a plush hotel situated just off the busy A66. The conservatory, patio and gardens are particularly pleasant on a warm summer evening.

PUBS ALONG THE WALKS

Swinside Inn, Swinside: 017687 78253

Braithwaite Walking Weekend
- Saturday Walk -
Braithwaite, Stonycroft Gill, Newlands Valley, Cat Bells & Swinside

WALK INFORMATION

Highlights: Old miners' tracks, a beautiful valley, German miners in search of gold, the tiny schoolroom, Lakeland's most popular fell and the Tale of Mrs Tiggy Winkle.

Distance: 9 miles (14.5 km)   Time: Allow 5 hours

Map: OS Explorer map OL4 - *always take a map on your walk.*

Refreshments: Pubs and shop at Braithwaite. Pub at Swinside.

Terrain: Clear paths, tracks and lanes all the way. There is a long and steady climb up to Barrow Door. A narrow path then heads across a steep slope to join a rough track that leads down through Stonycroft Gill. After crossing a small ford, a path skirts around the foot of Rowling End to join a road. This road is followed through the Newlands Valley to Little Town. A path then climbs quite steeply up onto the rocky summit of Cat Bells. The descent from Cat Bells is surprisingly steep in places with a number of rocky steps down along the ridge before a path winds down to join a road at Hawes End. This road is then followed to Swinside. A riverside path leads back to Braithwaite.

Highest point: Cat Bells - 451 metres above sea level.

Total ascent: 640 metres

Caution: There are steep drops to the side of the path up to Barrow Door, around the foot of Rowling End and across the Cat Bells ridge. The descent from Cat Bells to Hawes End is steep and rocky in places. Do not explore the old mine workings on the flanks of Cat Bells. Several small streams to cross. Take care walking along the roads.

Braithwaite

POINTS OF INTEREST

The steady climb out of Braithwaite up to the 'saddle' of land between Barrow and Stile End, known as Barrow Door, reveals wonderful retrospective views towards Skiddaw and Bassenthwaite Lake. These two hills are separated by the dramatic steep-sided ravine of Barrow Gill which, rather surprisingly, has been carved out by a small trickling stream that makes it way down from Barrow Door to join Coledale Beck. The name of Barrow is derived from an Anglo-Saxon word meaning a 'long ridge or hill'. The flanks of this hill are scarred with disused mine workings; indeed, the track that climbs up through the delightful cleft of Stonycroft Gill is an old mine road that once served a cobalt mine on the flanks of Outerside as well as a lead mine in its lower reaches.

The Newlands Valley is a hidden vale with green pastures, quiet country lanes and beautiful hamlets all enclosed by high fells. Newlands refers to the 'new lands' that were reclaimed back to agricultural use after Uzzicar Tarn was drained in the 14th Century. There are no villages as such in the Newlands Valley, only a few hamlets. Little Town can hardly be described as a 'town' as it is only made up of a handful of farms and cottages, but what it lacks in size it certainly makes up for in beauty. Beatrix Potter spent many happy childhood holidays in the Newlands Valley and loved this area so much that she used Little Town and Cat Bells as the setting for her children's book 'The Tale of Mrs Tiggy Winkle'. Just to the south-west of Little Town stands Newlands Church, a small and simple church that dates back to at least the 16th Century, although rebuilt on several occasions during the 19th Century. Attached to the side of the church is the old schoolroom, a tiny classroom that provided primary education for local children for over 150 years until it was closed in 1967. To the south of the church the valley divides into three main tributaries. Keskadale carries the road over Newlands Hause to Buttermere, a wonderful journey through some spectacular mountain scenery that once thrilled Victorian tourists who travelled along this road in horse-drawn carriages as part of the 22-mile Borrowdale-Buttermere-Newlands Round. The two other tributaries are Little Dale and the main Newlands Valley, both of which are hemmed in by the high mountains of Dale Head (753m), Hindscarth (727m) and Robinson (737m).

Cat Bells, also spelt Catbells, is one of the most famous fells in Lakeland, its distinctive profile rising high above Derwent Water. Thousands of walkers are drawn to its small rounded summit every year, for this is a Lakeland mountain in miniature and often the first 'peak' climbed by people visiting the Lake District for the first time. It is easy to see why, for there are superb views from its summit, which is flanked by steep and, in places, rocky slopes that give a tantalising taste of mountainous terrain. Its unusual name is believed to be derived from 'cat bields' or 'shelter of the wild cats' that once roamed these fells hundreds of years ago. Cat Bells actually forms the northern end of the High Spy Range, a continuous ridge of mountains and fells that forms a barrier between Borrowdale and the Newlands Valley all the way from Honister Pass to Derwent Water. This undulating ridge is made up of three main 'tops' - High Spy (653m), Maiden Moor (576m) and Cat Bells (451m), and the walk along this ridge is one of the finest in Lakeland. From Little Town, our route climbs up through Yewthwaite Gill to reach the crossroads of paths at Hause Gate, from where a wonderful view across Derwent Water unfolds; the name of Hause Gate is of Scandinavian origin and means 'the road (gate) across the mountain pass (hause)'. The fells that surround the Newlands valley, in particular Maiden Moor and Cat Bells, are scarred by centuries of mining as numerous shafts were driven into the flanks of these fells in search of minerals such as lead, copper, silver and even gold. These mines were first worked during the reign of Elizabeth I up until the late 19th Century, although one or two mines may date back as far as the 13th Century. The oldest and richest of all of these mines in this area was the Goldscope Mine. Goldscope does not refer to the gold deposits but actually means 'Gottesgabe' or 'God's gift', the name originating from the highly skilled German miners who were brought in to this area in Elizabethan times from Augsberg to develop the mines. German surnames still exist today in the Keswick area, the most notable of which is Fisher.

BRAITHWAITE SATURDAY WALK

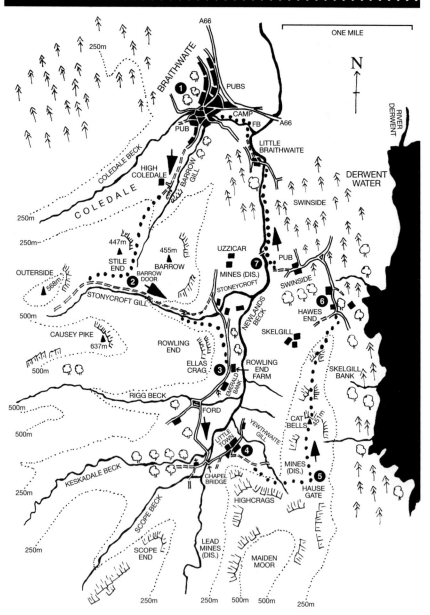

ONE MILE

N

A66

BRAITHWAITE

PUBS

CAMP

FB

A66

PUB

LITTLE
BRAITHWAITE

HIGH
COLEDALE

COLEDALE BECK

BARROW GILL

COLEDALE

250m

250m

SWINSIDE

DERWENT
WATER

RIVER DERWENT

447m

STILE
END

455m

BARROW

UZZICAR

PUB

OUTERSIDE

568m

BARROW
DOOR

MINES (DIS.)

STONEYCROFT

SWINSIDE

STONYCROFT GILL

NEWLANDS BECK

HAWES
END

500m

CAUSEY PIKE

637m

ROWLING
END

SKELGILL

500m

ELLAS
CRAG

ROWLING
END
FARM

SKELGILL
BANK

RIGG BECK

EMERALD BANK

500m

FORD

500m

YEWTHWAITE GILL

CAT
BELLS

451m

LITTLE
TOWN

KESKADALE BECK

CHAPEL
BRIDGE

MINES
(DIS.)

HAUSE
GATE

250m

SCOPE BECK

HIGHCRAGS

250m

SCOPE
END

LEAD
MINES
(DIS.)

MAIDEN
MOOR

250m

250m

500m   500m

250m

THE WALK

1. From the Royal Oak in the centre of Braithwaite (with your back to the pub), head left along the B5292 'Whinlatter Pass' road towards Cockermouth then, just before you leave the village, head left over a small stone-built bridge across Coledale Beck (sign 'Youth Centre, Coledale') and follow this lane bending to the right across Braithwaite Common then, where the road forks by the Methodist Church, bear left and follow the lane round to reach the Coledale Inn. Continue along the lane curving to the right passing in front of the Coledale Inn then heading gradually up (houses on your right) to reach a gate at the end of the metalled lane at the top of the village (houses end). Head through the gate and follow the stony track straight on rising steadily up, with a fence just to your right and the ravine of Barrow Gill falling away to your left, for 500 metres to reach a fork in the track (where the stony track bends to the right towards a gate and High Coledale barn set in a copse of woodland). Carry straight on along the track (fence bends away to your right) rising steadily up across the hillside, with Barrow Gill falling away to your left, heading up towards the small 'peak' of Stile End ahead. The track soon becomes a wide grassy path, which you follow straight on for 500 metres rising steadily up to reach the foot of the steep slopes of Stile End. Follow the path passing to the left side of Stile End across its steep eastern (left-hand) slope, with Barrow Gill falling away to your left, up to reach the 'pass' of Barrow Door between Barrow to your left and Stile End to your right, with the valley of Stonycroft Gill falling steeply away in front of you (NY 222 217).

2. As you reach Barrow Door (at the head of Barrow Gill) follow the path to the right *(do not head straight on steeply down into the valley)* skirting across the steep hillside (southern slopes of Stile End), with Stonycroft Gill falling away to your left, keeping roughly to the same contour at first then heading gradually down across the hillside to join the clear track (old mine road) running up through

the valley *(the path joins this track where the track bends to the left towards the head of the valley)*. Turn left along this track and follow it heading steadily down through the valley, with Stonycroft Gill to your right, for approximately 1.25 km then, just before the valley opens out into the Newlands Valley (150 metres before the track bends left), take the clear path back on yourself to the right that leads down to a ford across the stream set in a small rocky ravine (waterfalls). *NB: If stream impassable, continue down along the track to join the road.* Cross the stream then follow the path to the left, with the stream now down to your left, heading across the steep hillside for 500 metres to reach a fork in the path (as the valley opens out into the Newlands Valley). Follow the right-hand grassy path straight on then bending round to the right following the curve of the hillside (Rowling End) before heading very gradually down across the hillside to join the valley road just before Rowling End Farm (hidden by trees just down to your left) - NY 234 205.

3. Turn right along the road and follow this for 700 metres then take the stony track that branches off to the left down to reach a ford/FB across Rigg Beck then up to quickly re-join the road. Turn left along the road and follow this down to reach a small road-bridge across Keskadale Beck then continue along the road passing the turning for Newlands Church *(short detour to the church)* to reach Chapel Bridge across Newlands Beck. Cross this bridge and continue along the road up into Little Town.

4. As you reach Little Town ignore the first track to the right just before the buildings but continue along the road for 50 metres then take the next stony track to the right back on yourself that leads through a gate by the entrance to a house (SP 'Hause Gate leading to Cat Bells' and National Trust sign 'Yewthwaite'). Follow the track rising up above the house then swinging sharply left up to join a wall on your left (Little Town down to your left). Continue up along the track alongside this wall on your left for 300 metres then, where the wall gently curves left, take the path off to the right. Follow this path rising up along the foot of the steep slope (High Crags) for 400

metres then follow the path as it bends left and fords Yewthwaite Gill (stream), after which follow the path climbing quite steeply up across scree and boulders (cairns), at the top of which (where the gradient eases) you come to a path junction (cairn), with a stone-built sheepfold just across to your right. Carry straight on *(ignore path to left)* rising up to reach the top of the 'pass' of Hause Gate, with the steep slopes of Maiden Moor to your right and Cat Bells rising up across to your left (Borrowdale falling away in front of you down towards Derwent Water) - NY 244 192.

5. At Hause Gate, turn left along the clear path across the 'saddle' of land then climbing steadily up across the broad ridge for 0.75 km to reach the domed summit of Cat Bells. From the top of Cat Bells, continue straight on across the summit to quickly reach the start of the long, steep and rocky descent that leads down from the summit (heading down along the crest of the ridge). Follow the path straight down this steep, rocky ridge to reach a small 'saddle' of land and a junction of paths at the bottom of the steep, rocky section. Continue straight on along the crest of the fairly narrow, undulating ridge (Skelgill Bank) for 0.75 km to reach a 'short but steep' rocky section. Head down this rocky section *(memorial plaque to Thomas Arthur Leonard, 'father of the open air movement')* then follow the path straight on to soon reach the end of the ridge and an abrupt steep slope in front of you. Follow the clear path winding down the hillside then, as you approach the road at Hawes End and the path forks, follow the left-hand path down for 150 metres then turn right down a stone-pitched path to reach the road-turning towards 'Skelgill' by its junction with the hair-pin bend at Hawes End (NY 247 212).

6. Turn right to quickly reach the hair-pin bend where you carry straight on down along the road towards 'Portinscale, Keswick', over a cattle grid and winding down then continue straight on for 600 metres to reach a road junction where you head left (road sign 'Stair, Newlands Valley, Buttermere'). Follow this road straight on to quickly reach another road junction where you head left again to reach the Swinside Inn. Follow the road straight on down through

the hamlet passing the pub on your right (road sign 'Stair, Buttermere') then, where the road bends down to the left after 100 metres, take the enclosed track that branches off to the right (SP). Follow this track down and through a gate then straight on across the valley floor then, where the track opens out onto a field, head to the right along the unenclosed grassy track across the middle of the field. As you reach the other side of the field follow the grassy track bending sharp left alongside the fence/hedge on your right to reach Newlands Beck (NY 239 218).

7. As you reach the riverbank, head straight on along the clear path alongside Newlands Beck on your left *(ignore stone bridge after a short distance)* and follow this downstream for 1.25 km to reach a road bridge across Newlands Beck. Turn left over the bridge then walk on to quickly reach the cluster of farm buildings of Little Braithwaite. Just as you reach these buildings (as the road begins to rise up) turn right (SP 'Braithwaite') and follow the track through the farmyard passing a barn on your left, after which follow the track straight on alongside Newlands Beck on your right for 300 metres then curving round to the right (still with Newlands Beck on your right) to soon reach the confluence of Newlands Beck with Coledale Beck in front of you (hidden by bushes). Follow the track bending left up alongside Coledale Beck (leaving Newlands Beck behind) to soon reach a FB across Coledale Beck (where the track fords the stream). Cross the FB then turn left along the riverside path (Coledale Beck now on your left) to quickly reach a stile that leads into the caravan/campsite. Cross the stile and follow the riverside path through the campsite back into Braithwaite.

Braithwaite Walking Weekend
- Sunday Walk -
Braithwaite, Coledale Hause, Grisedale Pike & Sleet How

WALK INFORMATION

Highlights: A classic U-shaped glaciated valley, abandoned mines, crags and cascading cataracts, spectacular cliffs, ridge walking at its best, incredible views and an exciting descent.

Distance: 7 miles (11.25 km)   Time: Allow 4 hours

Map: OS Explorer map OL4 - *always take a map on your walk.*

Refreshments: Pubs and shop at Braithwaite. No facilities en route.

Terrain: A track leads gradually up into Coledale, at the head of which a rough stony track climbs steadily up to reach Coledale Hause (mountain pass). A path then heads up across the flanks of Sand Hill to reach the high-level ridge above Hobcarton Crag (cliffs). This ridge is then followed up onto the summit of Grisedale Pike (exposed to the elements) with steep slopes on virtually all sides and rough/rocky terrain. The path down from this summit is initially steep and rocky along a fairly narrow arête, however, the gradient soon eases and a clear path leads all the way back down to Braithwaite.

Highest point: Grisedale Pike - 791 metres above sea level.

Total ascent: 690 metres

Escape Route: From Coledale Hause, re-trace your steps back down to Force Crag Mines at the head of Coledale.

Caution: **Mountain Walk.** This is a strenuous walk to the summit of Grisedale Pike, with mountainous terrain for most of the walk. Coledale Beck is crossed via stepping-stones, which may be difficult after heavy rain. Do not explore the old mine workings. Coledale Hause may be confusing in mist. There are sheer crags on the northern side of the ridge above Hobcarton Crag leading to Grisedale Pike - keep to the path. The initial descent from Grisedale Pike is steep down an exposed and fairly narrow arête (loose rocks). OS map and compass essential. Do not attempt this walk in bad weather.

POINTS OF INTEREST

Coledale cuts deeply into the surrounding fells behind Braithwaite, a classic example of a glaciated U-shaped valley. It is a valley of stark beauty with steep slopes rising up to rocky fell-tops. An old miners' track leads straight into the heart of the mountains at the head of the valley, where you will find the crumbling remains of Force Crag Mine, with old spoil heaps, levels and buildings all around. Decades of mining, with little regard for the natural environment, have left their mark in quite a dramatic way; even the streams have turned orange! These mines were operational until relatively recently, extracting barytes from the surrounding hills that was used in the manufacture of paint and glass.

The impressive Force Crag rises up above these mines, the name of which literally means 'waterfall crag'. The main waterfall is Low Force (High Force tumbles down the crags above) where the delightfully named Pudding Beck cascades down the middle of these crags. A track climbs up across the southern side of Force Crag alongside the tumbling waters of the infant Coledale Beck to reach the mountain pass of Coledale Hause at the head of both Coledale Beck and Liza Beck in the shadow of Eel Crag (839m). From Coledale Hause it is a relatively short walk to the high-level ridge above Hobcarton Crag. This is one of those 'wow' moments with an incredible wall of crags in front of you plunging down into the valley of Hobcarton Gill. An excellent ridge walk now ensues up onto the summit of Grisedale Pike. This small rocky summit is a superb viewpoint with the Skiddaw range, Derwent Water, Causey Pike, High Spy, Dale Head, Grasmoor and Hopegill Head all in clear view. There are also expansive views of the vast Thornthwaite Forest, also known as Whinlatter Forest Park, which cloaks the hills on either side of Whinlatter Pass. This was one of the first forests to be planted by the newly created Forestry Commission after World War One when timber was in short supply. The forest is now managed primarily for recreation. Grisedale Pike rises up above four valleys, namely Coledale, Hobcarton Gill, Sanderson Gill and Grisedale Gill, although the mountain stands at the head of only one of them - Grisedale Gill - hence its name. The name means 'valley of the wild boar' and is one of three such named valleys in the Lake District.

BRAITHWAITE SUNDAY WALK

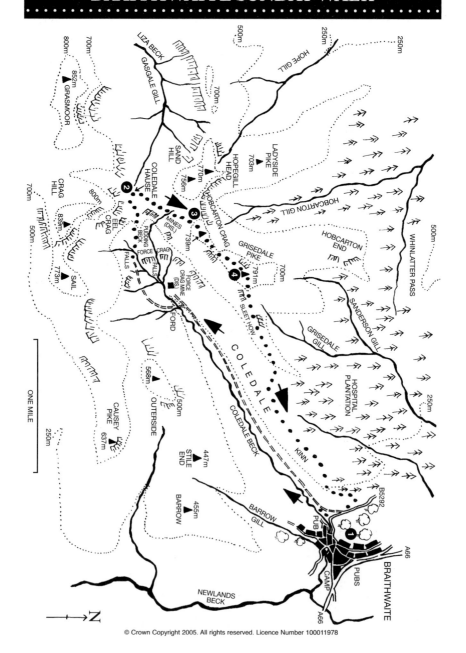

64

THE WALK

1. From the Royal Oak in the centre of Braithwaite (with your back to the pub), head left along the B5292 'Whinlatter Pass' road towards Cockermouth and follow this road up out of the village alongside Coledale Beck on your left. Just after leaving the village, as the road bends up to the right, take the wide footpath that leads up to the left, marked by an iron bench (SP 'Coledale Hause'). Follow this path climbing up across the steep hillside, with Coledale Beck down to your left *(steep drops to the side of the path)* to join a gravel track (miners' track). Turn left along this track and follow this for 3 km up into Coledale. As you approach the abandoned Force Crag Mines at the head of the valley (sheltering below the impressive outcrops of Force Crag) the track forks - follow the track down to the left to reach a ford/stepping-stones across Coledale Beck. After the stream, follow the rough track climbing up the hillside ahead then bending up to the right. The track now climbs steadily up across the hillside, with the head of Coledale down to your right, and leads up passing above Coledale Beck (waterfalls) down to your right (with Force Crag across to your right) and up onto the 'saddle' of land to the left of Force Crag (you emerge into a vast 'bowl' of land surrounded by mountains). As you reach the 'saddle' of land above the waterfalls, the track levels out and you soon reach a ford across the infant Coledale Beck. After the stream, follow the path straight on steadily climbing up through this mountainous 'bowl' then winding steeply up onto the col of Coledale Hause (mountain pass), with Eel Crag to your left (NY 189 212).

2. As you get to the top of the pass (with the col of Coledale Hause just across to your right) you come to a fork in the path (small cairn) - follow the path to the right down into the bottom of the col of Coledale Hause (between Sand Hill to the north and Eel Crag to the south) where you reach another path junction (at the foot of Sand Hill). Take the right-hand path and follow it, level at first then gradually rising up across the south-eastern slopes of Sand Hill to reach some fenced-off old mines shafts. Follow the path passing

these fenced-off shafts, just after which the path steepens and leads up to reach the path along the crest of Hobcarton Crag (cairn) and an old stone wall interspersed with rusty old fence posts, with the valley of Hobcarton Gill falling away in front of you (NY 193 220). *(Warning - sheer cliffs and crags beyond this old wall)*.

3. Follow the clear path straight on (to the right) alongside the old wall on your left rising up to quickly reach the 'summit' of Grisedale Pike's south-western subsidiary top (739 metres). From this subsidiary top, carry straight on along the ridge-top path dropping down at first then straight on along the top of the fairly narrow ridge (with the old wall on your left) before climbing up onto the conical summit of Grisedale Pike (791 metres), with the valley of Hobcarton Gill falling away to your left and Coledale to your right (NY 198 226).

4. As you reach the rocky summit of Grisedale Pike, carry straight on across the fairly narrow summit ridge for 75 metres then, where the old wall bends sharply away to the left (two old rusty fence posts), you come to a fork in the path (with a steep slope in front of you dropping down into Grisedale valley) where you follow the path to the right *(follow the slightly higher of the two paths to the right, although both lead to the top of the arête)* bearing down to quickly reach the top of the steep, rocky arête that leads (eastwards) down from the summit (Sleet How Ridge). Follow this arête steeply down *(take care)*, with Grisedale Gill falling steeply away to your left and Coledale to your right. The steep section is soon over (after about 300 metres), and a path leads straight on along the crest of the ridge (Sleet How) between Grisedale and Coledale to reach a fork in the path after a further 700 metres. Follow the path heading down to the right from the ridge, slanting down across the steep hillside (with Coledale falling away to your right). After a while, the path turns quite steeply to the right down the grassy slope onto a broad, grassy ridge of land (Kinn) where the path levels out. Follow the path straight on across this broad ridge, then gently rising up across the top of this ridge, with Hospital Plantation across to your left and Coledale down to your right, to reach a fence corner on your left

(NY 220 233). Follow the path straight on alongside this fence on your left gradually dropping down at first, then more steeply down and passing a plantation on your left *(ignore any paths off to the right)* down to reach a stile over a fence across your path (by a small clump of trees). Cross the stile and follow the path straight on with the plantation just across to your left *(Bassenthwaite Lake in the distance)* heading steadily down across the hillside for 400 metres then, where you reach the steep slope above the Whinlatter Pass road, follow the path bending sharp right, gradually slanting down across the hillside to join this road (by its junction with the Force Crag miners' track). Turn right down along the road back into Braithwaite.

BUTTERMERE

The village of Buttermere lies on a narrow strip of meadowland between Crummock Water and Buttermere (lake). A build-up of silts from Mill Beck and Sourmilk Gill over thousands of years has created this fertile alluvial plain, so dividing the once large lake that filled the Buttermere Valley following the last Ice Age. The name of Buttermere is probably derived from 'buthar's mere', Buthar being a long forgotten Norse chief who once ruled the surrounding area. It boasts an idyllic setting amongst high fells that soar skywards from the flat valley pastures and lapping waters of the lake. The village is a picturesque jumble of old farms, cottages, small church and two old inns set around Mill Beck. There was a third inn, the Buttermere Hotel, which was converted into a Youth Hostel many years ago. In Victorian times, these inns provided refreshments for travellers who came in search of 'Picturesque Nature'. It became a popular destination on the 22-mile Buttermere Round carriage excursion, a bone-shaking journey from Keswick via Honister Pass, Buttermere and Newlands Hause. Buttermere's tiny church is dedicated to St James, and stands on a knoll just above the village. It was built in 1840 in typical Lakeland style, replacing a smaller church, and has twelve steps leading up to it, one for each of the Apostles. On a window ledge inside the church is a memorial plaque to A. Wainwright, fell-walker and guidebook writer. The view from this window is one of tranquil beauty across Buttermere towards Haystacks in the distance where Wainwright's ashes are scattered. Up until the 18th Century the church was served by a reader, as the community was too small to warrant a clergyman. He earned a modest salary which was supplemented by the rights of whittle-gate (a meal at every farmhouse in the parish) and goose-gate (his geese to roam on the common) as well as a clog and clothing allowance.

THE VILLAGE

Buttermere has two inns, youth hostel, campsite, bed & breakfast, self-catering apartments, craft shop, ice cream parlour, cafe, car park, public payphone, toilets, and bus service.

ACCOMMODATION

Tourist Information Centre, Cockermouth   01900 822634

BUTTERMERE PUBS

Bridge Hotel, Buttermere   **017687 70252**
Converted from use as a corn mill to a hotel in 1735, the name changed for a while to the Victoria after Queen Victoria and the Prince Consort were entertained here in 1850. A comfortable two-roomed bar to the rear of the hotel caters for the many visitors to the area, with lots of memorabilia around the walls including an old advertising sign that offers the services of guides to take tourists to Scale Force and the surrounding mountains.

Fish Hotel, Buttermere   **017687 70253**
Originally known as the Inn at Buttermere, it became a popular destination for anglers drawn to the nearby lakes. Famed for its associations with the Maid of Buttermere, the old part of this hotel is now used as a lounge, bar and dining area for residents while a large open plan extension at the back of the hotel serves the needs of hungry and thirsty walkers.

PUBS ALONG THE WALKS

Kirkstile Inn, Loweswater: 01900 85219

Buttermere Walking Weekend
- Saturday Walk -
Buttermere, Scale Force, Red Pike, High Stile & Scarth Gap Pass

WALK INFORMATION

Highlights: The Beauty of Buttermere, Lakeland's highest waterfall, the red mountain, a high-level route between two valleys and a stroll alongside Buthar's mere.

Distance: 8.75 miles (14 km) Time: Allow 6 hours

Map: OS Explorer map OL4 - *always take a map on your walk.*

Refreshments: Pubs and cafe/shop at Buttermere. No facilities en route.

Terrain: A track/path leads to Scale Force, with boggy/rough ground in places. A pitched-stone path then climbs steeply up alongside this waterfall, above which the path heads up through the shallow valley of Scale Beck before turning up to the escarpment of Lingcomb Edge. A path follows this edge up onto Red Pike (755m) then along the broad, mountainous ridge up onto the rocky summit of High Stile. A rocky path then follows the undulating mountainous ridge all the way to Scarth Gap, with a steep descent down Gamlin End. From Scarth Gap a clear path (rough and rocky in places) leads down to join the lakeside path, which leads through Burtness Wood back to Buttermere.

Highest point: High Stile - 807 metres above sea level.

Total ascent: 805 metres

Escape Route:	From Red Pike, head east down into The Saddle (between Red Pike and Dodd) and down to reach Bleaberry Tarn from where a path leads down through Burtness Wood to the FB across Buttermere Dubs. *NB: The descent is steep with loose rocks.*
Caution	**Mountain Walk.** This is a strenuous walk up to and along the High Stile ridge, with mountainous terrain and rocky paths for most of the way. There are several steep sections, particularly Scale Force, Gamlin End and the descent from Seat. There are steep drops to the side of the path in places, especially Scale Force and the northern edge of the broad High Stile ridge between Red Pike and Scarth Gap (crags and gullies). OS map and compass essential. Do not attempt this walk in bad weather.

Buttermere

POINTS OF INTEREST

Over 200 years ago the Fish Hotel was at the centre of a scandal that gripped the nation. In 1792 a gentleman called Joseph Budworth stayed at the Fish Hotel whilst preparing a book entitled A Fortnight's Ramble to the Lakes. He was so struck by the beauty of Mary Robinson, the attractive young daughter of the landlord of the Fish Hotel, that he poetically described her good looks in his writings. She became something of a tourist attraction, much to her embarrassment! In 1802 a distinguished gentleman claiming to be the Hon. Colonel Alexander Augustus Hope MP, the younger brother of the Earl of Hopetoun, heard of this Beauty of Buttermere and came to the village in the hope of wooing her. Hope swept her off her feet and they were married within two months. Coleridge reported this whirlwind romance in the London Morning Post calling it the 'Romantic Marriage', for in those days it was very unusual for a country girl to marry into the gentry. Everything was going well until the Earl of Hopetoun saw the newspaper article and publicly declared that his brother was travelling around Europe and that the gentleman claiming to be his brother up in Cumberland must be an imposter. The police were waiting for Hope when he returned from his honeymoon. It turned out that this gentleman was actually John Hatfield, a liar, forger and bigamist. He was tried at Carlisle, not for bigamy and deserting his children, but for franking his letters as an MP; defrauding the Post Office then was a capital offence. He was hanged in 1803, whilst Mary married a local farmer and lived happily ever after at Caldbeck. This story has been the inspiration for many books and plays.

Scale Force is the highest waterfall in the Lake District, a slender cascade that plunges over 150-ft down through a dramatic rocky ravine with overhanging trees. The relatively easy walk from Buttermere to the foot of the waterfall is as popular today as it was when Scale Force was the highlight of the fashionable 'Buttermere Round' carriage excursion. The Victorian tourists would have strolled the short distance from Buttermere to the shores of Crummock Water and then paid a shilling to be rowed across the lake to walk the final leg up Scale Beck to the falls. The steep climb up alongside the ravine is superb, with the foaming waters of Scale Force plunging into the dark depths. Above the falls, a path leads up through the shallow valley before climbing across heather-covered slopes to the abrupt escarpment of Lingcomb Edge, with wonderful views down towards Buttermere village far below. This edge leads steadily up onto the domed summit of Buttermere's Red Pike (there is another Red Pike nearby, which towers above Wasdale), an unrivalled vantage point with far-reaching views. Red Pike marks the north-western end of the mountainous ridge that separates the Buttermere Valley from Ennerdale. This ridge runs for about two miles in a south-easterly direction, with the rocky summits of High Stile and High Crag punctuating the ridge along the way. Red Pike's northern and eastern slopes are scree-covered and fall steeply away into the cove that cradles Bleaberry Tarn. These scree slopes are tinged a pastel red colour, hence the name of the mountain, as the underlying rocks contain syenite, an igneous rock similar to granite. The cove of Bleaberry Tarn, along with its issuing stream of Sourmilk Gill, is a classic example of a hanging valley where glacial erosion during the last Ice Age scoured away the stream's natural watercourse and created a near-vertical drop down which Sourmilk Gill now cascades for over 1,000 feet churning into a white froth as it tumbles over rocks, hence its name. There are three coves, or combs, along the Buttermere side of this mountainous ridge (Ling Comb, Bleaberry Comb and Burtness Comb), separated by the three summits of Red Pike, High Stile and High Crag.

From the saddle of land to the south of Red Pike, high above Bleaberry Comb, a rough path climbs up onto the rocky crown of High Stile. This is not the true summit of High Stile, for this lies a short distance away on a fairly narrow mountainous spur of land that juts out from the main ridge into the Buttermere Valley, marked by the middle of three cairns (807 metres). From High Stile, a wonderful mountain walk ensues across the top of the fairly narrow ridge between Buttermere and Ennerdale all the way to the rocky rise of Seat at the end of the ridge. This is one of the finest ridge walks in Lakeland, with precipitous cliffs, crags and gullies falling away to your left down into Burtness Comb, including Eagle Crag and Comb Crags. Across to your right are the upper reaches of Ennerdale framed by the mountains of

Pillar, Kirk Fell and Great Gable. This is a remote and lonely valley where steps are being taken to bring it back to somewhere near its natural state through the selective felling of coniferous trees and planting of deciduous species, grazing management and generally allowing nature to do its work. This is the Wild Ennerdale Project, whose vision is *"to allow the evolution of Ennerdale as a wild valley for the benefit of people relying more on natural processes to shape its landscape and ecology."*

Scarth Gap Pass is an ancient packhorse route that starts at Gatesgarth Farm in the Buttermere Valley and heads over the fells into the upper reaches of Ennerdale. Scarth Gap is the 'saddle' of land between the mountains of High Crag and Haystacks; the word 'scarth' originates from Old Norse and means a 'notch in the ridge'. The contrast between the different rock types of the Lake District is shown to good effect from Scarth Gap, as the head of the Buttermere Valley is where the Borrowdale volcanics meet Skiddaw Slate. From here, the difference between craggy Haystacks (volcanic) and the smooth slopes of Robinson (slate) can be easily seen. Haystacks has an unusual name that is thought to be derived from the Old Norse words for 'high rocks'.

The lake of Buttermere is a tranquil sheet of water, its deep waters home to perch, pike, trout and char, a deepwater trout peculiar to the Lake District and a relic from the last Ice Age. Along its southern shoreline is Burtness Wood, an ancient mixed woodland owned and managed by the National Trust, who also own the lake. The National Trust are gradually felling the much maligned larch trees and replacing them with native oak.

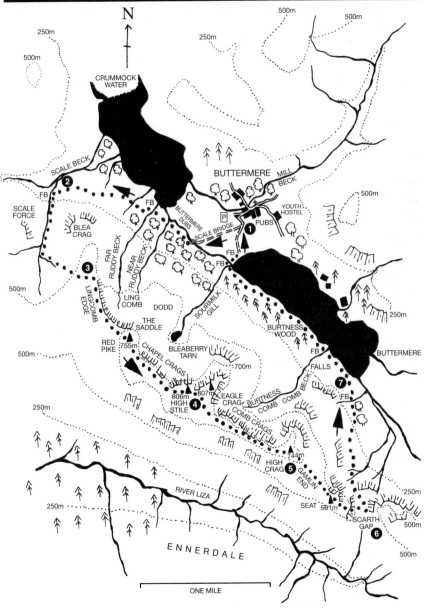

THE WALK

1. Leave Buttermere along the track passing to the left side of the Fish Hotel (SP 'Public Bridleway, Buttermere Lake, Scale Bridge, Private Road'). Just after you have passed the Fish Hotel follow the track bending sharp left then, just before the track bends sharp right, head right through a gate along an enclosed track. Follow this track straight on across fields then curving to the right to join Buttermere Dubs (stream) on your left which you follow to soon reach Scale Bridge across Buttermere Dubs. Cross Scale Bridge, after which turn right along the stony track heading along the foot of the steep wooded lower slopes of Red Pike (Buttermere Dubs just to your right) then, as you approach the head of Crummock Water, the path bears away from Buttermere Dubs (still skirting across the foot of the steep wooded hillside) and leads on to reach a wooden FB across Far Ruddy Beck (head of Crummock Water across to your right) - *ignore path off to the right just before this FB.* After the FB follow the stony path up to the left then bearing to the right and gradually rising up across the hillside. The path soon levels out for a short distance, then gently rises up for 250 metres to reach a path junction on a low 'shoulder' of land (lower northern slopes of Lingcomb Edge) marked by a large cairn. Turn sharp left at this path junction along a clear path heading up the hillside for 150 metres to reach the foot of the steep mountainside where you follow the rocky path to the right along the foot of this steep slope. Follow this path (cairns) bearing very gradually round to the left (boggy in places) into the side-valley of Scale Beck all the way to reach a small gate in a wall across your path (with Scale Beck beyond). *To view Scale Force, drop down to the FB and head left just before it.*

2. After the gate, turn immediately left up along a pitched-stone path climbing steeply up with the wall on your left at first. The path soon bends away from the wall and winds steeply up (pitched-stone path) with the ravine of Scale Force to your right. The gradient eases as you pass above the head of the waterfall just down to your right *(danger: keep to the path, steep drops)* - continue along the rocky path

heading gradually up through the sparsely wooded upper reaches of the ravine (stream on your right) passing more smaller waterfalls with some easy scrambling over rocks. Beyond this rocky/scrambling section, continue along the path heading up through the upper reaches of the valley *(ignore path that turns steeply up to the left)* alongside the stream on your right for 500 metres to reach a small side-stream where you follow the path turning sharp left heading up with this side-stream on your right (NY 149 164). Follow this stony path climbing steadily up across the hillside for 0.75 km to reach the escarpment of Lingcomb Edge above the cove of Ling Comb *(Buttermere village comes into view far below).*

3. As you reach the rim of Lingcomb Edge, turn right along the clear path (with Red Pike ahead) along the top of Lingcomb Edge climbing gradually up for 0.75 km *(take care, sheer drop - walk slightly to your right away from the edge)* before a final steep pull up across rocks zigzagging up to the summit cairn on Red Pike (NY 161 154). *Caution: sheer slopes on Red Pike's northern and eastern face).* As you reach the summit cairn, head to the right (south) gently dropping down from the summit across the broad ridge (grassy/rocky terrain), with the rim of the cove that encircles Bleaberry Tarn just across to your left, for 400 metres down onto the flat grassy 'saddle' between Red Pike and High Stile. Head straight on across this saddle of land *(in a south-easterly direction)*, keeping fairly close to the rim of Bleaberry Comb to your left, and then gently rising up across undulating, rocky terrain (still with the rim of the crags to your left). You then pass the head of a steep scree gully (Chapel Crags Gully), after which the path climbs steeply up (with Chapel Crags to your left) across rocks following a line of rusty old fence posts up onto the broad rocky crown of High Stile, marked by a large cairn (806 metres - NY 167 147). *NB: these old fence posts are your navigational guide across High Stile and High Crag.* Carry straight on following the line of old fence posts across the rocky summit (passing the summit cairn) to quickly reach the sheer cliffs above Bleaberry Comb in front of you, where you follow the old fence posts to the right (cliffs just to your left) then, after 50 metres, follow the fence posts curving to the left gently

rising up (line of cairns) to soon reach a cairn by a fence corner (where the fence bends sharp right). *The summit cairn of High Stile (807 metres) lies 150 metres straight on (east) from this fence corner midway along the fairly narrow mountainous spur that juts out into the Buttermere Valley (NY 170 148).*

4. As you reach the cairn by the fence corner near the summit of High Stile, head to the right alongside the old fence posts and follow these gently dropping down across rocky terrain then, after 100 metres, follow the fence posts bending to the right downhill. Head down for 100 metres then head left alongside the fence posts down onto the fairly narrow mountainous ridge of land between the Buttermere Valley (left) and Ennerdale (right). Follow the path straight on along the crest of this undulating mountainous ridge (still following the fence posts) for 1km, with the sheer crags and gullies of Comb Crags to your left, then steadily rising up onto the summit of High Crag, marked by a cairn (NY 180 141).

5. From High Crag's summit cairn, carry straight on *(south-easterly direction)* along a stony path winding steeply down Gamlin End, with scree and rocks at first and then a pitched-stone path that leads down onto the saddle of land between High Crag and Seat (small tarn just to your right). As you reach this saddle of land, carry straight on climbing up onto the small 'rise' of Seat (end of the High Stile ridge). Follow the path meandering across the left-hand side of the undulating rocky 'summit' of Seat then, as you reach the end of the summit (left-hand side), a pitched-stone path winds steeply down (rocky sections) to reach a 'crossroads' of paths at Scarth Gap (saddle of land between Seat and Haystacks), marked by a large cairn (NY 189 134).

6. As you reach this crossroads of paths (Scarth Gap) turn left along the clear path across rocky/heather terrain (cairns) for 200 metres to reach the brow of the steep descent back down into the Buttermere Valley (Scarth Gap Pass). Follow the wide rocky path quite steeply down (cairns) all the way to reach a gap in a wall across your path. After this wall gap the gradient eases and you follow the path

straight on heading gradually down across the hillside then more distinctly down towards the head of Buttermere (lake) to reach a bridle-gate in a fence across your path. Head through the gate and follow the path steadily down alongside an old wall on your right to reach a FB (wooden planks) across a small stream just by some woodland on your right. After the FB, follow the path down with the woodland on your right then, where this woodland ends (fence corner on your right), carry straight on bearing down across the hillside to join a broad level path alongside a wall overlooking the head of Buttermere (lake) at the bottom of the valley (NY 186 149).

7. Turn left along this path and follow it along the shore of Buttermere for 0.5 km to reach a FB across Comb Beck (waterfalls), after which carry straight on *(ignore bridleway off to the left after a short distance)* along the lakeside path (SP 'Permissive Path and Buttermere shore') to reach a gate in a wall that leads into Burtness Wood. Follow this clear path straight on through woodland along the shore of Buttermere (lake) for 1.5 km all the way to reach the end of the lake where you follow the gravel path to the right through a gate in the wall and over a FB across Sourmilk Gill (which feeds into the lake). After the FB, head on to quickly reach a larger FB across Buttermere Dubs (stream issuing from the lake), after which follow the gravel path straight on (hedgerow on your left) to join a track in the field corner where you head left through a gate. Follow the enclosed track straight on all the way back into Buttermere.

Buttermere Walking Weekend
- Sunday Walk -
Buttermere, Rannerdale, Crummock Water & Loweswater

WALK INFORMATION

Highlights: A bloody British battle, carpets of bluebells, the crooked lake, red squirrels, the town that never was and a beautiful lakeside path.

Distance: 8.5 miles (13.5 km)   Time: Allow 4 hours

Map: OS Explorer map OL4 - *always take a map on your walk.*

Refreshments: Pubs and cafe/shop at Buttermere. Pub at Loweswater.

Terrain: Lakeside path virtually all the way with rough pastureland, woodland and boggy ground in places. There are some quiet lanes around Loweswater and also a fairly steep climb at the start of the walk to the head of Rannerdale.

Highest point: (head of) Rannerdale - 300 metres above sea level.

Total ascent: 220 metres

Caution: The climb up out of Buttermere to the head of Rannerdale is steep. Take care walking along the roads around Loweswater. There are several small streams to cross and boggy ground around Scale Beck.

POINTS OF INTEREST

The high mountains that surround Buttermere offered protection from invading armies centuries ago. The Buttermere Valley was one of the few places in the North of England that the Celtic tribes kept from invading Normans, with a battle fought in Rannerdale. Following the Norman Conquest in 1066, Norman soldiers pushed northwards to crush the unruly tribes; however, as they made their way through the Buttermere Valley they were ambushed and defeated by British warriors. The valley is famed for its spring display of bluebells that, according to folklore, sprung up from the blood of the slain soldiers. Maybe there is some truth in this tale for the Lake District did not appear in the Domesday Book and remained an isolated area for centuries where ancient customs and dialect persisted.

The walk around Crummock Water is beautiful, with lapping waters, ancient woodland and towering mountains. The lake is almost twice the size of Buttermere and lies on Skiddaw Slate, the oldest of the Lakeland rocks at 500 million years old. This rock is responsible for the rounded fells of northern Lakeland and breaks up easily to form screes. Crummock Water is drained by the River Cocker, which flows through the pastoral Vale of Lorton before joining the Derwent at Cockermouth. The name of this lake is derived from the Celtic word for 'crooked'. Low Ling Crag juts out into the lake beneath High Ling Crag. This was where the rowing boats dropped off their passengers in Victorian times on their way to visit Scale Force.

The hamlet of Loweswater lies on an alluvial plain between Loweswater (lake) and Crummock Water. Loweswater is the smallest of the three lakes that grace the Buttermere Valley; indeed, following the last Ice Age all three would have been joined together as one large lake. The hamlet consists of a scattering of cottages and farms, with the focal point of the church and inn. There has been a chapel at Loweswater since the 12th Century, possibly established by the monks of St Bees Priory. The church was rebuilt in 1884 in preparation for the influx of people for the soon-to-be-opened mines at Godferhead. Plans were drawn up to build a village but the project never came to fruition.

lake heading very slightly inland across boggy ground (as the southern slopes of Mellbreak curve into the side-valley of Scale Beck) to reach a small FB across Scale Beck and a gate in a fence just beyond. After the gate, follow the path bearing slightly right then straight on through bracken to soon reach another FB across a stream *(also Scale Beck – the stream forks as it flows into Crummock Water)*. After this second FB, carry straight on along the indistinct grassy path gently rising up for 100 metres then bear left across boggy ground gently rising up (path becomes clearer) to soon cross another small stream after which the path gently drops down back towards Crummock Water. You soon join a much clearer stony path (Crummock Water down to your left) which you follow straight on for 750 metres across boggy ground (several small streams to cross) to reach a ford across Far Ruddy Beck *(FB just upstream)*, with the head of Crummock Water across to your left. Cross the stream and head straight on to quickly reach the well-worn Scale Force path. Follow this stony path straight on for 0.75 km to reach Scale Bridge to your left across Buttermere Dubs. Cross this bridge and follow the enclosed track to the right alongside Buttermere Dubs for a short distance then left away from the stream across fields to join a gravel track, which you follow to the left back into Buttermere.

CONISTON

With its feet dipping into Coniston Water and sheltered from westerly storms by mountains, Coniston has the appearance of an alpine village. Its idyllic setting has beguiled many writers and artists to settle here. It retains the character of a Lakeland village, with a thriving local community that manages to strike a balance between tourism and local life; it won the national 'Village of the Year Award 1997'. Coniston was part of Lancashire before Government reorganisation created Cumbria; however, a glance of the map will help to explain this oddity. Coniston appears to be 'cut off' from the rest of the Lake District by mountains and lakes and in the days before modern roads the quickest way to this region was across the treacherous sands of Morecambe Bay. The mountains that surround the village have been the source of its wealth for centuries. Slate has been quarried here since Roman times, although the boom period was during the 18th and 19th Centuries when the demand for roof slates rocketed as houses were built for the expanding urban population. The railway arrived in 1859 when a branch line was constructed between Coniston and the main coastal line at Foxfield Junction. Built by the Furness Railway to service the mines and quarries, it quickly developed into a popular tourist route for almost 100 years until the line closed to passengers in 1957. Along with slate, the area is also rich in mineral deposits, particularly copper. First developed in the 16th Century, the copper mines employed large numbers of men during its heyday in the 19th Century; however, competition from abroad meant that the mines had closed by 1915. Large-scale quarrying has also ended, although two small slate quarries remain.

THE VILLAGE

Coniston has B&Bs, hotels, self catering accommodation, two youth hostels (Coppermines Valley and Holly How) and four pubs. There is a garage, bakery, cafes, restaurant, general stores, small supermarket, outdoor shops, Post Office, newsagent, craft and gift shops, Tourist Information Centre, Barclays Bank, the Ruskin Museum and regular bus services. On Coniston Water you will find the steam-powered yacht 'Gondola', lake cruises on Coniston Launch as well as boat hire.

ACCOMMODATION

Tourist Information Centre, Coniston: 015394 41533

CONISTON PUBS

Black Bull Inn, Coniston   **015394 41335.**
This 16th Century coaching inn has had many famous guests over the years including de Quincey and Turner. The spacious lounge is full of character with oak beams as well as old photographs of Donald Campbell's fateful record attempt. Outlet for Coniston Brewing Co.'s award winning ales, whose brewery is situated at the rear of the pub.

Crown Inn, Coniston   **015394 41243**
This popular village pub has a central bar that serves the spacious and comfortable open-plan lounge, which is separated into distinct drinking areas with some cosy alcoves.

Sun Inn, Coniston   **015394 41248**
This 16th Century inn, with its adjoining Victorian hotel, is situated above the village. The small 'old' bar has a great deal of character with flagstone floors and a magnificent cast-iron range. Donald Campbell stayed at the hotel whilst attempting to break the world water speed record in January 1967.

Yewdale Hotel, Coniston   **015394 41280**
This well-appointed hotel and restaurant dates back to 1896 and was originally part guesthouse and part bank before becoming a hotel; the old bank counter now serves as the bar. Inside, it boasts some lovely carved woodwork, slate table tops and lots of old quarry photographs on the walls.

Coniston Walking Weekend
- Saturday Walk -
Coniston, Low Water, The Old Man of Coniston, Swirl How & Levers Water

WALK INFORMATION

Highlights: An ancient road, abandoned slate quarries, a mysterious mountain, a wonderful ridge walk, one of Lakeland's finest viewpoints, climbing down the prison wall and Elizabethan copper mines.

Distance: 8 miles (12.75 km)   Time: Allow 5 hours

Map: OS Explorer map OL6 - *always take a map on your walk.*

Refreshments: Pubs, cafes and shops at Coniston. No facilities en route.

Terrain: A lane and then a stony track lead up to the foot of the mines at Crowberry Haws. The track then becomes rough/rocky underfoot and climbs steeply up through old mine workings to reach Low Water set beneath The Old Man. A path then climbs steeply up the eastern shoulder of The Old Man (rocky) onto the summit. A path then heads across the top of the broad ridge, with cliffs to your right above Low Water, before dropping down into Levers Hawse (col). A steady climb then ensues across the top of Little How Crags and Great How Crags to the summit of Swirl How. A steep, rocky path then leads down Prison Band (arête) to Swirl Hawse from where a path turns down across boggy ground to Levers Water. A track leads quite steeply down before a path heads off down across the hillside to re-join the track beside Coppermines Youth Hostel. Clear tracks and paths lead back down to Coniston.

Highest point: The Old Man of Coniston - 803 metres above sea level.

Total ascent: 850 metres

Escape Route: From the summit of The Old Man, re-trace your steps back down to Walna Scar Road via Low Water and the old slate quarries.

Caution: **Mountain Walk.** This is a strenuous walk up to the summit of The Old Man, with mountainous terrain for most of the walk. There are a number of steep ascents and descents with rocky terrain, especially the descent down Prison Band. The broad ridge between The Old Man and Swirl How (802 metres) is exposed to the elements with few landmarks; there are also sheer cliffs along the eastern side of this ridge. OS map and compass essential. Do not attempt this walk in bad weather. Do not explore the old mine workings.

Coniston

POINTS OF INTEREST

Walna Scar Road links Coniston with the Duddon Valley and has been in constant use for well over 1,000 years. For centuries it was used as a packhorse route to transport copper ore from the Coniston mines to the port of Ravenglass via the Duddon valley and Eskdale and more recently to service the quarries on the flanks of The Old Man. For most of its length it is a rough and rocky track, although the metalled section out of Coniston allows quick access to the start of the summit climb. From Walna Scar Road, an old quarry track turns off across the foot of The Old Man to reach Crowberry Haws and the start of the steep climb through the old slate quarries. This is a fascinating area with abandoned levels, towering spoil heaps, ruinous buildings and the rusting remains of an aerial ropeway. Above these old quarries lies the mountain tarn of Low Water, which has a spectacular setting beneath imposing crags that rise sheer up to the summit of The Old Man.

The Old Man of Coniston dominates the southern area of the Lake District. It is a mysterious and mystical mountain that some people believe is charged with energy. Stories abound of goblins, fairies and ghosts that are said to shelter in the dark recesses on the side of the mountain, although such tales probably date back to the superstitions of the early Celtic people who lived in the vicinity. Indeed, its name comes from the old Celtic words 'Allt Maen' meaning 'High Rock'. The Old Man is one of the most climbed peaks in England attracting thousands of people every year up to the large summit cairn to enjoy the wonderful views. Stretched out before you is a scene that takes in Coniston Water, Morecambe Bay, Duddon Sands and even the Isle of Man and Blackpool Tower on a clear day, although more impressive is the breathtaking vista of mountain peaks looking northwards. Beware though, for there are sheer crags to the north-east down into the corrie of Low Water. From the summit, a wonderful mountain walk ensues across a broad ridge that takes in Brim Fell, Levers Hawse and Great How Crags all the way to the summit of Swirl How. The scenery is superb with plunging cliffs, deep corries and far-reaching views.

Swirl How lies at the centre of this group of high mountains that rise up to the west of Coniston, known as the Coniston Fells. From its summit water flows east, west and south into the rivers Brathay, Duddon or Coniston Water. There has been some question as to whether Swirl How was the highest of the Coniston Fells, but the official Ordnance Survey measurement now stands at 802 metres, one metre less than The Old Man. This is one of the finest summits in the Lake District with precipitous crags falling steeply away towards the Greenburn valley to the north and down towards Levers Water to the south-east. The views are superlative with almost every major Lakeland mountain in view. From the summit, a steep and rocky path heads down the fairly narrow ridge of Prison Band into the saddle of Swirl Hawse, from where it is a relatively easy walk down to Levers Water. Levers Water lies in a natural glacial combe, although a dam was constructed by the copper miners to provide waterpower for the thirteen waterwheels in the valley below. The issuing stream of Levers Water Beck cascades over impressive waterfalls on its steep descent into the Coppermines Valley.

The scarred landscape of the Coppermines Valley stands in silent tribute to the harsh life men faced centuries ago during the infancy of the Industrial Revolution. Mining has taken place in these hills since Roman times, although it was the skilled German miners brought here from Augsberg by the Company of Mines Royal during the 16th Century who developed the copper mines on a large scale. The heyday was during the mid 19th Century when over 900 men were employed, making it Europe's most important copper producing centre. Life was not 'copper-bottomed' for the miners, as conditions were harsh with frequent accidents caused by rock slips not to mention the backbreaking work carried out with the light of a tallow candle. Cheap imports heralded the terminal decline of the industry and by 1915 production had ceased. The gaunt decaying remains of buildings alongside Church Beck and Levers Water Beck date mainly from the 1800s, although some of these buildings have been given a new lease of life as holiday homes and a Youth Hostel.

CONISTON SATURDAY WALK

1. From the Black Bull Hotel in the centre of Coniston (with your back to the pub) turn right along the main road towards 'Broughton, Ulverston' and over the bridge across Church Beck then follow this road passing the garage on your left just after which take the turning to the right along Station Road (road-sign 'Coniston Old Man'). Follow this road rising steadily up *(ignore any turnings off)*, passing the turning with the Sun Inn down to your right just after which follow the road bending round to the left up to quickly reach a junction of road and lanes - carry straight on along the road ahead climbing quite steeply up through woodland (SP 'Walna Scar, Coniston Old Man'). After 300 metres, the road emerges from the trees and levels out *(Old Man of Coniston comes into view ahead)* then bends sharp left then right before gently rising up for a further 700 metres to reach a gate across the road at the end of the metalled road (start of a rough track - Walna Scar Road) with a parking area just beyond the gate. Head through the gate then turn immediately right (SP 'Old Man, 1.5 miles') along a stony track and follow this gently rising up across the foot of the steep slopes of the Old Man of Coniston. After 900 metres you cross Scrow Beck after which carry straight on up along the track for a further 300 metres then the track heads through a cleft in the low line of rocky/grassy outcrops (Crowberry Haws) just after which follow the track bending sharply round to the left *(views across Coppermines Valley)*. The track now becomes rough and rocky underfoot and climbs more steeply up *(ignore track that branches off to the right after a short distance)* winding up to reach some large spoil heaps of the former slate quarries where you carry on along the rough stony track climbing steeply up to reach another much larger spoil heap and the remains of buildings, rusting rail tracks and metal cables from an aerial ropeway (SD 279 981).

2. From these crumbling buildings on the large spoil heap, continue along the stony track climbing quite steeply up passing between the spoil heaps. The track soon bends up to the left to quickly reach a fork in the track (by an old mine entrance with the pulley system of the aerial ropeway just above) where you head sharp right and follow the rough, stony path climbing up above the spoil heaps. The path now leads steadily up to reach Low Water, set in a corrie beneath The Old Man of Coniston. As Low Water comes into view, head left along a clear rocky path and follow this on (Low Water down to your right) then, as you reach the head of the tarn, the path steepens and zig-zags up across the south wall of this corrie with a final steep climb along a pitched-stone path up onto the top of this south wall (eastern 'shoulder' leading up to the summit of The Old Man). As you reach the top of this 'shoulder', follow the path to the right heading quite steeply up across the top of this broad ridge with a final steep section across rocky ground, after which bear to the right rising up to reach the large cairn and Trig Point on the summit of The Old Man (SD 273 978). *Caution: sheer cliffs to your right.*

3. From the summit cairn, carry straight on (northwards) along the broad, eroded path across the top of the summit ridge, with the rim of the corrie above Low Water to your right *(caution: cliffs and crags)*. After 200 metres, follow the path as it drops down slightly from the summit and then continue straight on *(ignore the two paths off to the left that lead down towards Goat's Water)* along the wide cairned path across the top of the broad ridge (with the rim of the corrie just to your right) gently dropping down into a shallow 'saddle' of land before rising up to reach a small but well-built cairn on the top of Brim Fell (796 metres). From the top of Brim Fell carry straight on along the clear path across the top of the ridge, steadily dropping down for 1 km (ridge gradually narrows) into Levers Hawse, a narrow 'saddle' of land (views to right down to Levers Water and left down to Seathwaite Tarn). From Levers Hawse, follow the clear path straight on climbing steadily up across the top of the ridge (with crags falling away to your right towards the corrie of Levers Water) passing above Little How Crags (to your right) and up to reach the top of Great How Crags after 600 metres, where you follow the path gently curving to the left rising up across the

undulating ridge (Swirl Band) then up across the rocky summit plateau of Swirl How to soon reach the summit cairn, magnificently located above cliffs on its northern face that plunge down into the Greenburn Valley *(caution)* - NY 273 005.

4. A few paces before you reach the summit cairn head to the right (east) along a stony path that leads gently down to soon reach the top of Prison Band, a narrow and rocky arête that descends steeply down (eastwards) from the summit. Follow the rocky path heading steeply down Prison Band, with a number of rocky sections *(easy scrambling)*, all the way down to reach Swirl Hawse (col between Swirl How and Wetherlam). As you reach the crossroads of paths at Swirl Hawse (large cairn) turn right along a clear path heading for Levers Water. Follow this path straight on across the hillside, with the steep slopes of Black Sails rising up to your left. After 300 metres the path gradually drops down across the hillside *(indistinct path in places)* heading across boggy ground to eventually reach the northern shore of Levers Water. A clear path now heads along the left bank (east) of Levers Water all the way to reach the small dam where Levers Water Beck issues from the tarn (SD 282 993).

5. From the small dam, follow the stony track straight on heading down with Levers Water Beck to your right (waterfalls) for 500 metres then, where the track bends sharply round and down to the right, head straight on off this bend along a narrow grassy path (SD 285 989). Follow this path gently slanting down across the hillside (with the old spoil heaps down to your right in the valley of Levers Water Beck) to soon reach an old retaining wall *(course of an old mill race that fed the waterwheels in the Coppermines Valley)* where you head straight on through a breach in this retaining wall then follow the path straight on dropping down then gently curving round to the left following the curve of the hillside (Tongue Brow) then slanting down across rocky ground to join a track just to the left behind the large stone building in the Coppermines Valley. Turn right along this track passing the stone building on your right and follow it through the old workings passing crumbling building and spoil heaps to reach the old wrought-iron gates, beyond which you

join a track, with the whitewashed Coppermines Youth Hostel on your right (SD 289 986).

6. Turn left along this track and follow it heading down through the valley alongside Red Dell Beck on your left for 400 metres then cross a concrete bridge across this stream just by its confluence with Levers Water Beck (the stream now becomes Church Beck). Continue straight on along the stony track with Church Beck on your right to soon reach some impressive waterfalls (Coniston Hydro Electric Scheme) where you continue straight on heading down along the track for 200 metres then turn right over the stone-built Miners Bridge. Immediately after the bridge, turn left along a clear path heading down with the wooded ravine of Church Beck to your left (waterfalls) to reach a gate across the track. Head through the gate and follow the enclosed track straight on heading down, still with Church Beck to your left, to reach a bridge across the side-stream of Scrow Beck (just by a workshop). Cross the bridge and continue straight on along the track bearing away from Church Beck heading across a field to reach a gate across the track beside the farm buildings of Dixon Ground Farm on the outskirts of Coniston. After the gate, head straight on along the metalled lane to soon reach a road junction beside the Sun Inn where you turn left back down into the centre of Coniston.

Coniston Walking Weekend
- Sunday Walk -
Coniston, Coniston Water, Tarn Hows & Yew Tree Farm

WALK INFORMATION

Highlights: The World Water Speed Record, great minds of Victorian England, an idealised landscape, Lakeland's best-known beauty spot, spinning galleries and Beatrix Potter's legacy.

Distance: 7.5 miles (12 km)   Time: Allow 4 hours

Map: OS Explorer map OL7 - *always take a map on your walk.*

Refreshments: Pubs, cafe and shop at Coniston. Yew Tree Farm walkers' tea room.

Terrain: Clear paths and tracks all the way, alongside country lanes, across undulating fields, through woodland and around lakes. There are numerous ascents and descents along this walk.

Highest point: Tarn Hows - 230 metres above sea level.

Total ascent: 310 metres

Caution: This walk crosses a number of roads. Some sections of path may be muddy underfoot.

Coniston Water is the third largest of the lakes at over five miles long, and has a beautiful setting with a sylvan shoreline. It was this abundant timber that attracted the monks of Furness Abbey to come here and set up bloomeries for the smelting of iron-ore. There are two small islands on the lake, Fir Island and Peel Island otherwise known as 'Wild Cat Island' from Arthur Ransome's book 'Swallows and Amazons'. Ransome loved this area and was inspired by memories of boating on Coniston Water and Windermere. The lake has attracted artists and writers over years, none more famous than John Ruskin who moved into Brantwood in 1871 until his death in 1900. He was a remarkable and philanthropic man whose radical ideas influenced many people including Gandhi and Tolstoy. An artist, poet and social reformer who worked tirelessly to improve the conditions of the working classes, he was the most influential art critic of his time and later became the first Slade Professor of the Fine Arts at Oxford as well as founding several educational institutions. Ruskin was a pioneer of the conservation movement and counted Canon Rawnsley and Octavia Hill, co-founders of the National Trust, amongst his followers. Ruskin lies buried in St Andrew's churchyard at Coniston, preferring this quiet corner of old Lancashire to Poet's Corner at Westminster Abbey. The Ruskin Museum is worth visiting for its collection of Ruskin artefacts as well as exhibits relating to the local area. Coniston Water was the scene of a disaster on the 4th January 1967 when Donald Campbell CBE was killed in his boat 'Bluebird K7' whilst attempting to break his own world water speed record of 276.33mph. He reached an estimated 320mph but somersaulted into the air. The shattered boat sank into the lake and lay there undisturbed until divers found his body and the remains of Bluebird in 2001 and brought them to the surface. Donald Campbell now lies buried in the churchyard at Coniston and, when restored in 2010, his boat 'Bluebird K7' will go on display at the Ruskin Museum.

Tarns Hows is a famous beauty spot, its small lake fringed by woodland with the Langdale Pikes rising up in the distance. This area forms part of the Monk Coniston Estate. As the name implies, this area belonged to Furness Abbey in medieval times. During the 18th Century wealthy tourists and industrialists came to Lakeland in search of 'Nature', although their vision was often one of an idealised landscape. Several of these industrialists bought large estates, particularly around Windermere and Coniston Water, and built grand houses. In 1769 the Monk Coniston Estate was bought by the Knott family, who had made their fortune from iron-smelting. They 'improved' the landscape by planting trees, extended the house into a hall around which they laid out formal gardens. In 1835 James Marshall purchased the Monk Coniston Estate, which covered 670 acres stretching from Tarn Hows over to Little Langdale. The Marshall family came from Leeds and had made their money in the flax industry. James Marshall set about to create his own piece of idyllic Lakeland - what the landscape lacked, he simply created or remodelled, including Tarn Hows which is an artificial lake. In the 1920s, the Marshall family's wealth declined and so the estate was bought by Beatrix Potter, who subsequently sold part of the estate at cost price to the National Trust and bequeathed the remainder to them upon her death. Monk Coniston Hall is owned by the National Trust but leased to HF Holidays.

Our route passes the 17th Century Yew Tree Farm, once owned by Beatrix Potter and recently used in the film Miss Potter. It is noted for its spinning gallery as well as its scones for this farm is also a B&B and tearoom; indeed, Beatrix Potter helped set up this tea room as a way for her tenant to supplement his income. Beatrix Potter first came to Near Sawrey (near Hawkshead) in 1896 when she travelled up from London for a family holiday. She fell in love with Lakeland and returned time and again. She later bought Hill Top Farm at Near Sawrey with the royalties from her first book, *The Tale of Peter Rabbit*, published in 1900. She wrote several more books in this farmhouse including *Tom Kitten* and *The Tale of Jemima Puddleduck*. She was a keen conservationist and wanted to preserve the unique character of the Lake District and so, as her book royalties mounted up, she bought local farms and land to protect them from development. Through her friendship with Canon Rawnsley, Beatrix Potter played a key role during the early years of the National Trust and was instrumental in safeguarding the indigenous Herdwick sheep. When she died in 1943, she left over 4,000 acres of land and fifteen farms to the National Trust.

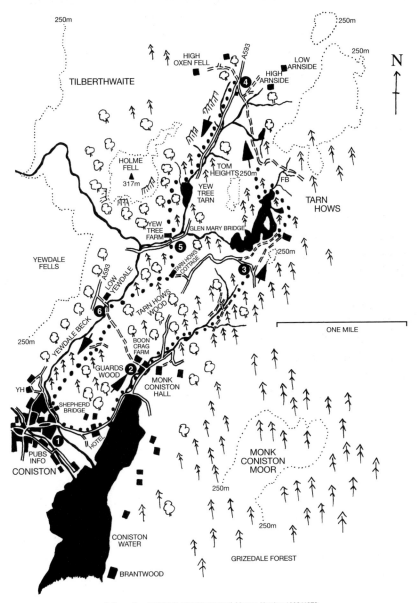

CONISTON SUNDAY WALK

250m

250m

250m

HIGH OXEN FELL

A593

LOW ARNSIDE

HIGH ARNSIDE

4

TILBERTHWAITE

HOLME FELL
▲
317m

TOM HEIGHTS 250m

FB

YEW TREE TARN

TARN HOWS

YEW TREE FARM

GLEN MARY BRIDGE

5

YEWDALE FELLS

A593

LOW YEWDALE

TARN HOWS COTTAGE

250m

3

TARN HOWS WOOD

6

YEWDALE BECK

BOON CRAG FARM

ONE MILE

250m

GUARDS WOOD

2

MONK CONISTON HALL

YH

SHEPHERD BRIDGE

HOTEL

1

PUBS INFO

CONISTON

MONK CONISTON MOOR

250m

250m

CONISTON WATER

GRIZEDALE FOREST

BRANTWOOD

N

THE WALK

1. Leave Coniston along the road towards 'Hawkshead' passing St Andrew's Church on your right and then the Crown Inn on your left. As you reach the edge of the village, carry straight on along the road over a bridge across Yewdale Beck ('Tarn Hows, Hawkshead'), after which follow the roadside path (SP 'Tarn Hows') straight on for 1.25 km *(passing the Waterhead Hotel after 0.5 km)* to reach a road junction at the head of Coniston Water (lake). Follow the roadside path bearing round to the left towards 'Hawkshead, Ambleside' and follow this for 400 metres to reach Boon Crag Farm (National Trust estate office and sawmill - SD 316 983).

2. Carry straight on along the main road *(ignore turning to the left between the farm buildings)* to quickly re-join the roadside path. Follow this roadside path (road on right) bearing very slightly away from the road, over a bridge across a stream and up to join a side-road across your path. Cross over and follow the wide path straight on rising up through woodland (SP 'Tarn Hows') with the stream on your right, passing a small dam/weir just to your right after 350 metres where you continue climbing more steeply up through the woods *(ignore path down to right)*, with the stream now set in a small ravine down to your right, to soon reach a bridge across the stream. After the bridge, follow the wide path straight on rising up through the woodland (stream now to your left) for 400 metres to reach a T-junction with another track. Head left (SP) along the track to soon reach a fork where you carry straight on along the right-hand track (SP 'Tarn Hows, Old Car Park') and follow this climbing quite steeply to join a wall on your left after 300 metres (open fields beyond this wall). Carry straight on up to soon reach a path junction where you head left (SP 'Tarn Hows') to reach the road at the top of the woods *(overlooking Tarn Hows with the Langdale Pikes in the distance)* - SD 330 994.

3. Cross over the road and head through the small parking area opposite to reach a gate at its far end, after which follow the track

straight on for 0.5 km *(views towards Tarn Hows to your left)* to reach a fork in the track. Bear left (SP 'Langdales, circular path') along the rough track down across the wooded hillside and through a gate that leads onto a gravel track. Turn right along this track (SP 'Langdales, circular path'), which rises gently up at first then soon levels and leads on meandering through the woods for 0.75 km *(keep to the clear path)* to eventually emerge from the woods to reach a small bridge (beside a bench) across a stream at the head of the tarn. After the bridge, follow the gravel path bending round to the left around the head of the tarn to soon reach a gate that leads back into woodland. After the gate, follow the path straight on (tarn on your left) for 250 metres to reach a path junction where you turn right along a clear path (SP 'Arnside, Langdales'). Follow this path straight on through the woods heading away from the tarn (path becomes rougher underfoot) to reach a gate that leads onto a walled stony track (NY 331 007). Turn left along this walled track (SP 'Oxenfell, Langdales') and follow it for 1 km to join a metalled lane leading to High Arnside Farm, which you follow straight on (to the left) down to reach the A593 main road.

4. Cross over the main road *(take care)* and take the lane opposite (National Trust sign 'Oxen Fell') then take the footpath immediately to your left through a kissing gate (SP 'Glen Mary Bridge'). After the kissing gate, follow the path straight on keeping close to the wall (and road) on your left and follow this path heading down through the shallow valley (Holme Fell rising up to your right) across boggy ground and down over a small stream after 600 metres, then continue straight on through woodland (still with the wall and road on your left) for a further 600 metres to eventually reach a bridle-gate in the wall to your left (National Trust sign 'Holme Fell') just before the road-bridge across the stream that feeds into Yew Tree Tarn. Do not head through this bridle-gate, but follow the path bearing gently up to the right to soon reach a gate in a wall (stream down to your left), after which head straight on along the wooded banks of the stream to reach a FB across the stream and a 'crossroads' of paths (Yew Tree Tarn just ahead). Do

not cross this FB but turn right (SP 'Holme Fell') through the woodland (tall pine trees) to soon reach a gate in a wall (NY 321 006). After the gate, bear to the left over a little stream then rising up through the trees to quickly reach another stream, after which the path all but levels out and leads on across the wooded hillside. After a while, the path emerges from the trees and passes some large boulders (waymarker post) just after which the path gently rises up to soon reach a gate in a fence on your left (waymarker-post). After the gate head straight on across the sparsely wooded undulating hillside for a short distance then bear round to the right through a narrow 'nick' between the low hillocks, after which carry straight on heading gently down through the shallow 'valley' between the hillocks then, as you approach a wall, the path becomes a track which you follow down to soon reach a kissing-gate beside a gate in this wall, with Yew Tree Farm just ahead. Head through the gate and follow the track down passing in front of Yew Tree Farm to join the main road (A593).

5. At the main road turn right *(take care)* then almost immediately left through a gate in a wall (SP 'Tarn Hows Cottage') then follow the path bearing slightly to the right heading up the fairly steep hillside (marker-posts) to reach a gate set in a fence that juts out into the field just beyond the line of old oak trees near the top of the steep bank. After the gate, head up alongside the fence/wall on your left to reach a gate in the top left corner of the field just below Tarn Hows Cottage. Head left through this gate then immediately right up alongside the wall on your right for a short distance then head right through the second gate (waymarker) that leads onto a track which you follow straight on to quickly reach a fork in the track in front of Tarn Hows Cottage (SD 321 994). Follow the right-hand track (SP 'Coniston, Low Yewdale') through two gates after which follow the path down through Tarn Hows Wood for 0.75 km to join the banks of Yewdale Beck on your right which you follow straight on to reach a kissing-gate at the bottom of the woods. After the gate, head straight across the field to join a stony track beside a bridge across Yewdale Beck (with Low Yewdale Farm just across the river).

6. Turn left along the track (SP 'Boon Crag, Coniston, Cumbria Way') alongside Yewdale Beck on your right then, where Yewdale Beck bends away, continue along the track gently rising up then winding up through a copse of trees, immediately after which head right through a gate (SP 'Coniston, Cumbria Way'). After the gate, head straight across the field to reach a gate in a wall across your path, after which bear left across the field (waymarker-post), over a grassy track then on to join a wall and woodland (Guards Wood) on your left. Carry straight on across the field with this wall/woodland on your left to reach a gate in a wall across your path that leads into woodland (SD 309 984). Follow the wide path straight on through the woods to soon reach a kissing-gate in a wall, after which follow the path leaving the woods behind heading down through gorse bushes *(Coniston comes into view)* then down across the field to reach a gate in a wall. After the gate, continue down alongside the fence on your left to reach a kissing-gate just to the right of the stone-built Dog Kennel *(information shelter)*. After the kissing-gate, follow the path on with the fence on your right down to reach Shepherd Bridge across Yewdale Beck. Head right over the bridge to join a road on the outskirts of Coniston where you head left to reach a road T-junction then right back along the road into the centre of Coniston.

GLENRIDDING

The village of Glenridding lies sheltered at the mouth of Glenridding valley where Glenridding Beck flows into Ullswater. This valley rises steeply up to its source amongst England's finest glaciated mountain landscape where deep corries have been scoured out of the towering east face of Helvellyn. It is this mountain that draws people to Glenridding, for the climb to its summit is one of the most popular in Lakeland, with the magnificent arêtes of Striding Edge and Swirral Edge providing adventurous routes to the summit. Glenridding is an old lead mining village. Greenside Mine first opened in the 17th Century, located in the remote valley of Sticks Gill beneath the steep slopes of Green Side. In 1825 the Greenside Mining Company was formed, which heralded a long period of prosperity and growth. New shafts were opened alongside Sticks Gill and Swart Beck, which tumbles steeply down from Sticks Gill valley to join Glenridding Beck. Mine buildings, dressing and smelting mills were built in the valley, some of which survive today as the Youth Hostel and two outdoor centres as well as rows of old miners' cottages in the village. This fast-flowing stream provided power, augmented by artificial water courses known as leats as well as three small reservoirs in Sticks Gill, Keppel Cove and Brown Cove. At its height the mine employed 300 people and was the largest in the Lake District producing over 1,000 tons of lead annually as well as some silver. In the late 19th Century it became the first mine in the country to use hydroelectric power to drive machinery. But there were setbacks. In 1927 heavy rain caused Keppel Cove dam to breach sending torrents of water down through Glenridding, washing away houses and bridges. Greenside Mine finally closed in 1962 as reserves were exhausted, although it did go out with a bang when the UK Atomic Weapons Research Establishment conducted two experimental explosions deep in the mine to see the effects of shock waves.

THE VILLAGE

Glenridding is a busy village that caters for walkers and climbers with hotels, B&Bs, pub, Youth Hostel (Greenside), bunk barn, campsite, outdoor shop, general stores, craft & gift shops, cafes, restaurant, health centre, garage, bus service, large car park, toilets, National Park Information Centre, Ullswater Steamers and boat hire.

ACCOMMODATION

National Park Information Centre, Glenridding 017684 82414

GLENRIDDING PUBS

Travellers Rest, Glenridding   **017684 82298**
The name of this traditional pub recalls the days when the bridleway over Sticks Pass to the west of Glenridding was a busy packhorse route. Inside this two-roomed pub, there is a comfortable wood-panelled lounge and a cosy bar with a log burning stove and low beams. Once busy with lead miners, it is often thronged with walkers who have just tackled Helvellyn. No accommodation.

Ratcher's Tavern (Glenridding Hotel)   **017684 82228**
Located downstairs in the heart of the Glenridding Hotel, this bar has flagstone floors, an open fire, beamed ceiling, pool table and a lively atmosphere.

Rambler's Bar (Inn on the Lake)   **017684 82444**
The Rambler's Bar adjoins this large lakeside hotel, which boasts extensive grounds, lakeside terrace and a private jetty on Ullswater. The comfortable bar has been furnished in traditional style with wooden floors, a large stone fireplace and an interesting old relief map of the Lake District that depicts the old railway lines.

PUBS ALONG THE WALKS

The Royal, Dockray: 017684 82356

Glenridding Walking Weekend
- Saturday Walk -
Glenridding, Grisedale, Dollywaggon Pike, Helvellyn, White Side & Keppel Cove

Highlights: Lancelot's lake, the valley of the wild boars, a brother's sad farewell, legend of the king's crown, magnificent mountains and amazing arêtes.

Distance: 11.5 miles (18.5 km)   Time: Allow 6 - 7 hours

Map: OS Explorer map OL5 - *always take a map on your walk.*

Refreshments: Pubs, shops and cafes at Glenridding. No facilities en route - take provisions with you.

Terrain: There is a short climb to Lanty's Tarn then down into Grisedale, from where a path heads up through this valley to reach Ruthwaite Lodge (climbing hut) from where the stony path climbs steadily up with a final pull up to Grisedale Tarn. A clear path (pitched-stone in places) zigzags steeply up onto Dollywaggon Pike. A wide path then heads across the top of the broad undulating summit ridge, with sheer crags to your right along its entire eastern edge, taking in the summits of High Crag and Nethermost Pike before a final steady climb onto Helvellyn (wind shelter). The path continues across the top of the summit ridge before dropping down onto Helvellyn Lower Man. A rocky path then drops steeply down its northern ridge (fairly narrow arête) into a saddle of land before rising up onto White Side. A wide path then skirts across the upper slopes of Raise high above Keppel Cove before zigzagging down into the Glenridding valley. A track then leads back down to Glenridding.

Highest point: Helvellyn - 950 metres above sea level.

Total ascent: 970 metres

Escape Route: If weather conditions are bad as you reach the summit ridge on Dollywaggon Pike, re-trace your steps back down to Grisedale Tarn and through Grisedale. *Striding Edge and Swirral Edge are not recommended as escape routes.*

Caution: **Mountain Walk.** This is a strenuous walk to the summit of Helvellyn, with mountainous terrain for most of the walk. There are several steep ascents and descents, as well as steep drops to the side of the path in places, particularly along the eastern edge of the summit ridge between Dollywaggon Pike and Helvellyn Lower Man. This eastern edge is prone to snow cornices in winter (overhanging snow lip) and should be avoided in winter conditions. There are few landmarks on the Helvellyn ridge, which may make navigation difficult. OS map and compass essential. Do not attempt this walk in bad weather.

Lanty's Tarn lies hidden amongst trees on Keldas, named after Lancelot Dobson who lived in Grisedale during the 18th Century. Beyond the tarn, a view unfolds of Grisedale, once the haunt of wild boar for its name is derived from the Old Norse for 'valley of the pigs'. As you head into Grisedale's upper reaches the landscape becomes wilder with the jagged crags of Dollywaggon Pike and High Crag dominating the skyline. Near the head of the valley is Ruthwaite Lodge, originally a shooting lodge but now a climbing hut, beyond which the path climbs up beneath Falcon Crag to reach Grisedale Tarn, which has a wonderful setting beneath Fairfield, Seat Sandal and Dollywaggon Pike. Just off the path is the Brothers Parting Stone where William and Dorothy Wordsworth said goodbye to their brother John in 1800, unaware this would be the last time they would see him. John drowned in 1805 when his ship sank off the Dorset coast. In the 1880s Canon Rawnsley arranged for the stone to be inscribed with a Wordsworth poem. According to legend, in AD945 a battle took place on the mountain pass between Grasmere and Thirlmere where Dunmail, King of Strathclyde, met the forces of King Edmund of England and King Malcolm of Scotland. During the 10th Century the ancient British kingdom of Strathclyde included Cumberland. Dunmail was defeated and his body buried under a cairn at what is now known as Dunmail Raise, however, his remaining soldiers threw his crown into Grisedale Tarn to keep it from enemy hands. Dunmail is often referred to as the last King of Cumbria, because soon afterwards Strathclyde came under Scottish control. The term 'Cumbrian' referred to the Celtic Britons who lived in the Kingdom of Strathclyde. They spoke Cumbric, a language related to Welsh.

From Grisedale Tarn, a path winds steeply up onto Dollywaggon Pike, which marks the southern end of the Helvellyn range of mountains that runs for several miles as a broad ridge between Thirlmere and Ullswater all the way to Clough Head, never dipping below 2,000-ft; Helvellyn lies at the centre of this range. The summit of Dollywaggon Pike lies just up to the right (east) off the main path, a mountainous spur that ends abruptly as an arête known as The Tongue that divides the corries of Ruthwaite Cove and Cock Cove. From Dollywaggon Pike, a path follows the broad ridge northwards up onto High Crag, the summit of which again lies just off the path to the east. The path across this broad ridge keeps on its left-hand (western) side. This western aspect falls away towards Thirlmere as rounded slopes. The contrast with its eastern aspect could not be starker for here is a defined rim of crags that plunge into deep corries, separated by narrow arêtes; a magnificent example of a glaciated mountain landscape. From High Crag, the path crosses the sloping plateau of Nethermost Pike skirting to the west of its 'summit' cairn, although this plateau can hardly be described as a 'pike'! Again, there is an arête on its eastern side that separates Nethermost Cove from Ruthwaite Cove, both examples of hanging valleys. In reality, High Crag and Nethermost Pike are one mountain, with High Crag forming its southern end.

The arrival at the windbreak on the summit plateau of Helvellyn is cause for celebration, for you have walked to the top of England's third highest mountain. From the windbreak, a short detour to the right (east) across the plateau brings you to the top of Striding Edge, the most famous arête in this country. Here you will find the memorial to Charles Gough who died in 1805 after falling from Striding Edge. His body lay undiscovered for three months and when found his faithful dog was still guarding his skeleton, an act of devotion described by Sir Walter Scott and Wordsworth. Far below is Red Tarn, a glacial corrie that lies between Striding Edge and Swirral Edge, its head wall rising 230 metres sheer up to the summit plateau. Helvellyn's summit Trig Point lies a short walk beyond the windbreak close to the eastern rim of the ridge. You have an overwhelming sense of walking on top of the world as you stride northwards across the summit plateau to reach its northern end where the ridge turns left (west) with Brown Cove falling away in front of you and the Swirral Edge path leading steeply down to the right. Our next objective is Helvellyn Little Man, which towers above Brown Cove. From Little Man, there is an exciting descent along an arête that protrudes northwards between Brown Cove and Helvellyn Gill. This arête offers the easiest (relatively speaking!) descent from Helvellyn of any of the eastern arêtes.

GLENRIDDING SATURDAY WALK

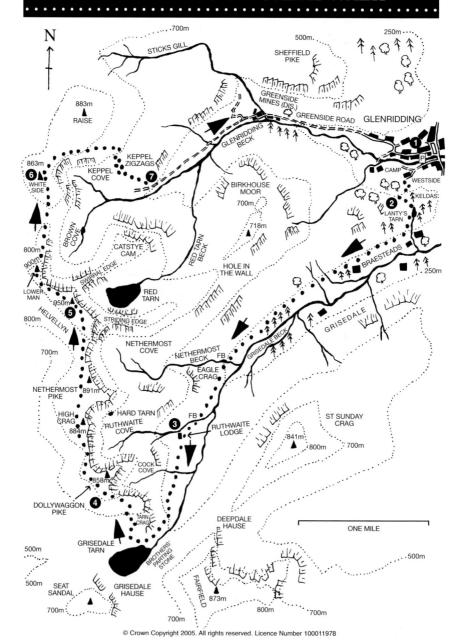

N

.700m

500m.

250m

STICKS GILL

SHEFFIELD
PIKE

GREENSIDE
MINES (DIS.)

GREENSIDE ROAD   GLENRIDDING

883m
RAISE

GLENRIDDING
BECK

863m

6

WHITE
SIDE

KEPPEL
COVE

KEPPEL
ZIGZAGS

7

CAMP

WESTSIDE

KELDAS

BIRKHOUSE
MOOR

700m

2

LANTY'S
TARN

BROWN
COVE

CATSTYE
CAM

718m

BRAESTEADS

250m

800m

900m

SWIRRAL EDGE

RED TARN
BECK

HOLE IN
THE WALL

GRISEDALE

LOWER
MAN

950m

5

RED
TARN

HELVELLYN

800m

STRIDING EDGE

GRISEDALE BECK

700m

NETHERMOST
COVE

NETHERMOST
BECK

FB

EAGLE
CRAG

NETHERMOST
PIKE

891m

HARD TARN

FB

ST SUNDAY
CRAG

HIGH
CRAG

884m

RUTHWAITE
COVE

3

RUTHWAITE
LODGE

841m

800m   700m

COCK
COVE

DOLLYWAGGON
PIKE

858m

4

TARN
CRAG

DEEPDALE
HAUSE

ONE MILE

500m

GRISEDALE
TARN

BROTHERS'
PARTING
STONE

500m

500m

SEAT
SANDAL

GRISEDALE
HAUSE

FAIRFIELD

873m

700m

800m   700m

700m

THE WALK

1. From the bridge across Glenridding Beck in the centre of Glenridding (near the entrance to the car park) take the lane along the left-hand side of the stream (SP 'Mire Beck, Helvellyn'). Follow this lane straight on with the stream on your right passing shops on your left and then between some houses/buildings to reach Eagle Farm on the edge of the village (circular chimneys). Carry straight on along the track leaving Glenridding behind, gently rising up through woodland (stream still on your right) to soon reach a fork in the track. Follow the left-hand track gently rising up away from the stream (SP 'Lanty's Tarn, Helvellyn') to reach a small group of houses (Westside). Carry straight on along the track passing these houses, then continue along the track for a short distance to quickly reach a small FB to your left (end of the track). Cross the FB and follow the pitched-stone path climbing quite steeply up the wooded hillside to reach a kissing-gate at the top of the woods, after which follow the path to the right gently slanting up across the steep hillside then, as you reach a small gate in a wall across your path, head sharp left back on yourself (SP 'Striding Edge, Grisedale') slanting up the hillside to reach a gate in a wall that leads into woodland surrounding Lanty's Tarn (NY 384 164).

2. Follow the path straight on passing Lanty's Tarn on your left to reach the small dam at its far end where you carry straight on dropping down into Grisedale. The path soon bears right down across the hillside then, as you reach the wall at the bottom of this field, you come to a path junction where you head right (SP 'Helvellyn') then, where this path forks after a short distance, follow the right-hand path gently rising up to reach a gap in a wall across your path *(ignore gate in the wall corner just down to your left)*. After the wall gap, head on for a few paces then, where the path forks, follow the left-hand level path keeping close to the wall on your left. Follow this narrow path straight on with the wall on your left heading up into Grisedale (with the valley sweeping away to your left) for 2 km then, just before you reach the end of Broomhill

Plantation on your left (last plantation as you approach the head of the valley), you reach a gate in a fence across your path (NY 365 148). Head through this gate and carry straight on across an area of small hillocks (glacial mounds), over a FB across Nethermostcove Beck to reach a kissing-gate in a wall. Head through the gate and carry straight on along the path climbing steadily into the upper reaches of the valley, with Grisedale Beck set in a rocky ravine to your left (Eagle Crag up to your right), to reach a FB across a stream (Ruthwaitecove Beck). After the FB, follow the path to the right climbing quite steeply up to reach Ruthwaite Lodge climbing hut (NY 355 136).

3. Pass in front of Ruthwaite Lodge and continue along the path heading steadily up through the upper reaches of Grisedale for 1.25 km, with a fairly steep pull up along a stony path passing below Falcon Crag and Tarn Crag, to reach Grisedale Tarn cradled between Fairfield to your left and Dollywaggon Pike to your right (NY 352 123). As you reach the top of the pass where Grisedale Tarn comes into view ahead (large cairn) the path forks - follow the right-hand path straight on across the hillside following the curve of the hillside gently round to the right, with Grisedale Tarn down to your left. The path soon begins to climb up the hillside to your right, steadily at first then zigzagging steeply up (pitched-stone path for most of the way) across the steep hillside all the way up onto Dollywaggon Pike. As you approach the top of the climb there are superb views to the right down into Cock Cove and Grisedale *(take care)* - carry on along the path rising up to soon reach the broad summit ridge (path levels out) and two old metal gate-posts (NY 346 128). *Detour to the right up onto Dollywaggon Pike summit (narrow domed mountainous spur jutting out between Ruthwaite Cove and Cock Cove). Re-trace your steps back to the old gateposts.*

4. As you reach the old gateposts, carry straight on *(north-westerly direction)* along the wide path skirting just to the west of the summit of Dollywaggon Pike (thus avoiding the crags along the eastern edge of the summit ridge) for 400 metres then follow the path curving round and down into a narrow 'saddle' of land between

Dollywaggon Pike and High Crag (Ruthwaite Cove falling steep away to your right). From this narrow saddle, follow the path straight on bearing up to the left climbing steadily up across the western (left-hand) side of High Crag. The path skirts around High Crag *(the summit of High Crag lies close to the eastern edge of the ridge marked by a large cairn)* then rises up onto the broad, flat summit plateau of Nethermost Pike (just to the north of High Crag) where you carry straight on along the path (series of cairns) for about 500 metres across the top of this broad grassy/rocky summit plateau passing the 'summit' cairn of Nethermost Pike just across to your right then down to reach a path junction (path from Thirlmere joins on your left) in a narrow 'saddle' of land (Swallow Scarth) between Nethermost Pike and Helvellyn (NY 343 144). From Swallow Scarth, follow the path straight on climbing steadily up to reach the windbreak on the summit plateau of Helvellyn. Walk straight on passing to the left-hand side of the windbreak gently rising up to soon reach the Trig Point on the summit of Helvellyn. *Warning: sheer cliffs just to your right (east).*

5. From Helvellyn's Trig Point, carry straight on along the summit ridge of Helvellyn for 150 metres to reach a cairn where the summit ridge bends distinctly to the left (with Brown Cove dropping away in front of you and the top of Swirral Edge down to your right). Follow the path to the left gently dropping down along the top of the ridge heading down from the summit, with Brown Cove falling steeply away to your right. The path soon levels out and leads on across the 'saddle' of land between Helvellyn and Lower Man to reach a fork in the path (cairn). Follow the right-hand path (with the escarpment on your right above Brown Cove) rising up onto Helvellyn Lower Man (NY 337 155). As you reach the summit of Lower Man, with Brown Cove down to your right, walk across the small summit then carry straight on (northerly direction) quite steeply down a rocky arête that leads from the summit into the col between Lower Man and White Side. From this col, carry straight on along the clear path (cairns) climbing up onto the summit of White Side (NY 338 167).

6. From the summit of White Side (small cairn and shelter), follow the path straight on (cairns) dropping down into the col between White Side and Raise to reach a fork in the path at the bottom of this col (with Keppel Cove down to your right). Take the wide path to the right that leads across the southern upper flanks of Raise, with the steep slopes of Red Screes and Keppel Cove falling away to your right. Follow this path straight on across the hillside then follow the path as it gradually drops down *(heading towards Glenridding village in the distance)* before winding steeply down the hillside in a series of zigzags all the way down into the valley of Glenridding Beck (fed by waters from Brown Cove and Keppel Cove) to join a track just above the stream (NY 352 166).

7. Follow this track to the left heading steadily down through the valley (Glenridding Beck down to your right) for 1.4 km to reach the old Greenside mining area where you follow the track winding down to reach the cluster of converted mine buildings (outdoor pursuits centre and then the Youth Hostel) alongside the track along the bottom of the valley (NY 365 174). Follow the track straight on down passing these buildings after which continue along the stony track (Greenside Road) heading down through the valley (Glenridding Beck just down to your right) for just over 1 km then, as you approach Glenridding village, you pass rows of cottages on your left and then the stony track becomes a metalled lane. Follow this lane winding back down into Glenridding.

Glenridding Walking Weekend
- Sunday Walk -
Glenridding, Aira Force, Dockray, Watermillock Common
& Glencoyne Head

WALK INFORMATION

Highlights: Lakeland's most popular waterfall, the legend of the sleepwalking lady, the Old Coach Road, a bird's eye view across Ullswater, the exciting Balcony Path around Glencoyne Head and collapsed mine workings.

Distance: 8 miles (12.75 km)   Time: Allow 4 - 5 hours

Map: OS Explorer map OL5 - *always take a map on your walk.*

Refreshments: Pubs, shops and cafes at Glenridding. Tea Rooms at Aira Force. Royal Hotel at Dockray.

Terrain: Narrow paths lead up through the wooded valley of Aira Beck, with its waterfalls, then across fields to Dockray. From Dockray, a grassy path (indistinct in places) heads up boggy ground to join a wall across Watermillock Common, with views across Ullswater. This wall guides you round into the Glencoyne Valley. The narrow path around Glencoyne Head (Balcony Path) traverses a high, steep slope with numerous small stream crossings and some rocky ground in places. Beyond Glencoyne Head, the path passes below some old collapsed mine workings down into the valley of Sticks Gill (disused mine workings). A clear path then leads down through this valley before winding steeply down into Glenridding valley from where a track leads back into Glenridding.

Highest point: Glencoyne Head - 620 metres above sea level.

Total ascent: 460 metres

Caution: There are steep drops to the side of the path around Aira Force. The path across Watermillock Common is boggy and indistinct in places. The Balcony Path around Glencoyne Head is narrow and quite 'airy' in places as it traverses a steep, high slope around the head of the valley - this section requires care and attention as well as a head for heights. Do not explore the old Greenside Mine workings. Do not attempt this walk in bad weather or winter conditions.

Linear Walk: This is a linear walk from Aira Force to Glenridding. There is a regular bus service between Glenridding and Park Brow Foot (Aira Force) from spring until autumn. To check bus times, call Traveline: 0871 200 22 33

Glenridding

POINTS OF INTEREST

Aira Beck is born on the flanks of Stybarrow Dodd (843 metres), a rounded grassy fell that forms part of a larger group of fells known as the Dodds that lie at the northern end of the Helvellyn range of mountains that separate Ullswater and Thirlmere. The landscape of the Dodds is more in keeping with the Pennines than Lakeland due to the rounded fells and deep valleys. Aira Beck flows north-eastwards through Deepdale to reach Dockray where it turns south, through a dramatic ravine before draining into Ullswater. It was around the confluence of Aira Beck and Ullswater that William Wordsworth walked through carpets of wild daffodils in 1804, an event that inspired him to pen perhaps the most famous poem in English Literature that begins *'I wandered lonely as a Cloud...'*.

The bridge that spans the stream below Aira Force affords a superb view of the waterfall. Above you, Aira Beck cascades some 70-feet through a narrow rocky chasm with overhanging trees. The top of the waterfall is spanned by a stone bridge, which creates a beautiful scene that no photographer can resist. The walk up through the steep-sided valley of Aira Beck is one of pure delight with a profusion of flowers, trees and birds. The environs of Aira Force were laid out as a pleasure garden by the Duke of Norfolk in the 18th Century, whose ancestors had inherited Greystoke Castle as well as Gowbarrow Park through marriage in the 16th Century. On the southern boundary of this old deer park lies Lyulph's Tower, a Georgian hunting lodge that stands on the site of a much older tower. According to legend, many centuries ago a beautiful lady called Emma lived in this tower. She was betrothed to a knight called Sir Eglamore, who was often away fighting battles. Emma was so distraught at not seeing Sir Eglamore that she would often sleepwalk at night to places that they had spent time together. One night, Sir Eglamore returned unannounced and went in search of Emma, only to find her near Aira Force. He touched her arm and woke her from her sleep, however, she was so startled that she fell into the waterfall and drowned. Sir Eglamore was broken-hearted and lived the rest of his life as a hermit in a cave beside the waterfall. This legend inspired Wordsworth to write the poem 'The Somnambulist'.

The path soon leads to the attractive village of Dockray where you will find an old coaching inn. This was once a busy place as the old road from Keswick to Penrith came this way before the railway was built. Known as the Old Coach Road, this route is now a fine track that meanders across the north-eastern flanks of Matterdale Common between Dockray and St John's in the Vale. From Dockray, our route heads up across the grassy moorland of Watermillock Common to join a wall on its southern side, from where there are superb views across Ullswater, with Place Fell rising up beyond. A path leads alongside this wall before curving round into the dramatic side-valley of Glencoyne. Your first view of Glencoyne Head is rather daunting with crags and scree slopes encircling the head of the valley. This is the start of the famous Balcony Path, an old lead miners' path that strikes a high-level course contouring around the head of this valley. The path is narrow, the slopes are steep and the valley bottom is a long way down; however, with care and attention it presents few difficulties.

Beyond Glencoyne Head, the path rises up onto easier ground at Nick Head, a saddle of land between Sheffield Pike and White Stones, from where the path drops down into Sticks Gill passing an enormous gash in the hillside along the way. This is not a disused quarry, as is marked on the map, but a collapsed lead mine that once formed part of the original Greenside Mine. Indeed, this whole valley is littered with old mine workings, spoil heaps and the remains of a dam that was built to provide water-power. The steep winding track that leads down into Glenridding is particularly impressive with mining devastation all around. The bridleway alongside Sticks Gill is known as the Sticks Pass, which climbs up to 750 metres on the saddle between Stybarrow Dodd and Raise. This is an old packhorse route across the fells from Patterdale to Keswick, the route of which would have once been marked by wooden posts across the high pass, hence its name. It was along this route that packhorses plodded over to Keswick laden with lead ore. This journey was made redundant after 1825 when a smelt mill was built in the Glenridding valley.

GLENRIDDING SUNDAY WALK

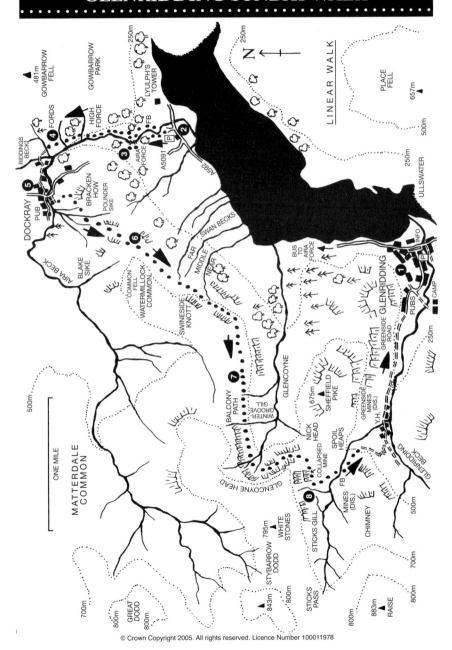

121

THE WALK

1. *Catch the bus from Glenridding to Aira Force car park (A592/A5091 junction).* From the bus stop along the A592 beside the turning towards 'Dockray, Matterdale, Troutbeck' (A5091), walk along the roadside path towards 'Penrith' to soon reach the National Trust Aira Force car park to your left.

2. Walk straight up through the car park to reach a stone archway in the wall at the top of the car park beside the information boards (sign 'Aira Force waterfall'). Head through the archway and follow the clear, wide path heading up, with Aira Beck just down to your right, to reach a bridlegate in a wall. After the bridlegate, follow the path through woodland and over a small bridge across a side-stream, after which carry straight on alongside a metal fence on your right that quickly leads through a gap in this fence and down to reach a large FB across Aira Beck. After the FB, follow the stone steps up and bending round to the left then, where the path forks, follow the left-hand level path heading straight on across the steep wooded slope with the stream down to your left. Follow this path straight on, level at first then undulating across the steep wooded slope *(take care)* heading up through this wooded gorge to reach a stone-built bridge at the foot of Aira Force set in a dramatic ravine (with a bridge spanning the ravine above the falls). After the bridge, follow the stone steps to the left climbing steeply up the hillside then bearing round to the right up to reach a junction of paths at the top of the climb where you head to the right (Aira Force down to your right) rising up then bending to the right to reach the stone bridge spanning Aira Force across the top of the ravine (NY 399 206).

3. Cross the bridge and follow the path straight on *(ignore path immediately to your left and then the path off down to your right)* through woodland heading away from the stream then, after 100 metres, take the path to the left (just before a bench) back on yourself slightly that quickly leads to a stile beside a gate on the edge of the woods. Follow the grassy path straight on across the bracken-

covered open fields (stream just out of sight across down to your left). The path soon becomes stony underfoot, which you follow straight on gently rising up to reach a stile across a fence that leads back into woodland. Follow the path straight on through the woods to quickly join a clearer path (joining from your left), which you follow straight on across the wooded hillside (stream down to your left) to reach a path junction (FB down to your left, which spans a narrow ravine). Carry straight on along the stony path *(ignore FB)* heading up through the wooded valley (stream to your left) to soon reach High Force (waterfall). Carry straight on along the rocky path up through woodland to soon reach a gap in a wall across your path (SP 'Dockray, Ulcat Row'). Head through this gap and carry straight on through sparse woodland (stream now across to your left) to reach a small gate through a fence just beyond a side-stream at the very edge of the woodland (NY 399 214).

4. After the small gate, follow the path straight on across the field to reach a gate in a wall across your path, after which the path bears down to the left over another small side-stream then straight on alongside the fence on your right for 100 metres then follow the path bearing left away from the fence (SP 'Dockray') to soon reach a gate across the path and a bridge across Riddings Beck (side-stream). After the bridge, follow the grassy track straight on passing a house on your right to soon join the stony driveway leading from this house, which you follow straight on (away from the house) to re-join Aira Beck on your left again. Follow this lane straight on to emerge onto the A5091 in the centre of Dockray (NY 393 216).

5. Turn left along the main road towards 'Ullswater, Patterdale' and over a bridge across Aira Beck just after which turn right (after a wooden hut and just by the 'phone box) along a lane (SP) passing some houses on your right to soon reach a gate at the end of the walled lane, with the open fell ahead (National Trust sign 'Watermillock Common'). Head through the gate and walk on for a few paces then, where the wall turns sharp left, head left off the track keeping close to this wall on your left *(no clear path)* gently rising up. Where this wall turns sharp left again, carry straight on gently rising up across the grassy hillside along an indistinct narrow grassy path heading towards the left-hand side of Bracken How (low craggy/grassy hill). As you reach the foot of the craggy/grassy slope of Bracken How you join a clearer grassy path that runs along the foot of this steeper slope (NY 393 213) - head to the right along this path skirting along the foot of Bracken How to your left. The hill of Bracken How soon bends away to the left - carry straight on along the path (leaving Bracken How behind) heading across the gently sloping grassy hillside to soon reach the stream of Pounder Sike set in a small valley (NY 391 212). Cross this stream then follow the path to the left heading up alongside this stream set in its small valley. Follow the clear path gently rising up across the hillside bearing very slightly away from the stream - the grassy path steepens and meanders up onto low outcrops/grassy slopes on the left-hand (north-eastern) shoulder of Common Fell (view of Ullswater opens out) and leads up to eventually join a stone wall on your left (NY 387 205).

6. The path now levels out - head straight on across the hillside alongside the wall on your left *(views to your left across Ullswater)* for 0.75 km to reach the small stream of Far Swan Beck across your path and then another two small streams in quick succession, after which the path rises up and passes below the protruding small hill of Swineside Knott (wall still on your left). After Swineside Knott, continue along the path up alongside the wall to soon reach another (unnamed) small hill on your right, where the path all but levels out. Follow this path straight on (wall on your left) below the steep slopes of this small hill, immediately beyond which the path bears right (away from the wall) and gently rises up at first, but soon levels out *(looking across the Glencoyne valley towards Glencoyne Head ahead)* and leads on across undulating grassy hillside (cairns) for 500 metres to reach a stile over a wall across your path (NY 371 192). *Caution: the next stage of this walk follows the Balcony Path around Glencoyne Head across a high, steep slope - take extra care.*

7. After the stile, head straight on along the narrow, level footpath (Balcony Path) across the steep valley side for 600 metres to reach

the small, rocky ravine of Wintergroove Gill across your path. After the stream, continue along the narrow path heading across the steep hillside (scree slopes) for a further 500 metres then, as you reach the steep crags of Glencoyne Head, you come to another stream (Deepdale Slack) set in a rocky cleft beyond which the rocky path sweeps round to the left around Glencoyne Head. The path becomes rocky and undulating underfoot and gently rises up to reach the top of a small craggy/grassy outcrop *(superb views)*, just beyond which the path traverses another high, steep slope and rises gently up to soon reach the end of the Balcony Path, with the 'col' of Nick Head down to your left (NY 362 184). As you reach the end of the Balcony Path, follow the grassy path bearing round to the right (following the curve of the hillside) heading towards the valley of Sticks Gill to soon reach a large, rocky gash in the hillside (collapsed mine workings). As you reach this rocky chasm, bear down to the left to safely cross below this gash after which follow the path winding down across spoil heaps to join the clear path along the floor of Sticks Gill valley (NY 357 183).

8. Turn left along this path and follow it heading down through the valley meandering between old spoil heaps (cairns) to reach a FB across Sticks Gill, after which head to the left along a clear path then follow this straight on (cairns), with Sticks Gill just across to your left, leaving the spoil heaps behind. The path soon leads gently down at first *(Glenridding village comes into view ahead)* before zigzagging steeply down across the hillside along a rocky path all the way down into the Glenridding valley to join a stony track as you near the bottom of the valley. Head left along this track and follow it winding down to reach the cluster of converted mine buildings (outdoor pursuits centre and then the Youth Hostel) on your right alongside the track along the bottom of the valley (NY 365 174). Follow the track down passing these buildings after which continue along the stony track (Greenside Road) heading down through the valley (Glenridding Beck just down to your right) for just over 1 km then, as you approach Glenridding village, you pass rows of cottages on your left and then the track becomes a metalled lane. Follow this lane winding down back into Glenridding.

GRASMERE

Grasmere lies at the very heart of the Lake District in the beautiful Vale of Grasmere, as the upper reaches of the Rothay Valley are known. It is encircled by mountains, woodland and tumbling streams with the quiet lapping waters of Grasmere (lake) a short stroll away, indeed its name is derived from the Old English for 'lake with grassy shores'. There has been a settlement here since at least the 13th Century and it remained a small farming community until the 19th Century when it became a popular tourist destination for wealthy Victorians who wanted to experience the wild and picturesque mountain scenery. Nowadays the majority of visitors are drawn to Grasmere because of its literary connections, most notably William Wordsworth who lived at nearby Dove Cottage and lies buried in the churchyard. St Oswald's Church dates back to the 13th Century although it stands on a pre-Conquest religious site where King Oswald of Northumbria once preached before battle. The churchyard is also the last resting-place for the Wordsworth family who lie buried in the shade of a yew tree planted by William Wordsworth. The church is unusual in that it once served three parishes and has an entrance for each into its churchyard. The floor of the church used to be made of beaten earth and every year rushes would be laid as a floor covering. The Grasmere Rushbearing Ceremony takes place every August as it has done for centuries. Adjacent to the church is the 17th Century schoolhouse where Wordsworth once taught, now home to the famous Sarah Nelson's Grasmere Gingerbread Shop. Another traditional annual event is Grasmere Sports, which was first held in 1852 and still features events such as Cumberland and Westmorland wrestling as well as fell racing.

THE VILLAGE

Grasmere offers numerous B&Bs, self catering accommodation, pubs and hotels as well as a youth hostel. There are cafes, restaurants, bakery, general stores, small supermarket, craft & gift shops, outdoor shops, art gallery, chemist, Post Office, car parks, bus services and the Wordsworth Museum and Art Gallery at Town End.

ACCOMMODATION

Tourist Information Centre, Ambleside: 015394 32582

GRASMERE PUBS

Dove & Olive Branch (Wordsworth Hotel)   015394 35592
This small pub forms part of the Wordsworth Hotel. It retains its own identity and is popular with visitors and locals. Slate floors, intimate seating and a roaring fire help create a cosy atmosphere.

Lamb Inn (Red Lion Hotel), Grasmere   015394 35456
Situated in the heart of Grasmere, this busy pub caters for the thousands of tourists who visit the village. The comfortable lounge bar is warmed by an open fire set in a large stone fireplace.

Swan Hotel, Grasmere   0844 879 9120
This old coaching inn dates back to 1650 and was even mentioned in one of Wordsworth's poems. The plush hotel bar boasts comfortable seating, open fires, polished floorboards and a refined atmosphere.

Travellers Rest, Grasmere   015394 35604
A 16th Century coaching inn situated at the foot of the pass over Dunmail Raise towards Keswick. This traditional Lakeland inn has plenty of 'olde worlde' character with exposed beams and several inter-connecting rooms on different levels. The stone-flagged bar boasts an open fire.

Tweedies Bar (Dale Lodge Hotel)   015394 35300
This pub adjoins the Dale Lodge Hotel and has its own character with a restaurant, games room and comfortable bar complete with stone-flagged floor and wood-burning stove.

Wainwright's Inn, Chapel Stile   015394 38088
Britannia Inn, Elterwater   015394 37210

Elterwater

Grasmere Walking Weekend
- Saturday Walk -
Grasmere, Easedale Tarn, Sergeant Man, High Raise & Greenup Edge

Highlights: Churning milky waters, hidden tarns, the Matterhorn of the Lake District, Lakeland's most central fell, an old packhorse route across the fells and the wild landscape of Far Easedale.

Distance: 9 miles (14.5 km)   Time: Allow 6 hours

Map: OS Explorer maps OL6 & OL7 - *always take maps.*

Refreshments: Pubs and shops at Grasmere. No facilities en route.

Terrain: Rough and rocky paths virtually all the way, with a number of steep sections. The sections from Blea Rigg to High Raise and Greenup Edge to Far Easedale follow indistinct paths across mountainous terrain with few landmarks, which may be confusing in mist. There are several streams to cross, and boggy ground in places.

Highest point: High Raise - 762 metres above sea level.

Total ascent: 710 metres

Escape Route: In bad weather, turn back at Easedale Tarn and re-trace your steps to Grasmere.

Caution: **Mountain Walk.** This is a strenuous walk up to the summit of High Raise. The walk heads across high and remote mountainous terrain with little shelter from the elements. The climb near Belles Knott is steep across stone slabs, which may be slippery when wet. OS map and compass essential. Do not attempt this walk in bad weather.

POINTS OF INTEREST

One of Lakeland's finest mountain walks, the 'Easedale Round' takes you to the summit of High Raise, Lakeland's most central fell. The initial part of this walk heads up through Easedale, an easy stroll from Grasmere. Beyond Brimmer Head Farm the valley divides with Sourmilk Gill cascading down from Easedale Tarn, hidden from view, to feed into Easedale Beck whilst the main valley, known as Far Easedale, strikes north-westwards towards its source amongst remote fells. We will save Far Easedale for the return leg of this walk, for our route heads up alongside Sourmilk Gill, so called because of the frothing churning waters, to reach Easedale Tarn that lies hidden in a corrie surrounded by towering crags. Beyond Easedale Tarn the crags close in as you climb up beneath Belles Knott, known as Lakeland's 'Matterhorn' due to its pointed profile, up to reach the broad ridge of Blea Rigg. This ridge provides a wonderful view of Stickle Tarn cradled beneath Pavey Ark and Harrison Stickle. Before long the summit of Sergeant Man beckons, a domed crown of crags that provides a wonderful viewpoint. Sergeant Man rises up as a rocky 'peak' when viewed from a distance, especially from the environs of the Langdale Pikes, however, in reality it is merely a protrusion on the south-eastern edge of High Raise's sloping plateau.

It is an easy walk onto the summit of High Raise, with the dramatic Langstrath Valley falling away beneath your feet. This summit has an additional name of High White Stones. A steady descent now ensues to Greenup Edge, a broad saddle of moorland between Ullscarf and High Raise that marks the high point along the pass between Borrowdale and Grasmere, once a busy packhorse route. From Greenup Edge, a path leads down into the upper reaches of Wyth Burn set in a mountainous bowl, although be wary not to follow this stream in the mistaken belief that it leads to Grasmere for it actually feeds Thirlmere - this is the notorious 'Wyth Burn trap'. Our route skirts around the head of the Wythburn Valley, and the infant Wyth Burn with its many feeder streams, to reach the head of Far Easedale from where it is a steady descent back to Grasmere. Far Easedale is the preserve of fell-walkers for the surrounding mountains are wild and remote punctuated by crags, with the tumbling waters of Far Easedale Gill close at hand.

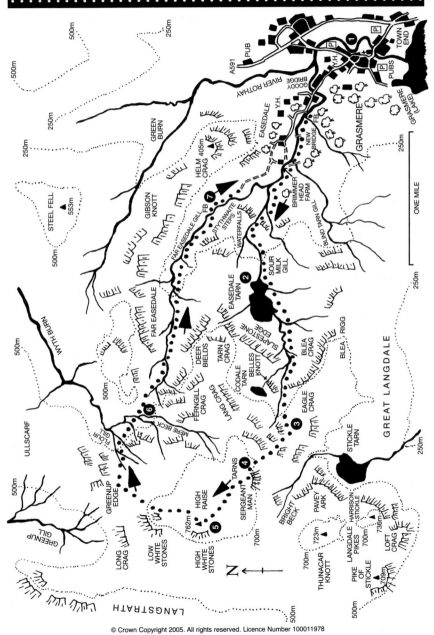

GRASMERE SATURDAY WALK

131

THE WALK

1. Leave Grasmere along Easedale Road (just to the right of the Heaton Cooper Studio) and follow this for 0.75 km passing Thorney How Youth Hostel and then guest houses and cottages to reach Goody Bridge across Easedale Beck on the edge of the village. Cross the bridge and carry straight on along the road then, where the road bends round to the right, take the footpath to the left over a FB across Easedale Beck (SP 'Easedale Tarn') and then over a smaller stone-slab FB after which follow the path straight on to quickly reach a gate in a wall (Easedale Beck on your right). Head through the gate and follow the path straight on across the field (heading up through Easedale) to soon join a wall on your left. Follow the stony path straight on alongside this wall on your left *(ignore the stone bridge across Easedale Beck)* to soon re-join Easedale Beck on your right which you follow straight on to reach a gate in a wall at the end of the enclosed path (NY 325 083). After the gate you join a farm track where you head right over a small concrete bridge across a side-stream then immediately branch off to the left along a clear path across the field (SP) - *do not continue along the track.* Follow the path across the field, which soon re-joins Easedale Beck on your right. A stony path now leads straight on, with Easedale Beck to your right, climbing steadily up (pitched-stone path for most of the way) then passing the waterfalls of Sour Milk Gill just to your right. The path steepens as you climb up alongside these waterfalls then, above the waterfalls, the gradient eases and you follow the path curving round to the left (heading away from the stream) then straight on across undulating terrain before rising up again to reach Easedale Tarn, set in a mountainous corrie (NY 311 087).

2. Follow the path straight on along the left side of Easedale Tarn (southern shore). As you reach the head of the tarn, follow the path straight on skirting below some small hillocks on your left (glacial moraines). The path joins the stream (feeding Easedale Tarn) on your right - carry straight on along the path skirting the hillocks on your left (with the stream just to your right) to reach the foot of a steep slope at the head of the valley, with Eagle Crag towering up in front of you to the left and the pyramidal peak of Belles Knott to your right. Our route heads steeply up through the 'pass' between Eagle Crag and Belles Knott (with the stream to your right), winding steeply up across rock slabs with some easy scrambling up to the top of the 'pass'. At the top of the steep climb, follow the rocky path straight on rising steadily up (stream on your right) to soon reach a fork in the path, where the ground levels out (with another mountainous corrie in front of you, but no tarn - NY 297 085). Take the left-hand path and follow this heading steadily up across the left-hand side of the corrie *(path to the right over the stream allows a short detour to Codale Tarn)*. Follow this rocky path heading gradually up across the left-hand (southern) side of the corrie for 500 metres to reach the line of crags at the head of the valley. Follow the path heading quite steeply up across boulders and rocks up through the 'nick' in the line of crags across the skyline that brings you up onto the broad undulating ridge of Blea Rigg (NY 292 084).

3. As you reach the top of the steep climb (with the undulating broad ridge of Blea Rigg in front of you), follow the path bending round to the right (cairns) for a short distance then curving left up along the foot of some low crags on your right then, after a few paces, turn right along a narrow path (small cairn) heading up between these crags. *NB if you can see Stickle Tarn and Pavey Ark then you have passed the path turning towards Sergeant Man.* Follow this narrow, rocky path rising steadily up *(initial compass bearing: 330 degrees)* across the rocky ground, with views back down to Codale and Easedale tarns at first, then skirting to the right of an unnamed but prominent crag, beyond which the stony path rises steadily up *(Sergeant Man comes into view ahead)* meandering up across the rocky hillside to eventually reach the prominent domed rocky summit of Sergeant Man. Follow the path steeply up onto the summit of Sergeant Man (NY 286 089). *Warning: sheer cliffs on its southern aspect.*

4. As you reach the summit of Sergeant Man, bear right *(north-westerly direction)* down from the rocky summit onto the broad

plateau of land *(compass bearing from the summit: 330 degrees)* skirting just to the left of the small tarns/low outcrops heading across boggy ground to soon pick up a clear, wide path that leads steadily up across the broad domed plateau of High Raise (following the line of rusty old fence posts). Follow this path gently rising up *(still heading in a NW direction)* then, where the path all but disappears, carry straight on passing to the left of a small tarn to reach the Trig Point and windbreak on the summit of High Raise (NY 281 095).

5. As you reach the Trig Point on the summit of High Raise, follow the path to the right heading in a north-easterly direction *(compass bearing: 58 degrees)* across the broad summit for 200 metres to reach a small cluster of rocks surmounted by a rusty fencepost. As you reach these rocks, bear left heading down across the middle of the broad ridge *(northerly direction)* for 400 metres to reach the scattered outcrops of Low White Stones. From these outcrops, follow the path in a NNE direction heading quite steeply down for 600 metres into the bottom of the saddle of land (Greenup Edge) between High Raise and Ullscarf (NY 286 105). As you reach the bottom of Greenup Edge walk straight on across this saddle of land to reach a 'crossroads' of paths just before the ground begins to rise up (with some low crags in front of you). Turn right along the narrow path, which soon drops steadily down to reach the small stream of Flour Gill on your right (which feeds Wyth Burn). Cross the stream and follow the rough path straight on across the hillside, with the 'bowl' of the upper reaches of the Wyth Burn *(which flows into Thirlmere)* down to your left. Follow this path straight on over some small streams dropping very gradually down across the hillside. The path soon turns quite sharply down to reach the foot of the steep, rocky hillside where you carry on along the clear path skirting along the foot of this steep hillside to your right, with the 'bowl' of the Wyth Burn to your left. The path keeps to the foot of this steep hillside and crosses a number of small side-streams and boggy ground (path indistinct in places) for about 500 metres then, as you reach the end of the steep slope and large crags on your right,

follow the path ahead bearing slightly left down over Mere Beck (which feeds Wyth Burn), after which head straight on up across boggy ground to pick up a stony path which you follow up to the right to reach the top of the 'pass' at the head of Far Easedale, marked by old fence posts and a cairn (NY 295 102).

6. Head straight on along the path heading down into Far Easedale (stone-pitched in places) to soon join a small stream on your right. The path leads steadily down then curves round to the right and crosses this small stream and continues steadily down to soon join another stream on your right. Follow the path down alongside this stream until you come to a small but deep rocky gorge (with some trees sheltering within) where you follow the path down alongside this gorge, just below which head to the right over the stream (just above a waterfall). After the stream, follow the path steeply down (stream now on your left) to reach the valley floor at the foot of the steep slope (head of Far Easedale). A clear path now leads straight on heading down through the broad valley of Far Easedale (stream across to your left). After just over 1 km the valley narrows and the stream flows through a steep-sided ravine, beyond which the valley opens out again and the path leads on to reach a junction with another path just before a wall across your path. Follow this path to the left to quickly reach the FB across Far Easedale Gill at Stythwaite Steps (NY 318 094).

7. Cross the FB then follow the path to the right heading down alongside Far Easedale Gill for 400 metres then, where the stream bends away to the right, follow the enclosed path bearing up to the left. Follow this enclosed track heading steadily down through the valley for 1 km (passing Brimmer Head Farm across to your right after 0.75 km) to reach a junction of tracks set amongst woodland where you carry straight on bearing slightly right towards 'Grasmere' *(ignore path up to Helm Crag to your left)* to quickly reach a gate (NY 327 085). Head through the gate and follow the track down passing between houses to emerge onto a metalled lane beside the entrances to these houses. Head along this lane and follow it (Easedale Road) for 1.5 km all the way back into Grasmere.

Grasmere Walking Weekend
- Sunday Walk -

*Grasmere, Silver How, Elterwater, Huntingstile Crag,
Loughrigg Terrace & Dove Cottage*

WALK INFORMATION

Highlights: A surprise view, digging for slate and gunpowder, one of Lakeland's loveliest villages, old coffin routes and the home of one of the world's greatest writers.

Distance: 6.25 miles (10 km)   **Time:**   Allow 3 - 4 hours

Map: OS Explorer map OL7 - *always take a map on your walk.*

Refreshments: Pubs at Grasmere, Chapel Stile and Elterwater.

Terrain: The climb over to Chapel Stile heads along rough paths across rocky moorland (boggy sections). The descent from Spedding Crag to Chapel Stile is steep. After a short section of road walking, a riverside path leads to Elterwater. A path then climbs back up over the moorland passing Huntingstile Crag before a woodland path cuts off across steep slopes to join Red Bank Road. Tracks and paths lead across Loughrigg Terrace before dropping down to reach the River Rothay at White Moss. A track then climbs up to join a lane which is followed back down to Grasmere.

Highest point: Spedding Crag - 260 metres above sea level.

Total ascent 420 metres

Caution There are several small streams to cross. This walk includes a number of steep sections. The moorland between Grasmere and Great Langdale is criss-crossed by paths, which may make route-finding confusing. Take care walking along lanes and crossing the A591.

POINTS OF INTEREST

From Grasmere, a path climbs up below the rocky slopes of Silver How across undulating moorland with fine retrospective views of Grasmere amidst its mountainous setting. Just beyond the low rise of Dow Bank is a 'nick' in the hillside and a surprise view as you reach the brow of the steep hillside overlooking Great Langdale, with Chapel Stile and Elterwater far below as well as the unsightly slate quarry. A steep path leads down to Chapel Stile, which once housed workers from the slate quarry and adjacent gunpowder works. The Elterwater Gunpowder Works operated from 1824 until 1928 providing explosives for the local quarries and mines. A hazardous job, especially when safety standards were not too stringent, with regular explosions and accidents. At its height six waterwheels, fed by the fast-flowing Great Langdale Beck, powered the Gunpowder Works and much of the surrounding woodland was managed to provide charcoal for the manufacturing process. A timeshare hotel has now been built on this industrial site, although Elterwater quarry continues to be worked for its green slate.

Elterwater is one of Lakeland's prettiest villages, with a small green shaded by a large old tree and overlooked by The Britannia, a traditional Lakeland inn that was originally a farm in the 17th Century. The village developed in the 19th Century to serve the nearby gunpowder works and quarries, hence the number of former miners' cottages. Close by lies Elter Water, the smallest of the sixteen lakes in Lakeland, which is fed by the River Brathay and Great Langdale Beck. Elter Water's irregular shoreline, sweeping in sinuous curves with the Langdale Pikes in the background, creates a scene of unrivalled beauty. This lake inspired Gainsborough to paint the Langdale Pikes seen across the lake when he visited this area in 1783; this was the only picture he painted of the Lake District. The lake attracts migrating whooper swans in winter, its name comes from the Old Norse word 'Elptarvatn' meaning 'swan lake'. The climb back over to Grasmere is one of delight, with another 'surprise view' of Grasmere framed beneath the distinctive Helm Crag. A path then leads up through woodland to reach the traverse known as Loughrigg Terrace across the steep slopes of

Loughrigg Fell, from where there are superb views across Grasmere.

William Wordsworth was born at Cockermouth in 1770, educated at Cockermouth and then Hawkshead Grammar School before leaving the region to travel through Europe, although he was always drawn back to his beloved Lake District. It was whilst travelling on foot through the Lake District with his friend Samuel Taylor Coleridge that Wordsworth spotted a cottage for rent just outside Grasmere. That building was Dove Cottage, home of William Wordsworth from 1799 until 1808. It was here that the famous poet produced some of his finest work, although much of his inspiration was gained outdoors amongst the fells and valleys. In particular, the poems contained within his published work *Lyrical Ballads* changed the course of English literature by exploring for the first time the lives of ordinary people, thus making poetry more accessible to the general public. The small whitewashed cottage was once an inn known as the Dove and Olive Branch and stands on the old Keswick to Ambleside road. William shared the house with his sister Dorothy and later his wife Mary and their three children. Here he composed perhaps the most famous poem in English Literature that begins *'I wandered lonely as a Cloud...'* in 1804 after seeing the wild daffodils on the banks of Ullswater. With a fourth child on the way, the Wordsworth family moved to a larger house at Grasmere called Allan Bank, although this was not suitable and so they moved again to the Rectory, but tragedy struck as two of their children died within a short space of time and so they moved away from the sad memories of Grasmere to Rydal Mount where they stayed until Wordsworth's death in 1850. The crowded conditions at Dove Cottage were exacerbated by a constant stream of literary visitors including Coleridge and Sir Walter Scott, all of whom often stayed for long periods. Dove Cottage is open to the public and is worth visiting to see the small stone-flagged rooms as well as the adjacent Wordsworth Museum. The church at Grasmere once served three parishes with parishioners having to travel from as far as Great Langdale and Ambleside for services. This walk follows two old Corpse Roads, one from Elterwater via Hunting Stile and Red Bank, and the other from Ambleside via Rydal and Town End. Look out for the old Coffin Stone at Town End.

For more information about William Wordsworth, please see Walking Weekend 1

GRASMERE SUNDAY WALK

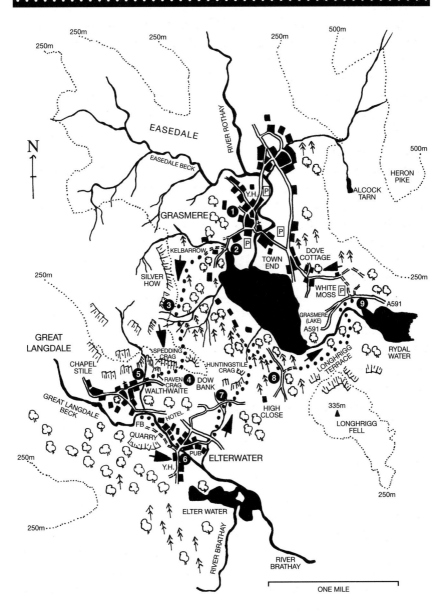

N

EASEDALE

RIVER ROTHAY

EASEDALE BECK

250m 250m 250m 250m 500m

500m

HERON PIKE

ALCOCK TARN

Y.H. P

GRASMERE

KELBARROW

SILVER HOW

GREAT LANGDALE

CHAPEL STILE

SPEDDING CRAG

HUNTINGSTILE CRAG

RAVEN CRAG

WALTHWAITE

DOW BANK

GREAT LANGDALE BECK

FB

QUARRY

HOTEL

HIGH CLOSE

PUB

Y.H.

ELTERWATER

ELTER WATER

RIVER BRATHAY

RIVER BRATHAY

DOVE COTTAGE

TOWN END

WHITE MOSS P

GRASMERE (LAKE)
A591

A591

LONGHRIGG TERRACE

RYDAL WATER

335m

LONGHRIGG FELL

250m

250m

250m

250m

ONE MILE

139

THE WALK

1. From the Red Lion Hotel in the centre of Grasmere (facing the hotel), take the road passing to the right side of the hotel (Langdale Road) and follow this down to a road junction. Turn right along Red Bank Road and follow this out of Grasmere, bending left just after the Gold Rill Hotel. Follow this lane *(take care)* straight on for a further 200 metres to a small bridge over the side-stream of Wray Gill (as you approach the lake) just after which turn right up through a gate and along a walled, stony track (SP) just before the entrance to Kelbarrow house (NY 334 072).

2. Follow this walled track climbing steadily up passing above the house to reach a kissing-gate at the top of the walled track, after which carry straight on up across the rough pasture to another kissing-gate in a wall across your path. Head through this kissing-gate and follow the rocky path straight on alongside a wall on your left climbing steadily up to reach a third kissing-gate *(with the steep rocky slopes of Silver How up to your right)*. Head through this kissing-gate and over a small stream just beyond then carry straight on along the rocky path rising steadily up alongside the wall on your left *(views soon open out across Grasmere and Rydal Water)* and follow this path up for 600 metres until you reach a crossroads of paths where the wall bends sharply away down to your left (small stream just in front) - NY 327 064.

3. Follow the wall bending down to the left (keep alongside the wall), over the small stream and continue down into an area of trees and undergrowth (juniper bushes), with woodland to your left over the wall. Follow the path through the trees/undergrowth crossing a number of small streams then, as you emerge from the trees/ undergrowth, you pass a gate and wall-stile in the wall just to your left - ignore this and continue straight on along the clear path for a short distance over another stream to soon reach a fork in the path (small clearing between the woodland over the wall to your left). Take the path up to the right and follow it climbing up across the

rough hillside (passing more juniper bushes) bearing slightly left. Just above these bushes the ground levels out slightly and the small 'twin peaks' of Dow Bank soon come into view ahead - continue straight on along the path towards these small 'peaks' to reach a junction of paths immediately before the first rocky 'peak' of Dow Bank (with a small roofless stone hut ahead). At this path junction at the foot of Dow Bank, turn right back on yourself slightly and follow the narrow path skirting around the foot of Dow Bank (with Dow Bank on your left) gently curving round to the left to soon reach a junction of paths *(ignore path off to the right)* where you carry straight on curving gently round to the left then straight on through a shallow 'saddle' of land. Follow this path straight on, over a boggy area then passing a solitary holly tree to soon reach a pronounced 'nick' in the hillside and the brow of a steep bank with a 'surprise view' overlooking Great Langdale, with Spedding Crag on your right (NY 328 057).

4. Follow the path straight on through this 'nick' in the hillside then gently curving round to the left across the steep hillside *(take care)* for 75 metres to reach a 'crossroads' of paths where you turn right along a clear path heading steeply downhill. Follow this path straight down the steep hillside (stone-pitched steps in places) to reach a narrow shelf of grassy land where the path levels out. Turn right and follow the path steadily down across the hillside to join a wall on your left which you follow straight on passing below Raven Crag to reach a road on the edge of Walthwaite (Chapel Stile).

5. Turn right along the road into the village to reach Holy Trinity Church where you take the turning down to the left to reach the main valley road. Turn left along this road *(take care)* passing Langdale Co-Operative Village Store on your left to reach Wainwright's Inn where you follow the road curving left passing the pub just after which take the bridleway to the right (SP) over a FB across Great Langdale Beck. After the FB, follow the wide riverside path to the left heading down with Great Langdale Beck on your left. Follow this path straight on passing slate spoil heaps on your right and then the timeshare hotel to your left across the river

(waterfalls) before rising up through woodland to quickly join a lane opposite a fenced-off slate mine entrance. Turn left along this lane and follow it down to join the road through Elterwater.

6. Turn left over the road-bridge across Great Langdale Beck to quickly reach a road junction by the village green just before the village shop (Britannia Inn to your left). Turn right towards 'Ambleside' just before the shop and follow this road out of the village and up across Elterwater Common to reach the main valley road beside an old stone guidepost. At the road, take the grassy path directly opposite and follow this up to quickly reach a wall corner by a gate. Head to the left along a grassy path just before this wall and over a small stream (stone slabs), a few paces beyond which you come to a crossroads of paths where you turn right along the clearer path heading up with the stream and wall just across to your right. Follow this path heading steadily up across the rough hillside gradually bearing slightly to the left away from the stream *(several paths to choose from - follow the clearer central path)* then passing a small roofless stone hut where you carry straight on (keep to central path) up to join a metalled road where a clear stony path branches off from the road (NY 333 052).

7. Turn right along the clear path (with the road just to your left) and follow this gently rising up for 150 metres then, just before you reach the wall on your right again, turn left up the bank to quickly reach the road at a signpost. Cross over and take the footpath opposite (SP) and follow this quite steeply up bearing slightly left across the hillside to join a clearer path at the foot of the steep slope of Huntingstile Crag. Follow this path to the right which quickly leads up onto the moor, with Huntingstile Crag on your left. Carry straight on along the foot of the steep slopes of Huntingstile Crag on your left *(lots of paths - keep straight on along the foot of the crags)* heading across the broad 'saddle' of moorland to soon join a wall on your left that leads down to a gate in a wall across your path (views of Grasmere ahead - NY 336 057). Head through the gate and follow the path heading down the hillside, enclosed by walls on either side some distance apart, then winding down through

woodland to reach a gate tucked away in the bottom corner of the enclosure just beyond a small stream. Head through the gate then, after a few paces, turn right through wrought-iron gate in a wall just by a bench (SP 'YHA, Loughrigg Terrace') and follow the level path straight on through woodland across the steep hillside following the contours of the wooded hillside round to reach a metal gate in a wall at the end of the woods. Carry straight on across the bracken-covered slope to join a road (Red Bank).

8. Turn right along the road for 100 metres then take the wide, stony path down to your left (SP 'Loughrigg Terrace'). Follow this clear track straight on through woodland and gently dropping down to reach a fork in the track where you head straight on through the metal kissing-gate beside a gate across the track, marked by a National Trust sign 'Loughrigg Fell' *(ignore gate to the left back on yourself)*. Head through this gate out of the woodland and over a small stream, just after which the path forks - follow the left-hand path *(ignore the steep pitched-stone path up to the right)*. Follow this gravel path straight on (Loughrigg Terrace) heading across the steep bracken-covered slopes of Loughrigg Fell dropping gently down for 0.75 km to join a wide stony path beside a wall (NY 347 060). Turn right along this path and follow it winding down alongside this wall to soon reach a junction of paths where you turn left through a kissing gate in the high stone wall (stone sign set into the wall 'Rydal'). After the kissing-gate, follow the path heading down through woodland (White Moss Wood) to reach a FB across the River Rothay. After the FB, follow the wide path ahead bearing round to the right then straight on (River Rothay bends away to the right) to reach a distinct fork in the path just before a small FB and ford across the side-stream of Dunney Beck. Follow the left-hand path up towards another FB across this side-stream (toilet block just ahead) - do not cross this FB but turn left along a path just before it that leads up to reach the A591 main road (SP), with White Moss car park just across to your left (NY 349 065).

9. Cross over the road *(take care)* along the track opposite (SP 'Public Bridleway') and follow this bearing up to the left through woodland

climbing steadily up for 400 metres to join a metalled lane. Turn left along this lane and follow this straight on through woodland then winding down to reach a road junction (small tarn on your right). Follow the road to the right *(ignore turning to the right after the tarn)* and follow this road straight on down into Town End, passing Dove Cottage on your right to reach the road junction with the A591 at a mini roundabout on the outskirts of Grasmere. Cross over this main road *(take care)* and follow Stock Lane straight on back into Grasmere.

Grasmere

GREAT LANGDALE

Old Dungeon Ghyll

Great Langdale is Nature in all its glory on a vast scale. At Stool End Farm, the upper reaches of Great Langdale divides into two valleys known as Oxendale and Mickleden with a craggy spur known as The Band rising up between them. Great Langdale is enclosed by some of Lakeland's most famous mountains including Crinkle Crags, Bowfell and the Langdale Pikes. The five summits of the Langdale Pikes, Harrison Stickle, Pike o' Stickle, Thorn Crag, Loft Crag and Pavey Ark, have been popular expeditions since Victorian times. On the flanks of Pike of Stickle lie the remnants of one of the earliest known factories in the world that dates back several thousand years. Here, Neolithic people discovered a hard band of volcanic rock and developed an 'axe factory' exporting axe heads as far afield as Ireland and Brittany. The rocks of Great Langdale were laid down 450 million years ago when volcanoes spewed ash and lava into the atmosphere over a period of a million years. This volcanic debris cooled and compressed into layers of hard rock known as the Borrowdale Volcanics that were then folded and uplifted by tectonic plate movements some 50 million years ago to create a mountainous dome that now forms the central Lakeland fells. Rivers then eroded valleys into this dome, which were subsequently scoured by glaciers during a succession of Ice Ages that lasted over a million years, the last one being 10,000 years ago. These glaciers changed V-shaped river valleys into U-shaped glaciated valleys, including Great Langdale. Corries were formed high in the mountains, now often filled by tarns. As the glaciers retreated, soil and rock were dropped in the form of moraines and drumlins, which often trapped meltwater thus forming the sixteen major lakes and hundreds of smaller tarns of today including Elter Water, Great Langdale's only remaining lake. Below Stool End Farm, the flat valley floor, now criss-crossed by walls, was once filled by a glacial lake but stream debris has gradually silted it up.

THE VILLAGE

There are two hamlets in the upper reaches of Great Langdale situated just one kilometre apart. Old Dungeon Ghyll (ODG) boasts a pub (hotel), B&Bs, car park, bus service and campsite. The New Dungeon Ghyll (NDG) offers a pub and hotel, B&B, camping barn, car park, bus service and toilets.

ACCOMMODATION

Tourist Information Centre, Ambleside   015394 32582

GREAT LANGDALE PUBS

Old Dungeon Ghyll, Great Langdale   015394 37272
Situated beneath the Langdale Pikes, the ODG is a famous walkers' pub. The building dates back to the 13th Century and was originally a farm, only becoming a hotel in the 1850s. It was bought by the National Trust in 1929 using funds donated by G.M. Trevelyan, the famous historian, and continued to run as a farm and inn until 1949, when the barn was converted into the Hikers Bar.

New Dungeon Ghyll, Great Langdale   015394 37213
This Victorian hotel was built to cater for those early tourists who came to see Dungeon Ghyll Force which cascades through a ravine on the flanks of the Langdale Pikes. Inside, there is a comfortable Walkers' Bar with an open fire, as well as a residents' lounge, whilst outside is a delightful patio area.

Sticklebarn Tavern, Great Langdale   015394 37356
This pub was a barn for one of the local farms until the 1970s when it was converted into a pub. Popular with walkers and climbers, this pub has a large downstairs bar with a tiled floor and wood burning stove, whilst upstairs is the Hayloft bar with live entertainment at weekends.

PUBS ALONG THE WALKS

Three Shires Inn, Little Langdale   015394 37215
Britannia Inn, Elterwater   015394 37210
Wainwright's Inn, Chapel Stile   015394 38088

Great Langdale Walking Weekend
- Saturday Walk -
ODG, Rossett Gill, Esk Pike, Bowfell, Three Tarns & The Band

WALK INFORMATION

Highlights: A prehistoric axe factory, glacial erosion that has left a basket of eggs, hidden tarns, the wettest place in England, two magnificent mountain summits and a slanting slab of stone.

Distance: 8.5 miles (13.5 km)   Time: Allow 6 hours

Map: OS Explorer map OL6 - *always take a map on your walk.*

Refreshments: ODG at Great Langdale. No facilities en route - take plenty of provisions with you.

Terrain: A stony path leads up into Mickleden (valley) to reach Rossett Gill at its head, from where a steep climb ensues (pitched-stone path for most of the way) to reach Angle Tarn. Stony paths then lead steadily up to the path junction at Esk Hause shelter, from where it is a short walk up to Esk Hause. The path from Esk Hause to Esk Pike and then Bowfell is rough, rocky and steep in places; there are also cliffs and crags on Esk Pike's north-eastern aspect and Bowfell's north-eastern and southern slopes. The descent from Bowfell to Three Tarns is steep along a rocky slope, whilst the descent along The Band is long and steep in places.

Highest point: Bowfell - 902 metres above sea level.

Total ascent: 955 metres

Escape Route: From Ore Gap, head left (north) down to reach Angle Tarn then re-trace your steps back down Rossett Gill.

Caution: **Mountain Walk.** This is a strenuous walk to the summits of Esk Pike and Bowfell, with mountainous terrain for most of the way. The paths are generally well-trodden, although rocky in places with a number of steep sections as well as steep drops to the side of the path in places. There are few landmarks on the mountain summits and high fells, which may make navigation difficult. OS map and compass essential. Do not attempt this walk in bad weather.

Connecting route: This walk starts and finishes at the Old Dungeon Ghyll (ODG). For the connecting route between the New Dungeon Ghyll and ODG see Point 8 of the Sunday walk's route description. *This connecting route will add an additional 2.5 km (1.5 miles) to the Saturday walk.*

POINTS OF INTEREST

Mickleden cuts a deep trench between Bowfell and the Langdale Pikes, a perfect example of a glaciated valley. A path leads up through this valley towards the wall of crags that encircle its head; however, as you reach the imposing Rossett Crag the path splits with the well-graded Stake Pass path zigzagging up alongside Stake Gill over to the Langstrath Valley and Borrowdale or, as our route takes us, winding steeply up alongside the boulder-strewn gully of Rossett Gill en route to the mountain pass of Esk Hause and, ultimately, Wasdale. These paths were once busy packhorse routes across the fells to Keswick and the coast, although the route up Rossett Gill has been in constant use for a thousand years as early Norse settlers would have come this way to get to their summer grazing lands on the fells. The Rossett Gill route had become badly eroded in recent years as impatient walkers had taken the direct line through the gully. However, the original packhorse route has recently been repaired, which makes the ascent easier. The strange hillocks at head of Mickleden are mounds of glacial debris known as drumlins left by the retreating glacier. Here, the small rounded drumlins are clustered together to create an unusual landscape known as 'basket of eggs topography'.

The steep climb up alongside Rossett Gill brings you out into a mountainous world, with Angle Tarn cradled beneath the crags of Hanging Knotts, which form the northern shoulder of Bowfell. Angle Tarn feeds Angletarn Gill that tumbles down into the Langstrath Valley. Beyond Angle Tarn, the path crosses Tongue Head and then drops down to reach the head of Allencrags Gill and an area of boggy ground that would have once held a small tarn, from where there is a wonderful view down into the Langstrath Valley. It is now a short climb up to reach the Esk Hause shelter. This stone cross-shaped wind break lies slightly to the north-east of the true Esk Hause in a saddle of land between Esk Hause and Allen Crags alongside the main Great Langdale to Wasdale path. It is a short climb from the shelter to the 'proper' Esk Hause, a sweeping saddle of land between Great End and Esk Pike that marks the watershed between Eskdale and Borrowdale. This is the heart of the

Lake District with nothing but mountains and valleys as far as the eye can see; it is the highest mountain pass in the Lake District (for pedestrians) and reputedly the wettest place in the country.

Esk Pike is a magnificent mountain that stands proudly above the source of the River Esk, hence its name, although it also towers above the head of the Langstrath Valley. It stands at the centre of a broad horseshoe of England's highest mountains that form a great arc around the head of Eskdale including Scafell, Scafell Pike, Great End, Esk Pike, Bowfell and Crinkle Crags, most of which are over 900 metres in height. Its summit crags offer magnificent views down Eskdale and across towards the Scafell massif. The saddle of land between Esk Pike and Bowfell is known as Ore Gap, as a vein of iron ore (hematite) runs across this col that is said to send your compass needle spinning!

Reaching the summit of Bowfell is a moment for celebration, for this famous mountain offers one of the most extensive viewpoints in the Lake District with a commanding panorama in all directions from its conical summit of shattered rocks and awkward boulders. Seen from a distance, Bowfell grabs your attention, its pyramidal peak rising above all of its near neighbours and dominating the upper reaches of three major valleys - Great Langdale, Eskdale and Langstrath. From the summit there is a view south-eastwards down towards the saddle of Three Tarns set between Bowfell and Crinkle Crags, but do not be tempted by this seemingly straight-forward route for dangers lurk at Bowfell Links where cliffs await the unwary, making this direct route hazardous. The path from Bowfell to Three Tarns skirts to the east of the summit passing above the top of Great Slab, one of Lakeland's geological wonders where a massive slab of flat volcanic rock lies at an inviting angle; do not be tempted to walk on this slab as it slants away to fresh air at its base! Great Slab forms part of an impressive array of crags on Bowfell's north-eastern slopes high above Mickleden, including Bowfell Buttress and Cambridge Crag. Beyond Great Slab, the path heads steeply down to Three Tarns. This small cluster of tarns marks the start of the descent along The Band, a surprisingly long ridge of land that eventually leads down to Stool End Farm. The views from this broad ridge down into Oxendale are magnificent.

GREAT LANGDALE SATURDAY WALK

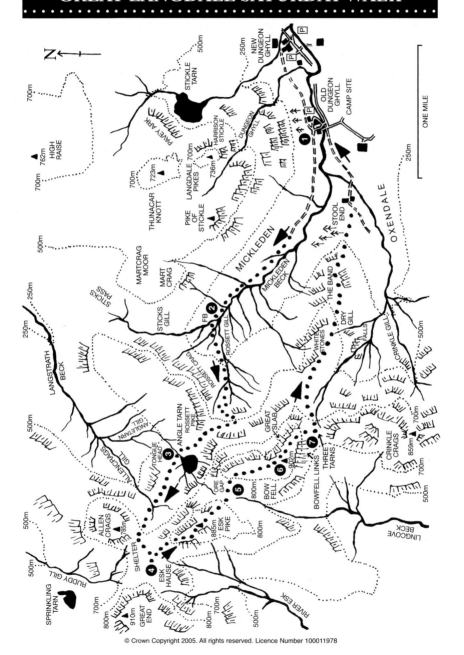

151

THE WALK

1. From the car park beside the Old Dungeon Ghyll (ODG), head along the lane passing to the right of the hotel's 'Hikers Bar' and follow this curving left behind the pub then, where the lane bends sharp right, carry straight on along the stony track to quickly reach a gate in a wall. After the gate, follow the stony track straight on alongside the wall on your left (National Trust sign 'Mickleden') for 0.75 km to reach a gate in a wall across the track (stone-built sheep pens on your left just beyond the gate). Head through this gate and continue straight on to quickly reach another gate, after which carry straight on along the track heading up into the valley of Mickleden with the wall on your left (Pike of Stickle rising steeply up to your right) then, where the wall ends after 0.5 km, carry straight on along the clear, wide path walking towards the head of the valley (Mickleden Beck to your left) for a further 1.5 km to reach a FB across Stake Gill near a circular sheepfold *(just upstream from its confluence with Rossett Gill which then forms Mickleden Beck)* at the foot of Stake Pass, with Rossett Crag towering above (NY 262 074).

2. Cross the FB, after which carry straight on along the rocky path (stone sign 'Esk Hause') that soon crosses a small stream (Little Gill) then continue straight on gently rising up for 450 metres to join the banks of Rossett Gill (rocky ravine) on your left. Carry on along the clear path (pitched-stone path for most of the way) climbing steeply up alongside the stream (gradient steepens) then, as you approach the foot of the steep crags, you come to a fork in the stream where you cross over the right-hand stream (which comes down from the rocky cleft of Rossett Gill up to your right). After this stream, follow the pitched-stone path bending up to the right climbing steeply up with Rossett Gill to your right then winding steeply up between the crags, above which the gradient eases slightly (Rossett Gill on your right) where you follow the path swinging sharply round to the left (halfway up the climb). The path leads on across the steep hillside (cairns) gently rising up for 300 metres before the path climbs steeply up to the right then bends round to the right slanting up across the steep rocky hillside (pitched-stone path) then, as you reach the top of the steep section, the gradient eases and the path leads on, with Rossett Gill falling away to your right, before rising steadily up to reach the top of the pass at the head of Rossett Gill. Carry straight on across the top of the pass. Angle Tarn soon comes into view ahead below - follow the path down to reach stepping stones across the outflow stream (Angletarn Gill) from Angle Tarn (NY 245 078).

3. After you have crossed the stream (Angletarn Gill), carry straight on along the pitched-stone path climbing up the hillside ahead (Tongue Head). The path climbs quite steeply at first then rises up onto the top of Tongue Head. Head straight on along the stony path across Tongue Head then down to reach a small stream (Allencrags Gill) that issues from a small reed-choked bog/tarn (head of the Langstrath valley). Cross the stream and carry straight on along the pitched-stone path climbing quite steeply up for 0.5 km to reach a 'crossroads' of paths beside an X-shaped wind shelter set in a 'saddle' of land with Allen Crags up to your right and the northern shoulder of Esk Pike to your left (NY 235 083) *NB: This is not Esk Hause.* Turn left at this 'crossroads' passing the wind shelter on your left and follow the broad path rising up *(ignore path that branches off to the right after 150 metres)* then, as you reach the top of the pass, the path bends slightly to the right to quickly reach a path junction (marked by a cairn) at the top of the pass of Esk Hause *(saddle of land along the watershed between Eskdale and Borrowdale, with Great End across to your right, Esk Pike to your left and the head of Eskdale in front of you - NY 233 081).*

4. As you reach Esk Hause, turn left (back on yourself) along the broad, rough path across the col of Esk Hause *(south-easterly direction)* then, after a short distance, follow the path climbing up across crags and rocks with some easy scrambling *(clear path for most of the way - look for polished, boot-worn rocks)* then, as you approach the summit, you head across a fairly wide grassy/rocky shelf of land before a final climb up the rocks and crags onto the summit of Esk Pike *(small stone-built shelter beside the summit crags).* From the

rudimentary shelter beside the summit crag on Esk Pike, head straight on across the rocky summit in a south-easterly direction *(compass bearing: 130 degrees)* down from the summit passing to the left-hand side of some rocky outcrops just on the southern side of the summit then continue along the path down across rocky ground *(still heading south-east)* to reach the bottom of the col of Ore Gap *(saddle of lane between Esk Pike and Bowfell - NY 241 072)*.

5. From Ore Gap carry straight on *(compass bearing: 104 degrees)* climbing up across the rocky, boulder-strewn hillside ahead (cairned path) for 200 metres then, as the ground begins to steepen (crags of Hanging Knotts), follow the cairned path bearing to the right *(compass bearing 165 degrees)* then straight on climbing steadily up towards the summit of Bowfell, with a final scramble across boulders and rocks up onto the small, domed rocky summit of Bowfell (NY 245 064). *Although Three Tarns can be seen from the summit of Bowfell set in the col between Bowfell and Crinkle Crags, do not walk directly to them as the crags of Bowfell Links lie between.*

6. As you reach the summit cairn on Bowfell (with the col of Three Tarns ahead of you far below), turn left (north-east) down from the small domed summit peak to quickly pick up a clear cairned path on the shelf of rocky land on the north-eastern side of the summit *(this path passes to the east of the summit peak in a south-easterly direction)*. Follow this cairned path to the right *(south-easterly direction; compass bearing 126 degrees)* passing immediately below the small domed summit of Bowfell then gently down across rocky terrain passing the top of the large sloping slab of rock (Great Slab) on your left, just after which you pass a small unnamed tarn. After the small tarn, the path drops very steeply down across scree to reach Three Tarns set at the bottom of the col between Bowfell and Crinkle Crags (NY 248 061).

7. As you reach the bottom of the col of Three Tarns (foot of the steep descent) the path forks - follow the left-hand rocky path (cairns) to quickly reach the top of a pitched-stone path that leads quite steeply down through the head of a gully alongside a small stream (Buscoe

Sike). The path soon opens out from this gully. Carry straight on along the pitched-stone path (leaving the stream to bear away down to the right) heading steadily down across the steep hillside (with the valley of Buscoe Sike sweeping away to your right). After approx. 0.5 km the path all but levels out (pitched-stone path ends) and leads straight on gradually dropping down across the top (right-hand side) of the broad ridge of land known as The Band *(which projects into Great Langdale with Oxendale down to your right)* for 1.3 km then, where a view of Great Langdale reveals itself as you approach the end of the ridge, the path becomes much steeper (pitched-stone path in places with some rocky sections) and winds steeply down across the end of The Band to eventually reach a kissing-gate in a wall across your path at the bottom of The Band *(2.5 km from Three Tarns - NY 273 057)*. Head through the gate and continue along the path down to reach a track which you follow to the left down to reach Stool End Farm. Head through the gate into the farmyard and follow the track bearing to the right (SP) skirting around the stone-built barn, after which the track becomes a metalled lane which you follow straight on across fields for 1 km to reach a road junction beside a post-box. Head straight on along the road for a short distance then left over the bridge across Great Langdale Beck then bear right at the fork back to the ODG.

Great Langdale Walking Weekend - Sunday Walk -

ODG, Blea Tarn, Little Langdale, Elterwater, Chapel Stile & Oak Howe

WALK INFORMATION

Highlights: A beautiful tarn where red squirrels abound, the path of the stallion that follows a Roman road, a Viking meeting place, a picturesque quarryman's bridge and swan lake.

Distance: 9 miles (14.25 km)   Time: Allow 4 - 5 hours

Map: OS Explorer maps OL6 & 7 - *always take a map on your walk.*

Refreshments: Pubs at Great Langdale (ODG & NDG), Little Langdale, Elterwater and Chapel Stile. Cafes and/or shops at Elterwater and Chapel Stile.

Terrain: A mixture of field paths, rough pastureland, quiet country lanes, stony tracks and riverside paths, with rough or rocky ground in places as well as some boggy areas. The route is undulating, with a short but steep climb from ODG up to the top of the pass over to Little Langdale.

Highest point: Pass between Great and Little Langdale - 224 metres above sea level.

Total ascent: 350 metres

Caution: Take care walking along the roads through Little Langdale and Great Langdale. This walk involves one short but steep climb.

POINTS OF INTEREST

This walk explores the valleys of Great Langdale and Little Langdale by way of a circuitous route around Lingmell Fell, which separates the two valleys. Great Langdale is the larger of the two valleys both in size and stature for its flat valley pastures are hemmed in by lofty mountains with the mighty Langdale Pikes soaring above, silent sentinels that draw your eyes skywards. Great Langdale is drained by Great Langdale Beck, which meanders across the valley floor skirting the villages of Chapel Stile and Elterwater before draining into Elter Water, the smallest of Lakeland's sixteen lakes This lake is also fed by the River Brathay, which drains Little Langdale. The emerging river is the Brathay, meaning 'broad river' in Old Norse, which then flows eastwards to swell the deep waters of Windermere.

From the Old Dungeon Ghyll, a path leads up to join the narrow road over to Little Langdale before skirting the shores of Blea Tarn, one of the most picturesque tarns in the Lake District with a classic view back towards the Langdale Pikes. Keep an eye out for red squirrels in the woodland around its shores. Beyond the tarn, the path follows the delightful Bleamoss Beck, with its small waterfalls, before heading across rough and boggy ground to join the road at the foot of the Wrynose Pass. This is one of the most famous mountain roads in Lakeland with sharp bends and steep drops; indeed, its name is derived from the old word 'Wrayene' meaning 'path of the stallion' as good strong horses were needed to make it to the top. The Three Shire Stone stands at the top of the pass, erected in 1816 on the spot where the old boundaries of Westmorland, Lancashire and Cumberland came together until Cumbria was created in 1974. The Roman road from Ambleside to Ravenglass came this way and is still visible in places next to the modern road, a tribute to the skill of those long forgotten road builders.

Little Langdale is a delightful valley, quieter than neighbouring Great Langdale and with a totally different character. It is hemmed in by craggy hills rather than mountains, although Wetherlam (762 metres) overlooks the head of the valley. Many of these hills have been quarried for green slate, especially around Tilberthwaite and on Lingmoor Fell above Elterwater. This slate was formed during the volcanic eruptions many millions of years ago that threw up fine ash into the atmosphere that then fell into a shallow sea where it was compressed to form these highly-prized slates. The picturesque footbridge of Slater Bridge that spans the River Brathay just to the east of Little Langdale Tarn was built to provide easy access for the quarrymen to get to the Tilberthwaite quarries from the hamlet of Little Langdale.

Just behind Fell Foot Farm at the head of the valley stands the Ting Mound, a rare example of a Viking meeting place where courts were held, law and order administered and disputes settled. These mounds were often artificially built, circular in shape with terraces leading up in steps to the top of the mound, where people could stand or sit to hear the pronouncements. These administrative meeting places were often centrally located within their area of jurisdiction; indeed, Little Langdale's Ting Mound is situated beside the old Roman road across the hills to the coast. This form of administration continued from those early Norse settlers in pre-Conquest times through the early medieval period until courthouses began to be built in towns as population levels grew during the 13th Century. Beyond Fell Foot Farm, our route follows an old stony track towards the former slate quarries of Tilberthwaite, passing Bridge End Farm along the way. The view back towards this farm with the magnificent Langdale Pikes as a backdrop is one of the most famous views in the Lake District. The farmhouse is a superb example of vernacular architecture with farmhouse and barn all under one roof. This design is known as a 'long house', a tradition that dates back to the Viking settlers as the animals would have provided heat in the house - an early form of central heating, albeit quite smelly!

For more information about Elterwater and Chapel Stile,
see Walking Weekend 7

GREAT LANGDALE SUNDAY WALK

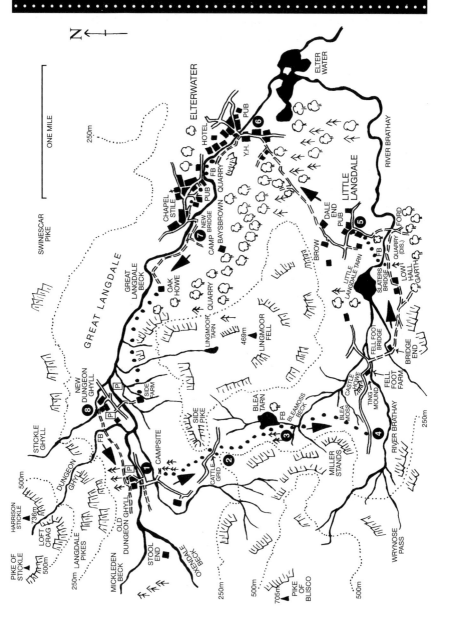

ONE MILE

250m

ELTER WATER

ELTERWATER

RIVER BRATHAY

HOTEL

PUB

Y.H.

6

SWINESCAR PIKE

CHAPEL STILE

NEW PUB

CAMP BRIDGE

BAYSBROWN QUARRY

LITTLE LANGDALE

DALE END PUB

5

FB

BROW

QUARRY (DIS.)

FORD

7

GREAT LANGDALE BECK

OAK HOWE

LINGMOOR TARN

QUARRY

LINGMOOR FELL

LITTLE LANGDALE TARN

SLATERS BRIDGE

LOW HALL GARTH

GREAT LANGDALE

469m

FELL FOOT BRIDGE

BRIDGE END

STICKLE GHYLL

NEW DUNGEON GHYLL

P

P

SIDE FARM

SIDE PIKE

BLEA TARN

FB

BLEAMOSS BECK

CASTLE HOWE

FELL FOOT FARM

250m

8

P

P

FB

CAMPSITE

CATTLE GRID

2

3

BLEA MOSS

TING MOUND

4

RIVER BRATHAY

HARRISON STICKLE

500m

736m

1

DUNGEON GHYLL

MILLER STANDS

WRYNOSE PASS

PIKE OF STICKLE

LOFT CRAG

500m

250m LANGDALE PIKES

500m

OLD DUNGEON GHYLL

P

STOOL END

MICKLEDEN BECK

OXENDALE BECK

250m

500m

705m

PIKE OF BLISCO

500m

© Crown Copyright 2005. All rights reserved. Licence Number 100011978

159

THE WALK

1. From the Old Dungeon Ghyll (with your back to the hotel), walk along the driveway away from the hotel, bearing left over the bridge across Great Langdale Beck to quickly reach a T-junction where you turn right then follow the road bending sharp left (by the post-box) to reach another bridge across a stream. After this bridge, turn left through the gate (SP) and follow the track across the campsite parking area then, after a short distance, take the path to the right over a small FB (following the curve of the wall on your right) then straight on across the campsite to reach a kissing gate at the foot of a small wooded bank (end of campsite). Follow the path up through another kissing gate then between two old stone gateposts in a wall and out onto a field. Bear to the right up across the field to a kissing gate that leads into woodland, then follow the path up to another kissing gate at the top of the woods, after which follow the path winding steeply up the hillside (wall on your right) to reach the top of the 'pass' and a road on your right. Carry straight on alongside the wall/road on your right to soon reach a ladder stile that leads onto the road by a cattle grid *(top of the pass between Great Langdale and Little Langdale)*.

2. After the ladder stile, head straight across the road (passing the cattle grid on your left) then carry straight on alongside the wall on your left to quickly reach a bridle-gate in this wall on your left (NY 289 051). Head through the bridle-gate and follow the stony path straight on heading gently down through the valley (with crags rising up to your right) for 0.75 km to reach a bridlegate in a fence that leads into coniferous woodland, with Blea Tarn just across to your left. Head through the gate and follow the path straight on through woodland skirting the shores of the tarn to reach a bridlegate across your path beside Bleamoss Beck at the bottom end of the tarn *(ignore FB to your left)*.

3. After the bridlegate, follow the rocky path straight on alongside Bleamoss Beck on your left, crossing over a small side-stream after 100 metres then continue on for a further 50 metres to reach

another side-stream where Bleamoss Beck bends distinctly to the left into a small, rocky ravine (NY 293 040). Cross this side-stream and follow the path bending to the left alongside this rocky ravine (waterfalls) then, after about 100 metres, follow the path bearing gradually away from the stream following the curve of the hillside on your right (Miller Stands) to join a wall on your left. Follow the path straight on alongside this wall on your left then, where the wall bends away, continue straight on following the gently curving hillside (crags of Miller Stands to your right) to reach the unfenced moorland road at the foot of the Wrynose Pass (NY 292 032) - *as you approach this road the path disappears as you head across boggy ground.*

4. Turn left along the road and follow it down to reach Fell Foot Farm. Follow the road passing in front of the farmhouse, just after which the road bends round to the left and joins the infant River Brathay on your right then, after 100 metres, turn right over a stone bridge across the river (Fell Foot Bridge). Follow the track straight on across fields to reach a bridge across Greenburn Beck with Bridge End Farm just beyond (NY 301 029). From Bridge End Farm follow the track straight on then curving round to the left (wall on your left) and gently rising up for 600 metres to reach a fork in the track. Follow the left-hand track down to soon reach a gate in a wall at the start of a walled track (with High Hall Garth farm just ahead). Follow the enclosed track passing High Hall Garth then steeply down to reach another old farmhouse of Low Hall Garth (climbing hut). Follow the track bending to the right around the buildings (track levels out) then continue straight on along the track for 250 metres then turn left through a kissing-gate (and wall-stile) down to reach Slater Bridge (stone FB) across the River Brathay. Cross the bridge then, after a few paces, turn right through a wall-gap and follow the path gently rising up across the hillside, through a gap in an old wall then carry on up to reach a kissing-gate in a fence at the top of the low hill. Head through the kissing-gate and walk straight on bearing slightly to the right down to reach a kissing gate that leads onto an enclosed lane beside some houses (NY 315 032). Turn left up along the lane to reach its junction with the main valley road *(Three Shires Inn detour to right).*

5. Turn left along the road and follow it up through the hamlet then continue along the road for 200 metres (Little Langdale Tarn comes into view ahead) then turn right along a farm lane (sign 'Unsuitable for Motor vehicles') and follow this up to reach Dale End Farm (at the end of the metalled lane). At the farm, carry straight on along the clear enclosed stony track and follow this for 600 metres across the hillside *(ignore any paths/tracks off this main track)*, with Howe Banks rising up to your left, to reach a gate across the track that leads into woodland (NY 321 041). Carry straight on down along the track through the woodland for a further 600 metres to join a track coming in from your left (near a house). The track now becomes a lane, which you follow straight on for 250 metres down to join a road. Turn left along the road down into Elterwater.

6. As you reach the road-bridge across Great Langdale Beck in the centre of Elterwater turn left immediately before this bridge along a lane ('Dead End' sign and sign on wall 'Chapel Stile') and follow this up out of the village with Great Langdale Beck on your right. Follow this lane for 400 metres *(caution: quarry traffic)* then, as you reach a fenced-off slate mine entrance on your left, head right along a clear path (SP 'Chapel Stile') that leads down through woodland to join Great Langdale Beck on your right (NY 325 051). Follow the path straight on passing a large spoil heap on your left just after which you reach a FB across Great Langdale Beck. Cross the FB to quickly join the road beside Wainwrights' Inn. Turn left along the road passing the pub, a short distance after which take the path to the left (SP 'Baysbrown Campsite') and follow the path round to quickly join a wall on your right and follow this wall bending round to the right then head straight on (wall on your right) for 150 metres to join a road across your path. Turn left along this road for a few paces then, where this road forks by the entrance to the house, head to the right along the narrow lane and follow it into the yard of Thrang Farm. Pass to the right of the buildings along an enclosed path and follow this to join a stony track, which you follow to the left (SP 'Baysbrown Campsite') round to reach New Bridge across Great Langdale Beck (NY 317 053).

7. After the bridge follow the track bending sharply round to the right then straight on alongside Great Langdale Beck on your right *(campsite to your left – ignore track up towards the farm)* for 600 metres then follow the track as it very gradually bears away from the river across the middle of the field then sweeping round to the left to reach Oak Howe Farm (at the foot of Lingmoor Fell). Carry straight on passing in front of the house then follow the path curving round to the right around the stone barn on your right to quickly reach a path junction. At this path junction, carry straight on (SP 'New Dungeon Ghyll') along the stony path alongside a wall on your left then, after 125 metres, follow the path bending sharp left (waymarker-post). Follow this path straight on *(Langdale Pikes ahead of you in the distance)*, enclosed by walls on either side, then drop down to reach a gate in a wall across your path. After the gate, carry straight on along the stony path alongside a wall on your right heading across the hillside for 0.75 km to reach a stream (which drains Lingmoor Tarn high on the fell-side) just beyond which you reach a small gap in the wall corner (set in a small enclosure). Head through this wall gap and follow the path gradually down across the hillside at first then more steeply down a pitched-stone path (heading towards Side House Farm) to reach a gate in the bottom corner of the field (NY 297 061). Head through the gate and follow the path straight on to reach Side House Farm. As you reach the farm buildings, cross the small FB to the right across the stream and through a gate beside the stone barn that leads into the farmyard. Bear to the right down through the farmyard and out along the enclosed farm track and follow this across fields, over a bridge across Great Langdale Beck and up to join the road at New Dungeon Ghyll.

8. Turn right along the road for 200 metres then left up into the heart of the hamlet (New Dungeon Ghyll Hotel on your right and Stickle Barn Tavern on your left) where you carry straight on up passing to the right-hand side of Stickle Cottage (SP) and through a bridle-gate, after which follow the path up alongside the fence/hedge on your left to quickly reach a gap in a wall in the top left corner of the field. After the gap, follow the rocky path straight on gently rising

up and through a small belt of trees, immediately after which the path forks - head left along the rocky path rising up with the wall on your left to reach a kissing-gate beside a field gate in a wall across your path. Head through the gate and follow the path straight on alongside the wall on your left for 0.75 km back to reach the cluster of buildings at Old Dungeon Ghyll. You pass above a whitewashed house (just above the ODG) to reach a kissing-gate in a wall across your path, after which head down to the left to quickly join a stony track which you follow to the left through a gate in the bottom corner of the field then head straight on down passing behind the ODG back to the car park.

Great Langdale

KESWICK

Keswick lies in the Vale of Keswick along the banks of the River Greta with Derwent Water close by. It has an enviable position with valleys and mountains on all sides, including Skiddaw to the north and Borrowdale to the south. Its history can be traced back to AD554 when St Kentigern travelled to this area from Scotland and established a church at Crosthwaite, which means 'cross in a clearing'. Nothing remains of this ancient church, although fragments remain of its 12th Century replacement. In medieval times the church belonged to Fountains Abbey (Yorkshire) and was rebuilt in the 14th and 16th Centuries. Keswick was first mentioned in the 13th Century and means 'cheese farm' as the monks of both Furness and Fountains abbeys owned grazing land in this area. Keswick gained a market charter in 1276, which still continues to this day. This small, rural trading centre was transformed in the 16th Century when the Company of Mines Royal was founded by Elizabeth I to exploit mineral reserves in Borrowdale and the Newlands Valley, particularly lead, copper and silver. A pure deposit of graphite was discovered during this time at Seathwaite. Graphite had a variety of uses, most notably in the production of pencils. Writing instruments have been around since at least Roman times, but it was the discovery of this graphite that heralded a new era for writers and artists across the world. The Cumberland Pencil Company opened the UK's first pencil factory at Keswick in 1832, and is still making pencils under its 'Derwent' brand. The mines continued to be worked into the 19th Century, when cheaper imports heralded their terminal decline.

This decline coincided with the growth of tourism, helped by the arrival of the railway as well as the Lakes Poets whose romantic writings put the Lake District on the tourist map. Southey and Coleridge both lived at Keswick during the early 19th Century.

THE TOWN

Keswick offers plenty of facilities, including hotels, B&Bs, lots of pubs, a Youth Hostel, campsites, restaurants, cafes, bakers, delicatessens, sandwich shops, supermarkets, newsagents, outdoor shops, chemist, Post Office, several High Street banks, toilets, garage, bus station, hospital (minor injury unit) as well as the Theatre by the Lake, various museums, boat hire and the Keswick Launch (Derwent Water).

ACCOMMODATION

Tourist Information Centre, Keswick   017687 72645

KESWICK PUBS

There are over a dozen pubs in Keswick. These are two of my favourites:

George Hotel, Keswick   **017687 72076**
George Hotel is Keswick's oldest inn where the Earl of Derwentwater called in for ale before embarking on the ill-fated 1715 Jacobite Rebellion, a cause that would cost him his life. This historic inn has plenty of character with several rooms, old beams, open fires and an old coaching horn above the fireplace.

Dog and Gun, Keswick   **017687 73463**
The Dog and Gun is situated just off the top of the Market Place along the old Lake Road. This is a great traditional pub with a stone-flagged bar, open fire, extensive range of local real ales and a buzzing atmosphere. It is famous for its Hungarian Goulash. No accommodation.

Keswick Walking Weekend
- Saturday Walk -
Keswick, Jenkin Hill, Skiddaw, Bakestall, Skiddaw House & Lonscale Crags

WALK INFORMATION

Highlights: An unusual clock, pony routes and tourist trails, a 3,000-ft high ridge, the Back O' Skiddaw, Britain's highest Youth Hostel and a high-level path above Glenderaterra Beck.

Distance: 14 miles (22.5 km)   *shorter route: 16 km (10 miles)*

Time: Allow 7 - 8 hours

Map: OS Explorer map OL4 - *always take a map on your walk.*

Refreshments: Pubs, shops and Tea Rooms at Keswick. No facilities en route - take provisions with you.

Terrain: Clear lanes, tracks and paths leave Keswick and climb up through woodland and across the slopes of Latrigg to reach the top of Gale Road. A well-trodden path (tourist route) then leads up onto Skiddaw, steep in places. The summit is rocky, with steep slopes on either side of the broad summit ridge. The descent heads across Open Access land with a clear path for most of the way alongside a fence, and a steep descent along Birkett Edge. A track then leads through upland valleys to Skiddaw House from where a path heads across the steep slopes of Lonscale Fell high above Glenderaterra Beck back to Gale Road.

Highest point: Skiddaw - 931 metres above sea level.

Total ascent:	990 metres
Escape route:	From the summit of Skiddaw, re-trace your steps back down along the 'tourist route'.
Shorter route:	Start from parking area at the top of Gale Road, NY 281 254 (Point 2 of the walk). This will save 6.5 km (as well as 200 metres of climbing).
Open Access:	The section from Skiddaw to Dash Beck heads across Open Access land **www.openaccess.gov.uk**
Caution:	**Mountain Walk.** This is a strenuous walk to the summit of Skiddaw, with mountainous terrain in places. The path is clear for most of the way to the summit. There are a number of steep sections, especially the climb from Whit Beck to Jenkin Hill and the descent down Birkett Edge. There are steep drops to the side of the wide path across Lonscale Crags - care is required on this section as well as a head for heights. The path also fords Whit Beck. OS map and compass essential. Do not attempt in poor weather.

POINTS OF INTEREST

Keswick's large Market Place is lined with elegant Georgian and Victorian houses, shops and inns, at the centre of which is the historic Moot Hall. A market building has stood here since at least the 16th Century, although the present building dates from the early 19th Century and has been used over the years as a covered market, court house, prison and town hall; it is currently used as the Tourist Information Centre. Of particular note is the Moot Hall clock, which only has an hour hand as local folk were only interested in hours, not minutes! From the Market Place, our route follows Station Road across the River Greta to reach the former Keswick Railway Station. The Cockermouth, Keswick and Penrith Railway was built in the 1860s to provide a rail link between industrial County Durham and west Cumberland. The line was busy with freight throughout its history, and also brought tourists to the Northern Lakes. Despite fierce local opposition, the line succumbed to Beeching's infamous axe. In 1964 freight services were stopped and in 1966 the section from Keswick westwards to Workington was closed, leaving the Penrith to Keswick section open as a branch line. This was not sustainable and in 1972 the line was closed completely. There are efforts to re-open the Penrith to Keswick section.

From Keswick, a delightful path climbs up across the flanks of Latrigg to reach the top of Gale Road, just beyond which is the Hawell Memorial, a carved Celtic cross in memory of two local shepherds and noted Herdwick breeders. This memorial marks the start of the steep climb up onto Jenkin Hill on the south-eastern shoulder of Skiddaw Little Man. This wide path, known as the tourist route, leads all the way to the summit and has been in use for well over 100 years, making it one of the oldest recreational paths in Lakeland. Ponies used to take intrepid Victorian visitors from Keswick's railway station all the way to the summit, with a refreshment hut halfway up. Beyond Skiddaw Little Man, the path climbs up onto Skiddaw's South Top where a dramatic view unfolds of Carl Side, Longside Edge and Southerndale. An easy walk across the top of the broad summit ridge leads to Skiddaw's summit, known as the Main Top. The summit ridge extends for half a mile in a north-south direction and exceeds 3,000-ft along its length, with four 'tops' along the ridge - South Top, Middle Top, Main Top and North Top. Skiddaw has the distinction of being one of only four mountains in England above 3,000-feet, the other three being Scafell Pike, Scafell and Helvellyn. Skiddaw actually forms the highest mountain in the centre of a large mountain range with several lesser tops radiating out along descending ridges. The slopes of these mountains are generally more rounded than the volcanic rocks of central Lakeland. This is due to its underlying Skiddaw Slates, which are layers of sedimentary rock laid down around 500 million years ago at the bottom of a sea where silt and mud were compressed to form layers of soft shale and slate that erode easily.

From the summit, our route leaves the crowds behind as we head down the northern ridge passing above Gilbratar Crag that juts out above Barkbethdale to reach Bakestall from where there are far-reaching views across northern Cumbria towards the Solway Firth and the hills of southern Scotland. From Bakestall there is a steep descent along Birkett Edge into the valley of Dash Beck to join a track known as the Supply Road. A short detour down to the left brings you to the slender waterfall of Whitewater Dash. You are now on the north-western edge of the unfrequented fells known as the 'Back O' Skiddaw', which are reminiscent of the Pennines with rolling hills and heather moorland. The Supply Road leads through the valley of Dash Beck, which feeds into Bassenthwaite Lake to the west, passing its source amongst Candleseaves Bog on the slopes of Skiddaw before crossing the watershed to reach the headwaters of the River Caldew, which flows north-eastwards to swell the waters of the River Eden. Here is the lonely Skiddaw House, the highest youth hostel in the country. It was originally built in the early 19th Century by the Earl of Egremont as a shooting lodge and home for his gamekeeper and shepherd. This whole area is known as Skiddaw Forest, although the only trees to be found are the ones that shelter Skiddaw House; 'forest' is a historic term that was applied to hunting preserves. From Skiddaw House, the final part of this walk follows an exciting high-level path across the eastern slopes of Lonscale Fell, with sheer drops down into the valley of Glenderaterra Beck.

KESWICK SATURDAY WALK MAP A

© Crown Copyright 2005. All rights reserved. Licence Number 100011978

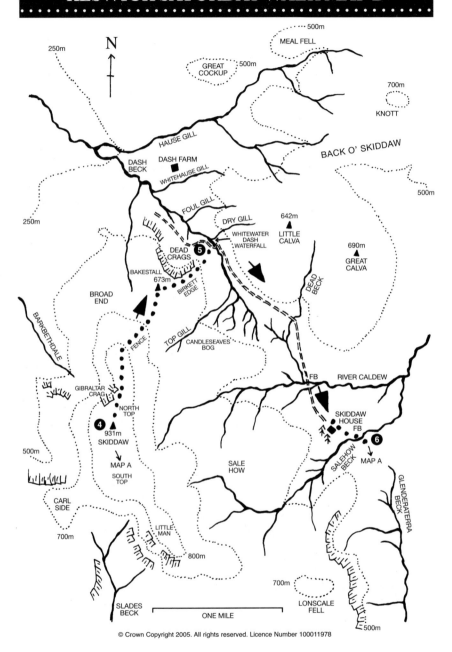

172

THE WALK

1. From the Moot Hall in the centre of Keswick, head out of the top left-hand corner of the Market Place to quickly reach a road junction where you turn left along Station Street and follow this to reach a crossroads with Penrith Road. Continue straight on along Station Road and follow this over a bridge across the River Greta then passing Keswick Museum & Art Gallery and Fitz Park then, just after the museum, follow the road bending sharp right along Brundholme Road. Follow this road straight on passing beneath an old railway bridge then curving round to the left to reach a mini roundabout where you head to the right along Brundholme Road, which merges into Briar Rigg Road *(ignore turning towards Windebrowe and Brundholme)*. Continue along this road *(use roadside path)* passing a small housing estate on your left. As the road drops down a gentle slope, take the stony track (Spooney Green Lane) to the right (SP 'Skiddaw') and follow this track straight on across a bridge above the A66 then on to reach a gate across the track just after Spooney Green House (NY 270 244). Head through the gate and follow the track straight on up through Latrigg Woods with the edge of the woods on your left *(ignore track off to the right)* climbing quite steeply up for 500 metres then follow the track bending sharp left over a small stream then on to quickly reach the promontory of Ewe How (viewpoint). At Ewe How, follow the track bending sharply round to the right *(ignore path off to the right just beyond Ewe How)* then straight on heading up across the wooded hillside (small valley falling away to your left) then bending sharply round to the left over a small stream to reach a gate across the track. Head through the gate and follow the path straight on then curving to the right to join the corner of a plantation on your left (Gale Gill Woods). Continue straight on alongside the plantation/fence on your left then, where this plantation ends, continue along the path (head of Gale Gill valley down to your left) all the way up to reach the top of Gale Road beside the parking area (NY 281 254).

2. Turn right along the road (Gale Road) through the parking area to quickly reach a gate at the top end of the road (track ahead), immediately after which turn left (SP 'Skiddaw, Bassenthwaite, Mosedale') along a path alongside the wall on your left (wall becomes a fence) then follow the fence bending left to reach a gate across your path. Head through the gate and follow the path alongside the fence on your left rising steadily up to soon reach the Hawell Memorial Cross. Carry straight on along the path and down into a slight dip before climbing steeply up (valley of Whit Beck falling away to your right) to reach a gate in the fence/tumbledown wall on your left. Head through the gate and follow the wide path heading steeply up with the fence now on your right then, after about 400 metres, the path bends to the left away from the fence climbing up for a further 200 metres before the path bends distinctly to the left and the gradient eases. Follow this path straight on across the hillside steadily rising up for 1 km *(twin peaks of Skiddaw Little Man come into view ahead)* to reach a bridlegate/stile in a fence and a fork in the path on Jenkin Hill, at the foot of Skiddaw Little Man (NY 272 275).

3. Head through the bridlegate (sign on gate 'Skiddaw Summit') and follow the path straight on contouring across the steep upper (north-eastern) slopes of Skiddaw Little Man (with its summit up to your left), with the head of Salehow Beck falling away to your right. After 600 metres the path curves to the left skirting around the northern side of Skiddaw Little Man and rises up to reach a gate in a fence across your path in the saddle of land between Skiddaw and Skiddaw Little Man, with the summit ridge of Skiddaw rising in front of you *(same fence you passed through on Jenkin Hill)*. Head through the gate and follow the wide path straight on climbing quite steeply up onto the southern end (South Top) of Skiddaw's summit ridge, marked by a cairn. As you reach this cairn, head to the right *(northwards)* for 500 metres along the top of the broad, rocky summit ridge (cairns and shelters), with two very slight 'down and ups' along the ridge as you head across the Middle Top, to reach the Trig Point, viewfinder and shelter on the summit of Skiddaw (NY 261 291).

4. From the summit of Skiddaw, carry straight on along the top of the summit ridge *(heading northwards)* to soon reach the North Top at the northern end of the ridge (shelter) where you head straight on dropping steadily down the northern ridge *(keep to the path down the middle of the ridge -crags across to your left)* then, where the path levels out and the ridge widens out as you reach the flat grassy expanse of Broad End (path disappears), head to the right to quickly join a fence on your right *(same fence as you passed through on Jenkin Hill)*. Head straight on alongside this fence on your right *(keep alongside this fence all the way down off the mountain)* to soon reach a fence corner (where the ridge begins to drop down again at the end of Broad End - NY 262 300). Head to the right alongside this fence and follow this steadily down for 0.75 km before levelling out then gently rising up onto Bakestall *(summit of Bakestall short detour ahead)*. As you reach the top of Bakestall, follow the fence to the right heading steeply down the hillside (Birkett Edge) passing above the crags of Birkett Edge just off the path to the left *(keep away from these crags)* all the way down to join the Supply Road (track) in the valley of Dash Beck, with Little Calva rising up in front of you (NY 273 313). *Short detour to left down along track to Whitewater Dash waterfalls.*

5. Turn right along the track (Supply Road) and follow this to soon cross over Dash Beck then winding slightly up before levelling out heading up through the valley, with Dash Beck down to your right. After a while, the track leaves Dash Beck behind (which bends away to its source on the flanks of Skiddaw) - continue straight on along the track crossing the 'watershed' between Dash Beck and the River Caldew. After 1.5 km the track crosses the small stream of Dead Beck (which feeds into the Caldew) then bends slightly to the right and drops down for a further 0.75 km to reach a ford/FB across the infant River Caldew. Cross the ford/FB and continue straight on along the track rising up to reach Skiddaw House (Youth Hostel). As you approach Skiddaw House (just before the gate that leads into the enclosed garden in front of Skiddaw House), bear left off the track (waymarker-post) and through a gap in the wall then carry

straight on alongside the wall on your right (following the wall enclosure around the front of Skiddaw House). After you have passed Skiddaw House (wall ends on your right), carry straight on gently dropping down and bearing slightly left to reach a FB across Salehow Beck (NY 291 289).

6. After the FB, follow the path straight on across the heather moorland to reach a gate across your path (where a fence joins a wall). Head through the gate and follow the path bearing slightly right at first then straight on across the hillside with the head of the valley of Glenderaterra Beck just down to your left *(heading towards the crags of Lonscale Fell ahead of you)* for 400 metres to join an old wall on your left (NY 293 284). Carry straight on alongside this wall on your left then, where this wall begins to bend away down to the left after 500 metres, you come to a fork in the path - carry straight on along the right-hand fork (leaving the wall to bend away down to the left) to soon reach a FB across a side-stream. Cross the FB and carry straight on along the path heading across the steep slopes of Lonscale Fell, with the valley of Glenderaterra Beck falling steeply away to your left. As you approach the end of the valley after 1.75 km, the path crosses crags and rocks (Lonscale Crags) beyond which it bends to the right onto easier ground leaving the Glenderaterra valley behind to quickly reach a gate in a fence (NY 294 261). Head through the gate and follow the path straight on across the hillside (following the curve of the hillside) for 1 km to reach a ford across Whit Beck set in a ravine. Cross the stream and follow the path bending sharp left then rising up across the valley side, with Whit Beck down to your left. The path soon levels out and curves slightly to the right across the field (away from the stream) to join a fence on your right and a gate across your path (near the Hawell Memorial Cross). Carry straight on alongside this fence on your right and follow it curving to the right then straight on back to the parking area at the top of Gale Road.

7. Walk down through the small parking area then, after 50 metres, take the footpath to the left through a gate (SP 'Keswick'). Re-trace your steps along the path back down across the lower slopes of

Latrigg *(keep to the clear path heading downhill all the way)* passing Gale Gill Woods on your right then down to reach Ewe How (viewpoint) before heading down through Latrigg Woods back to reach Spooney Green House where you carry on along the track over the A66 back to join the road on the outskirts of Keswick. Turn left along this road (Briar Rigg Road which merges into Brundholme Road) and re-trace your steps back into Keswick.

Keswick

Keswick Walking Weekend
- Sunday Walk -
Keswick, Walla Crag, Ashness Bridge, Derwent Water & Friar's Crag

WALK INFORMATION

Highlights: Far-reaching views across Derwent Water, fleeing with the family jewels, the most photographed bridge in Lakeland and a beautiful lakeshore path.

Distance: 6.5 miles (10.5 km) Time: Allow 3 - 4 hours

Map: OS Explorer map OL4 - *always take a map on your walk.*

Refreshments: Pubs and shops at Keswick. No facilities en route.

Terrain: A mixture of quiet lanes, woodland, moorland and lakeside paths. Walla Crag is exposed to the elements, with sheer cliffs and steep drops. There are also a number of small streams to cross. *You may shorten this walk by catching the Keswick Launch (boat) from Ashness Gate Jetty back to Keswick.*

Highest point: Walla Crag - 379 metres above sea level.

Total ascent: 290 metres

Caution: There is a fairly steep climb up to Walla Crag. There are steep drops to the side of the path across Walla Crag; if in doubt, follow the path that keeps to the left-hand side of the wall across the top of Walla Crag. If the lakeside path along Derwent Water is flooded, follow the roadside path (B5289) for 1 km from Ashness Gate to Calfclose Bay where, at the bus stops just before Great Wood car park, head left down to re-join the lakeside path. Alternatively, follow the roadside path all the way back to Keswick.

POINTS OF INTEREST

Walla Crag dominates Derwent Water and the lower reaches of Borrowdale, a long line of crags that rise up above the tree canopy of Great Wood. Seen from Keswick, these crags look quite daunting, but the climb to its crest is surprisingly easy. The top of Walla Crag is carpeted with heather and affords one of the finest views in Lakeland with Keswick framed by the Skiddaw massif, Derwent Water spread out before you and Cat Bells rising up beyond. Just beyond the highest point is a ravine that cuts into the crags known as Lady's Rake. It is named after Lady Radclyffe, wife of James Radclyffe, the 3rd Earl of Derwentwater. The Radclyffe family were devout Catholics and supporters of James Stuart, the Old Pretender. However, the Earl was executed following his part in the Jacobite Uprising of 1715. This 'Fifteen Rebellion' was an attempt to restore the Catholic Stuart kings to the British throne and displace the Hanoverians; however, the Jacobite forces were defeated at the Battle of Preston and the rebellion collapsed in 1716. When Lady Radclyffe returned to Lord's Island many local people, upset at the Earl's execution, blamed her for his fate and so she fled to the top of Walla Crag via Lady's Rake, taking the family valuables with her! The Earl of Derwentwater owned land and estates around Keswick, including a house on Lord's Island, as well as Dilston Hall in Northumberland, but these were forfeited to the Crown following the 1715 uprising.

The walk from Walla Crag to Ashness Bridge is superb, with the path skirting around the head of the deep ravine of Cat Gill then above Falcon Crag before a gradual descent to reach Ashness Gill, with beautiful views across the head of Derwent Water. Ashness Bridge is a wonderful example of a single-arched packhorse bridge, although it has been widened over the years to accommodate the motor road. This road was once a busy packhorse route up to the hidden hamlet of Watendlath, from where routes radiated out across the fells over to Rosthwaite, Armboth and Wythburn. These packhorse trails were the motorways of medieval England, with the packhorses carrying panniers full of commodities such as lead, wool, coal and salt. This picturesque bridge is probably the most photographed in Lakeland, with the tumbling waters of Ashness Gill flowing beneath the bridge framed by Skiddaw in the distance.

The lakeshore path from Ashness Gate all the way back to Keswick is a delight with sweeping bays, woodland copse and fine views across the island-studded lake towards Catbells. The highlight is Friar's Crag, a tree-capped outcrop that juts out into Derwent Water between Derwent Isle and Lord's Island. The crag is said to be named after the monks who would make pilgrimages from this outcrop out to St Herbert's Island on Derwent Water. John Ruskin was brought here as a five-year-old child by his nurse, a moment he remembered for the rest of life. He later described the experience as *"the creation of the world for me"* and claimed the view to be one of the finest in Europe. There is an inscribed memorial stone to John Ruskin at Friar's Crag. Alongside the path between Friar's Crag and the Landing Stages is a memorial to Canon Rawnsley (1851 - 1920), one of the Lake District's most prominent and influential campaigners who saw beauty in the landscape and realised this beauty needed protection. He was vicar of St Margaret's Church at Low Wray near Ambleside and then St Kentigern's Church at Crosthwaite; in 1912 he was appointed as Chaplain to the King. Throughout this time he campaigned to conserve and preserve the beauty of the Lake District whilst improving public access to it. He was also concerned about uncontrolled industrial development threatening and destroying the countryside and coastline of the British Isles. In 1895 he co-founded The National Trust along with Octavia Hill and Sir Robert Hunter to permanently preserve beautiful or historic land and buildings for the benefit of the nation. Today, The National Trust has over 3.5 million members and owns 612,000 acres of countryside, 700 miles of coastline and more than 200 important buildings and gardens. He was also a close friend of John Ruskin and Beatrix Potter. Canon Rawnsley lies buried in the churchyard at Crosthwaite.

For more information about Derwent Water and Borrowdale,
see Walking Weekend 11

For more information about John Ruskin and Beatrix Potter,
see Walking Weekend 5

KESWICK SUNDAY WALK

RIVER DERWENT

A66

A66

RIVER GRETA

① FITZ PARK

DISMANTLED RAILWAY

KESWICK

STONE CIRCLE

CAMPING

CROW PARK

P

THEATRE

JETTYS

FRIAR'S CRAG

B5289

SPRINGS FARM

MAST

FB

THE INGS

SPRINGS WOOD

FB

CASTLERIGG

FB

② RAKEFOOT

FB

N

A591

STABLE HILLS

CALF CLOSE BAY

GREAT WOOD

WALLA CRAG

③

BROCKLE BECK

P

CAT GILL

250m

FALCON CRAG

④

CASTLERIGG FELL

BLEABERRY FELL

FB

ASHNESS BRIDGE

DERWENT WATER

ASHNESS GILL

ASHNESS WOOD

BORROWDALE

RIVER DERWENT

250m

ONE MILE

608m
▲
HIGH SEAT

500m

500m

⑤ STABLE HILLS

THE WALK

....

1. From the Moot Hall in the centre of Keswick, head out of the top
    left-hand corner of the Market Place to quickly reach a road
    junction where you carry straight on along St John's Street heading
    out of the town centre, passing the George Hotel on your left then
    St John's Church on your right. Continue straight on along this road
    (becomes Ambleside Road) then, as you reach the edge of Keswick
    where the road begins to climb quite steeply up (Manor Brow), turn
    right along Springs Road. Follow this road straight on, with houses
    on your left and fields to your right, for 700 metres to reach a bridge
    across Brockle Beck at Springs Farm (end of metalled lane). Carry
    straight on along the stony track bearing to the left (Brockle Beck
    to your left) through a gateway just to the right of a small barn and
    up to reach a gate across the track that leads into Springs Wood (NY
    276 226). Follow the track gently rising up through the woods
    (stream to your left) to reach a fork in the track (FB just to your left)
    where you turn sharp right (sign 'Rakefoot Farm, Walla Crag,
    Castlerigg Stone Circle') then bending round to the left heading up
    along the edge of the woodland (fields on your right). Follow this
    path up along the edge of the woods, with the stream down to your
    left, passing a transmitter mast to reach a path junction where you
    carry straight on (sign 'Castlerigg, Walla Crag') rising up, with the
    wooded stream down to your left, to eventually reach a FB across
    Brockle Beck. Cross the FB and head up to quickly join a road
    (NY 283 223).

2. Turn right along the road and follow it up to reach a fork in the road
    just before Rakefoot Farm where you follow the right-hand lane
    (sign 'Walla Crag') to soon reach a FB to your right just before the
    end of the metalled lane. Cross this FB (SP 'Walla Crag') after
    which head left up along the stony path alongside the wall on your
    right (Brockle Beck down to your left) to reach a gate in a wall
    across your path. After the gate, carry straight on along the path
    heading up alongside the wall then, after 100 metres, follow the wall
    bending up to the right - follow the path heading quite steeply up

alongside this wall (leaving Brockle Beck behind). After 300 metres the path levels out and drops down very slightly over the source of a small stream before climbing gradually up bearing slightly left (with the wall now just across to your right - *the path cuts off this slight 'kink' in the wall)* then, where the path re-joins the wall, head through the kissing-gate in a section of fence set in this wall that brings you out on the top of Walla Crag (NY 279 215).

3. After the kissing-gate, follow the clear, undulating path straight on along the top of Walla Crag *(caution - steep drops to side of path)* for 400 metres to reach the highest point on Walla Crag, marked by a small cairn. From this highest point, carry straight on along the path across the top of the crags dropping very slightly down to reach a stile set in the wall to your left (NY 276 211). Cross the stile, after which turn right to immediately reach a fork in the path where you head left (away from the wall) along the wide grassy path across the flat open moorland. Follow this path straight on for 250 metres then gently curving round to the right *(ignore path that branches off to the left)* across this shelf of moorland, with Castlerigg Fell rising up across to your left, to soon reach Cat Gill (stream) at the head of its ravine. Cross this stream and follow the path straight on to soon reach another stream (feeder stream into Cat Gill), after which follow the path as it skirts around the head of another (southern) feeder stream into Cat Gill ravine. Beyond the head of this ravine, continue along the path heading across the shelf of moorland for approximately 150 metres then gently curving left passing a small boulder beside the path *(views open out ahead of the Jaws of Borrowdale ahead).* The path now leads straight on dropping gently down across the hillside, with Borrowdale in the distance, for 0.75 km to reach a bridle-gate in a wall across your path, and Ashness Bridge down to your right (NY 272 198). Head through this gate and carry straight on down across the hillside to reach a FB across Ashness Gill (stream), after which follow the path to the right (alongside this stream) down to join the road beside Ashness Bridge. Turn right over Ashness Bridge and follow the road down to reach the main Borrowdale Road (B5289) just above Derwent

Water (NY 269 204). *You may shorten this walk by catching the Keswick Launch (boat) from Ashness Gate Jetty back to Keswick.*

4. Cross over the road *(take care)* and down through the squeeze-stile opposite that leads down onto the shore beside Ashness Gate Jetty (Keswick Launch landing stage).* Turn right along the narrow shoreline (Derwent Water on your left) and follow this for 500 metres (parallel with the road on your right) then, where the shore opens out, follow the path straight on through woodland (Derwent Water now just across to your left) to emerge out onto Calfclose Bay. Follow the shoreline path skirting round to the left around Calfclose Bay (heading away from the road). As you reach the far end of the bay you cross a small stream, after which follow the path heading to the left (alongside a fence on your right), with Derwent Water to your left, to reach a small rise of land (capped by tall fir trees) which juts out slightly into the lake (NY 267 215). Follow the path across this small rise of land to reach a small gate in a fence, after which follow the path straight on along the edge of the field (lake to your left) to soon reach Stable Hills (house). * *The lakeside path between Ashness Gate Jetty and Stable Hills is a permissive path.*

5. As you approach the house, follow the path bearing to the right (away from the lake) to join the access track from the house. Follow this track to the right then curving round to the left to reach a cattle grid. Carry straight on along the enclosed lane passing the entrance to the house then, where the lane bends right after 200 metres, take the path to the left through a gate that leads into woodland (The Ings). Follow the path through the woodland/marshland for 300 metres then, as you approach the end of the woods, follow the path round to the left over a FB across Brockle Beck then carry straight on through the woods to reach a gate at the end of the woods (NY 266 222). After the gate, follow the path straight on across the sparsely wooded pastureland following the shoreline of Derwent Water again to soon reach a gate that leads onto Friar's Crag *(rocky rise of land capped by pine trees)*. After the gate, head left up stone steps to reach the Ruskin Memorial and the Friar's Crag viewpoint. As you reach the

Memorial, head right and follow this clear path through woodland with Derwent Water on your left. This path joins a metalled road beside the entrance to a house - follow this road straight on to reach the boat houses and landing stages (Keswick Launch) on the outskirts of Keswick. After these landing stages, follow the road straight on (away from the lake) passing the Theatre by the Lake back up into the centre of Keswick.

PATTERDALE

The village of Patterdale lies at the head of Ullswater with the craggy heights of Place Fell to the east and Helvellyn to the west. The village is named after the valley in which it lies, one of Lakeland's finest. From its source high on Kirkstone Pass to the south, Kirkstone Beck tumbles down from the flanks of Red Screes to soon reach the flat valley floor and Brothers Water. The issuing stream is Goldrill Beck, which follows a meandering course across pastures before draining into Ullswater. The valley is named after St Patrick, who came this way after his ship was wrecked off Morecambe Bay on his return from Ireland in the 5th Century. It is believed that St Patrick was born along the Cumbrian coast in the late 4th Century, although Scotland and Wales also lay claim to his birthplace. As a teenager, he was captured by pirates and taken to Ireland where he worked as a shepherd for six years. He escaped and returned to Britain on board that ill-fated ship. It was as he was heading home through Lakeland that he stopped at what is now Patterdale and baptised local people at a roadside spring that still bears his name. Patterdale's church is dedicated to St Patrick, one of Lakeland's finest Victorian churches designed by Anthony Salvin in 1853. The church is noted for its tapestries, embroidered by Ann Macbeth who lived in the village in the early 20th Century. Born in Lancashire, Ann studied at Glasgow School of Art and was an associate of Charles Rennie Mackintosh, world famous designer in the Arts and Craft Movement. Near the church stands Patterdale Hall, built by the influential Mounsey family in the 17th Century, who gained the title 'Kings of Patterdale' after fighting off Scottish raiders at Stybarrow Crag in 1648. The Mounsey family remained at the Hall until the early 19th Century when it was sold to the Marshall family. It is now an outdoor centre.

THE VILLAGE

Patterdale offers a wide range of facilities including several B&Bs, a hotel, Youth Hostel, campsite, village store and Post Office, toilets, car park, bus service, payphone and the White Lion Inn.

ACCOMMODATION

National Park Information Centre, Glenridding 017684 82414

PATTERDALE PUBS

White Lion Inn, Patterdale   017684 82214

This long and narrow roadside inn dates back over 200 years, and still provides hospitality for travellers before the arduous journey over Kirkstone Pass. Wordsworth used to pop in for a drink; indeed, he was in the bar when news came through that Admiral Lord Nelson had been killed at the Battle of Trafalgar in 1805. Inside, there is a long and comfortable lounge with a small raised snug area as well as a stone-flagged bar.

Patterdale Hotel Patterdale   017684 82231

This imposing hotel has a comfortable lounge bar. At the front of the hotel is a large beer garden that offers wonderful views of Place Fell.

Patterdale Walking Weekend
- Saturday Walk -
Patterdale, Angle Tarn, High Street, Thornthwaite Beacon & Hartsop

WALK INFORMATION

Highlights: A hidden mountain tarn, the red deer of Martindale, England's last golden eagle, walking in the footsteps of Romans, a windswept racecourse and Lakeland's most impressive cairn.

Distance: 11.5 miles (18.5 km) Time: Allow 7 hours

Map: OS Explorer map OL5 - *always take a map on your walk.*

Refreshments: Pubs, shop and Tea Rooms at Patterdale. No facilities en route - take provisions with you.

Terrain: From Patterdale there is a steady climb to Boredale Hause from where a path leads up to Angle Tarn, with steep drops to the side of the path around Dubhow Beck. From Angle Tarn, the path climbs steadily up across the high fells, with boggy and rocky terrain, passing Satura Crag and The Knott to reach the Straits of Riggindale (fairly narrow col). A path then climbs up onto the broad grassy summit of High Street, with steep drops to the side of the path across its western flanks, before heading round to reach Thornthwaite Beacon. There is then a steep descent into the col of Thresthwaite Mouth, from where a pitched-stone path leads steeply down into Thresthwaite Glen. A path heads down through this valley to join a track that leads into Hartsop village. Tracks and lanes lead back to Patterdale.

Highest point: High Street - 828 metres above sea level.

Total ascent: 765 metres

Escape route: On the ascent of The Knott (after the wall beyond Sulphury Gill), take the path to the right (west) down to join Hayeswater Gill, which you follow down into Hartsop.

Caution: **Mountain Walk.** This is a strenuous walk to the summit of High Street, with mountainous terrain in places. The descent from Thornthwaite Beacon to Thresthwaite Mouth is very steep across a steep and rocky slope, whilst the descent into Thresthwaite Glen is also steep. There are steep drops to the side of the path in places, as well as several streams to cross through Thresthwaite Glen. There are few landmarks on High Street, which may make navigation difficult. OS map and compass essential. Do not attempt this walk in bad weather or winter conditions.

Angle Tarn lies beneath Angletarn Pikes high above Patterdale, only revealing itself at the last moment. It has a beautiful setting with two small islands, a sinuous shoreline and fine views towards Fairfield and Helvellyn. From Angle Tarn, the path leads up to Satura Crag from where there are sweeping views northwards into remote Bannerdale. This valley forms part of the historic Martindale Deer Forest, an area that includes the valleys of Bannerdale and Ramps Gill as well as the protruding ridge of The Nab that separates them. This deer forest is home of the oldest native red deer herd in England, as well as wild fell ponies; it forms part of the Dalemain Estate. From Satura Crag, the path skirts across the upper flanks of Rest Dodd before climbing onto the eastern shoulder of The Knott, a rounded prominence on the high ridge of land overlooking the valley of Hayeswater Gill (south-west) and the head of Ramps Gill (north). Beyond The Knott, the ridge narrows into the col of the Straits of Riggindale, with airy views down into Hayeswater Gill (west) and Riggindale (east) with the head of Haweswater Reservoir in the distance. The crags that tower above Riggindale are home to England's only golden eagle, a lone male who lost his partner some years ago.

The Straits of Riggindale lead southwards up onto the broad grassy summit of High Street. It is along this narrow saddle that we join the Roman road of High Street that gave its name to this mountain. The route of this Roman road can still be clearly seen as a grassy track across the upper western flanks of High Street - we follow this route as far as the head of Hayeswater Gill near Thornthwaite Crag. It was built around AD90 to connect the Roman forts at Ambleside and Brougham near Penrith, via the Troutbeck Valley, High Street, High Raise and Loadpot Hill before dropping down to the low-lying ground between the rivers Lowther and Eamont. It followed the route of an existing prehistoric road across the mountains which avoided the thickly wooded and dangerous valleys. The mountain of High Street is a broad grassy ridge, one of Lakeland's biggest and most imposing, which forms the spine of a vast range of mountains that lie between Patterdale and

Mardale with valleys radiating in all directions. The views from the top are not the best; however, a short detour to the east will bring you to the crags above Blea Water, a magnificent glacial corrie that holds a deep lake. The summit of High Street is also known as Racecourse Hill. Centuries ago, the shepherds of Mardale came up onto High Street once a year to exchange stray sheep. This developed into the Shepherds' Meet with fell running, wrestling, horse racing and much merriment. The last event took place in 1835. The village of Mardale Green was controversially submerged beneath Haweswater Reservoir when the level of the natural lake was raised in the 1930s to provide Manchester with drinking water.

Our route follows the western edge of the High Street plateau as it sweeps around the head of Hayeswater Gill up to reach Thornthwaite Crag and the impressive Thornthwaite Beacon. This substantial cairn stands atop some low outcrops on a narrow ridge of land at the head of four valleys, with commanding views down the length of the Troutbeck Valley towards Windermere. The descent from Thornthwaite Beacon into the col of Thresthwaite Mouth is steep and rocky, although the views from this narrow saddle are impressive with the Troutbeck Valley and Thresthwaite Glen on either side. The steep descent into Thresthwaite Glen takes you into a landscape of towering crags and tumbling becks, with Hartsop Dodd and Gray Crag enclosing the valley. A wonderful walk ensues down through this valley all the way to Hartsop where Thresthwaite Glen feeds into Patterdale. Near the confluence of Pasture Beck and Hayeswater Gill are the remains of Myers Head Lead Mine, with its well-preserved pit that once housed a waterwheel as well as stone pillars that supported an aqueduct. This lead mine was only worked for about ten years during the 1870s until flooding halted production. William Wordsworth visited Patterdale and Ullswater on many occasions, to visit friends and to admire the rugged beauty - it even inspired him to compose perhaps the most famous poem in English Literature that begins 'I wandered lonely as a Cloud...' in 1804 after seeing the daffodils beside Ullswater. He loved this area so much that he bought an old cottage at Rooking, now known as Wordsworth Cottage, with the intention of building his dream home on nearby land, but for reasons unknown this house was never built.

PATTERDALE SATURDAY WALK

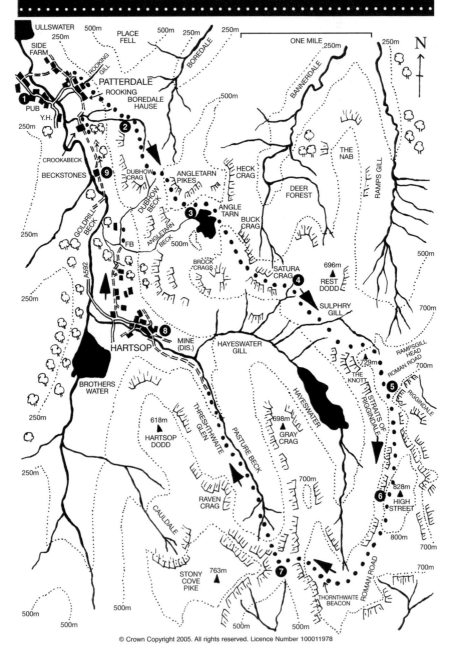

192

1. With your back to the Patterdale Hotel, turn left along the main road and follow this passing the school on your right a short distance after which turn right (sign 'Side Farm') along a track passing to the left side of the George Starkey Hut (SP 'Howtown, Boredale'). Follow this track straight on over a bridge across Goldrill Beck then across fields and up to reach Side Farm. Walk up through the farmyard passing between the barn and farmhouse to reach a T-junction with another track (immediately after the farmhouse). Turn right along this track (sign 'Patterdale, Hartsop') passing behind the farmhouse and through a gate that leads out onto a field. Follow the track straight across the top of the field, passing Side Cottage on your left to reach another gate across the track *(track now becomes a metalled lane)*. Immediately after this gate, turn left through the first gate on your left (SP 'Angle Tarn, Boredale Hause') and follow the path winding quite steeply up the hillside at first then, where the path forks, follow the clearer stony path bending sharply round to the right. The path now leads straight on gently rising up across the hillside, with a wall (as well as woodland and cottages) just down to your right, to reach a fork in the path after 200 metres (bench just up to your left). Follow the right-hand (level) path alongside the wall (and woodland) on your right to soon reach a small copse of larch trees where you follow the path bearing left away from the wall passing these trees. The path now climbs quite steeply up across the hillside (pitched-stone path in places) for 600 metres then curves round to the left to reach the junction of paths at Boredale Hause, where the path levels out (NY 407 156).

2. As you reach the small cairn at Boredale Hause beside the water mains inspection cover and two water signs 'AV' and 'SV' *(small rectangular sheepfold just across the stream to your right)*, follow the path bearing to the right to quickly cross Stonebarrow Gill (stream) just upstream of this sheepfold. After the stream, follow the path up to the left alongside the stream passing a small waterfall after a short distance, then follow the path bearing up to the right away from the

stream. Follow the path heading gradually up across the hillside for 400 metres to re-join the stream, which is now set in a small ravine down on your left, where you continue heading up through this ravine. The path leads up alongside the stream through the head of this ravine ('nick' in the hillside), beyond which you reach a large cairn at the head of the stream (NY 409 152). Continue straight on rising up and bearing slightly up to the left across the hillside *(Brothers Water comes into view down to your right)* to reach a fork in the path just before the head of the ravine of Dubhow Beck. Take the left-hand path *(both paths lead to Angle Tarn)* straight on rising up the hillside for 50 metres then bending round to the right across the very head of Dubhow Beck. After the stream, continue straight on along the fairly level path heading across the hillside skirting below Angletarn Pikes up to your left, just after which Angle Tarn comes into view. Follow the path curving down to the left to reach Angle Tarn (NY 416 145).

3. As you reach Angle Tarn, follow the path curving to the right skirting around the shoreline then, as you round the tarn, the path climbs up bearing very slightly left leaving the tarn behind. The path soon levels out and leads straight on *(with Buck Crag above the head of Bannerdale to your left)* before gently rising up to reach a gateway in a wall across your path. Head through the gateway and follow the undulating path straight on across craggy ground, keeping close to the wall on your right, heading across the top of Satura Crag *(head of Bannerdale to your left)* then, where the path forks after 300 metres, follow the right-hand path up and over some low crags (wall just across to your right). Beyond these low crags (several small pools/tarns), follow the path straight on with the wall and then a fence on your right *(views of Hayeswater to your right)*. The path soon joins the fence on your right, which you follow straight on dropping down to reach the head of Prison Gill (stream) where the fence turns to the right and meets the bottom end of a wall (slopes of Rest Dodd rising up in front of you - NY 427 136).

4. Follow the path bending round to the right across this stream (passing the bottom end of the wall) then straight on alongside the

fence on your right for 400 metres then, where the fence becomes a wall, follow the path bearing left away from the wall up across the hillside, over Sulphury Gill (stream) to reach another wall across your path just beyond this stream (foot of the steep slopes of The Knott). Head across the wall and follow the rocky path straight on steadily climbing up then, as you approach a wall just below the summit of The Knott, follow the path bending up to the left (with this wall just up to your right) rising steadily up to reach an old wall across your path (beside where it joins the wall on your right - NY 436 128). Head through this wall and follow the path ahead gently rising up and curving round to the right to join a wall on your right *(same wall you have just walked through)*, with the summit of The Knott a short detour up to your right. Continue along the path gently rising up alongside this wall on your right *(views down to your right towards Hayeswater)*. The path soon levels out then drops down onto the Straits of Riggindale (narrow col), with views to your left into Riggindale (NY 439 123).

5. At the bottom of this 'col', head through the gap in the wall to your right, immediately after which the path forks - follow the (right-hand) wide path (Roman road) straight on bearing slightly away from the wall *(ignore path to the left up alongside the wall)* heading steadily up across the right-hand (western) side of the broad ridge, with Hayeswater down to your right, up onto the summit plateau of High Street. After 1 km, the path levels out and becomes much narrower as you head across the western edge of High Street's broad summit plateau, with steep drops to your right towards Hayeswater (NY 439 110). **Short detour to the summit of High Street:** *just as the path levels out, head left along a narrow path across the broad plateau for 150 metres to reach the Trig Point on the summit of High Street. Re-trace your steps back to the narrow path along the western edge of the summit plateau.*

6. Carry straight on along the narrow path across the western edge of the summit plateau. The path soon broadens *(still following the line of the Roman Road)* and leads across the western side of the summit plateau (bearing slightly away from the steep slopes above Hayeswater) then drops gently down across the broad ridge

(heading in a south-westerly direction away from the summit) to reach an old wall across your path (NY 437 103). Head over this wall and follow the broad path straight on gradually curving to the right around the head of Hayeswater Gill then up to reach the stone-built Thornthwaite Beacon (cairn) on Thornthwaite Crag (NY 432 101). Head through the wall-gap beside this beacon then follow the grassy path straight on bearing to the right gently dropping down across the hillside *(Ullswater comes into view)*. The path soon bends more distinctly to the right and heads across a steep and rocky slope, gradually dropping down across scree *(take care)* before winding steeply down along a rocky path into the col of Thresthwaite Mouth (between Stony Cove Pike and Thornthwaite Crag), at the head of the Troutbeck Valley (south) and Thresthwaite Glen (north) - NY 426 103.

7. Walk across the col of Thresthwaite Mouth then, as you reach the foot of the steep crags of Stony Cove Pike in front of you, turn right over an old wall and follow the narrow path down into Thresthwaite Cove (head of Thresthwaite Glen). The path soon winds steeply down (stone-pitched path) into the head of the valley (Thresthwaite Cove) then crosses a small stream (Pasture Beck) to your left, after which the path all but levels out. Follow this narrow, undulating path straight on heading down through the valley along its left-hand (western) side, with the stream just to your right. After 0.5 km, the path heads across a steep slope below Raven Crag, with the stream now flowing through a ravine down to your right, beyond which the path heads down across a boulder-strewn slope to reach a wall across your path (NY 421 115). After this wall, head straight on heading down through Thresthwaite Glen, over a side-stream then down to join the banks of the stream on your right. Follow the path straight on alongside the stream heading down through the valley - the path soon becomes a track which you follow straight on to reach a ladder stile beside a gate across your path, with the stream on your right (NY 417 123). After the gate, follow the track straight on heading down through the valley with the stream on your right at first then gently rising up to join a wall on your right. Continue along the

track heading down through the valley with the wall on your right (passing above the confluence of Pasture Beck and Hayeswater Gill just down to your right) then, after 0.75 km, the track bends to the right over a ladder stile beside a gate. After the ladder-stile/gate, follow the track down to reach a stone bridge across the river on the edge of Hartsop. Cross the bridge and head up through a gate that leads onto a stony track, which you follow to the left into Hartsop (track becomes a metalled lane).

8. Follow the lane through Hartsop and continue along the lane down out of the hamlet then, just before you reach the junction with the main road (A692), turn right immediately before Hayesdale Lodge (adventure centre) along an enclosed lane (NY 406 132). Follow this lane straight on passing Crossgates Farm on your right after 400 metres, just after which the lane forks where you carry straight on along the walled stony track *(ignore lane up to right towards Hartsop Fold)*. Follow this enclosed track meandering down through the valley for 0.5 km to reach a gate at the end of the enclosed track, with a ford/FB across Angletarn Beck just beyond the gate. Head through the gate and cross Angletarn Beck then head straight on along the path alongside a small stream (Dubhow Beck) and a wall/fence on your left. After a while, the path fords this stream and continues on alongside the wall on your left and the stream now on your right. You soon leave Dubhow Beck behind *(which comes down a ravine from its source high above)* - carry straight on along the wide path with the wall on your left *(ignore track climbing steeply up to the right after 300 metres)* then follow this path down to reach a junction of tracks where you carry straight on (SP 'Patterdale') to reach Beckstones Farm (NY 403 150).

9. Walk through the farmyard passing in front of the farmhouse, just after which head through the two wooden gates just ahead then follow the track straight on heading down through the valley across the sparsely wooded hillside to reach the next farm of Crookabeck (NY 402 155). Just as you reach the gate that leads into the farmyard head up the steps to the right (SP 'footpath to Patterdale, permissive path) and follow this permissive path skirting to the right

of the farm buildings then across a small field and over a FB across Stonebarrow Gill to re-join the track just beyond Crookabeck Farm opposite a large barn *(NB: The Right of Way heads straight through the farmyard - follow the permissive path around the farm)*. Turn right along this track (SP 'Patterdale') and follow it straight on passing the houses of Rooking (track becomes a lane) to reach a T-junction opposite Wordsworth Cottage. Follow the road to the left to reach a bridge across Goldrill Beck and the main road (A592) just beyond. Turn right along the main road back into Patterdale.

Patterdale

Patterdale Walking Weekend
- Sunday Walk -
Patterdale, Chapel-in-the-Hause, Boredale, Sandwick, Ullswater & Silver Bay

WALK INFORMATION

Highlights: A ruinous chapel, the valley of the wild boars, Ullswater's secluded southern shore, Donald Campbell's first world water-speed record and the most beautiful path in Lakeland.

Distance: 8 miles (13 km)   Time: Allow 4 hours

Map: OS Explorer map OL5 - *always take a map on your walk.*

Refreshments: Pubs and shop at Patterdale. Tea Room at Side Farm. No facilities en route.

Terrain: Stony paths climb quite steeply up to Boredale Hause to reach a crossroads of paths. A rocky path then heads down into Boredale, steep at first but then gently dropping down to reach Boredale Head Farm. A quiet farm lane then leads down through the valley before field paths cut off to re-join the lane at Sandwick. A stony path follows the shoreline of Ullswater skirting across the lower slopes of Place Fell back to Patterdale.

Highest point: Boredale Hause - 400 metres above sea level.

Total ascent: 410 metres

Caution: The climb up to Boredale Hause is quite steep, whilst the descent into Boredale is initially steep along a rocky path. Take care at Boredale Hause as the maze of paths may be confusing in mist. There are some small streams to cross, which may be difficult after heavy rain.

POINTS OF INTEREST

This walk circumnavigates Place Fell, taking in Boredale as well as the lakeshore path alongside Ullswater, arguably England's most beautiful lake. The climb to Boredale Hause is superb, with wonderful retrospective views across the glaciated valley framed by mountains. The path swings round into Boredale Hause, a grassy col between Place Fell and Angletarn Pikes. Here, beside the path, are the scant remains of the medieval Chapel in the Hause, once used by people following the old packhorse trail between Martindale and Patterdale. Beyond the hause you reach a rocky gully where a wonderful view unfolds of Boredale. The next stretch of the walk is superb with an overwhelming sense of walking into the view as you descend into the valley. The old name for Boredale is Boardale, a much more romantic title that conjures up images of the wild boars that once roamed here. This vast area of fells and valleys to the south of Ullswater, including Boredale, Martindale, Bannerdale and Ramps Gill, are quiet and unfrequented, hidden away from casual visitors thanks to the 'dead end' roads that lead into them.

The highlight of this walk is the beautiful lakeside path between Sandwick and Patterdale that contours around the base of Place Fell, undulating across the fellside and through woodland with the rippling waters of Ullswater to your right. The views across Ullswater are supreme and the variety of terrain unsurpassed, with Scalehow Force and Silver Bay a particular highlights. Ullswater is England's second largest after Windermere, but remains unspoilt and undeveloped. The name of this lake is probably derived from Ulfr, a Norse farmer who settled here over a thousand years ago. It was on Ullswater in 1955 that Donald Campbell set the first of several world water-speed records in Bluebird K7, reaching speeds of 202 mph. Campbell was killed on Coniston Water in 1967 whilst attempting to break his own records. In the early 1960s Manchester Corporation put forward a bill to take water from Ullswater, but this controversial plan was rejected by the House of Lords after an impassioned speech by Lord Birkett of Ulverston. Ullswater is home to schelly, an endangered freshwater fish and survivor from the last Ice Age.

PATTERDALE SUNDAY WALK

201

1. With your back to the Patterdale Hotel, turn left along the main road and follow this passing the school on your right a short distance after which turn right (sign 'Side Farm') along a track passing to the left side of the George Starkey Hut (SP 'Howtown, Boredale'). Follow this track straight on over a bridge across Goldrill Beck then across fields and up to reach Side Farm. Walk up through the farmyard passing between the barn and farmhouse to reach a T-junction with another track (immediately after the farmhouse). Turn right along this track (sign 'Patterdale, Hartsop') passing behind the farmhouse and through a gate that leads out onto a field. Follow the track straight on across the top of the field, passing Side Cottage on your left to reach another gate across the track *(track now becomes a metalled lane)*. Immediately after this gate, turn left through the first gate on your left (SP 'Angle Tarn, Boredale Hause') and follow the path winding quite steeply up the hillside at first then, where the path forks, follow the clearer stony path bending sharply round to the right. The path now leads straight on gently rising up across the hillside, with a wall (as well as woodland and cottages) just down to your right, to reach a fork in the path after 200 metres. Follow the left-hand path (passing a bench 'VR 1897') climbing up across the steep hillside (parallel with the lower path just down to your right) for about 500 metres then, where the path levels out for a short distance (25 metres before you join the lower path), turn up to the left back on yourself slightly along a grassy path (beside a solitary hawthorn tree). After a few paces, follow the path bending sharply round and up to the right (with the two paths now down to your right) then rising up across the hillside, with the valley falling away to your right, to soon reach a small stream. Just after the stream the path bends round to the left heading up across the hillside to reach the top of the climb (small cairn). The broad grassy path now leads straight on very gently rising up to soon reach a 'crossroads' of paths beside a small rectangular ruin (Chapel in the Hause) set in the mountain pass of Boredale Hause (NY 408 158).

2. At this 'crossroads' of paths (Chapel in the Hause), carry straight on along the grassy path gently rising up. The path soon levels out and leads straight on across the broad grassy col of Boredale Hause then, as you reach the other side of Boredale Hause, the path gently drops down to reach a pronounced V-shaped gully at the head of Boredale *(Boredale comes into view)*. Follow the stony path down through this gully to soon reach two water inspection covers (Hayeswater pipeline) where you follow the rocky path steeply down into Boredale (with the valley spread out before you). The gradient soon eases - continue along the wide path heading steadily down into the valley for 0.75 km to join a wall on your right along the bottom of the valley. Carry straight on along the track with this wall on your right to reach Boredale Head Farm (NY 419 170).

3. Follow the lane straight on passing in front of the farmhouse, beyond which carry straight on along the metalled lane heading down through Boredale for 1.25 km to reach a road-bridge across Boredale Beck (just after Nettleslack Farm). Cross the bridge, and follow the road winding round for 0.5 km to reach the white-washed farms at Garth Heads either side of the road (NY 428 186). Turn left along an enclosed grassy track immediately after the white-washed farmhouse on your left (SP) and follow this track down to reach a ford across Boredale Beck *(stone-slab FB just upstream of the ford)*. After the ford, follow the track up then curving round to the right to reach a gate in the top right corner of the field, after which continue straight on along the track gently rising up (wall on your right) curving up to the left to quickly reach a barn. As you reach the barn, head off the track passing to the left side of the barn (waymarker-post) heading straight up the field *(do not continue along the track through the gate)* up to reach a stile in the top right corner of the field, after which turn immediately left over another stile across a wall. After this stile, turn right and follow the undulating, grassy path alongside the wall on your right for 600 metres *(ignore gates through this wall on right)* then, where the wall bends sharply away to the right down towards the road (view of Ullswater ahead) follow the path straight on gradually slanting down across the hillside to join this unfenced road (NY 424 195).

Turn left along this road for a short distance then, just before the road drops down into the hamlet of Sandwick, turn left along a rutted track (SP 'Public Bridleway Patterdale').

4. Follow this rough track up to quickly join a wall on your right where you follow the broad, stony path straight on alongside this wall on your right *(views of Ullswater across to your right)*. Follow this path very gradually rising up for 0.75 km to reach a barn beside the path, just beyond which the path fords a small stream. Cross the stream then continue along the stony path (wall still on your right) gently dropping down to soon reach a FB across Scalehow Beck set in a dramatic wooded ravine (NY 415 192). *Scalehow Force waterfall just upstream.*

5. After the FB, follow the path to the right to re-join the wall on your right where you carry on along the clear, stony path rising up with this wall on your right. As you reach the top of this rise, follow the rocky path (and wall) bending to the right heading steadily down then, where the wall curves away to the right and the path all but levels out, carry straight on along the clear path across the sparsely wooded hillside, with Ullswater just down to your right. Follow this path straight on across the hillside *(wonderful views unfold across the lake)* very gradually dropping down across the hillside (lower slopes of Low Birk Fell) almost to lake level at the foot of Long Crag. Carry straight on along the lakeside path, which quickly rises up across the steep wooded slopes (Ullswater just down to your right). The path soon levels out - follow this undulating path straight on across the steep wooded hillside for 0.5 km to emerge from the trees onto a rocky promontory, with views across Ullswater ahead. From this promontory, continue straight on along the path through woodland across the steep wooded slopes. After a while, the path leads steadily down to reach lake level again before rising quickly up again across the steep wooded hillside. Follow this undulating path straight on across the steep wooded slopes (Ullswater down to your right) until you emerge from the trees to reach a fork in the path, with Silver Bay just down to your right and Silver Crag rising up in front of you (NY 397 183).

6. As you reach the fork in the path, carry straight on along the stony (level) path *(ignore path up to left)* and follow this curving round to the right hugging the steep craggy slopes of Silver Crag. The path skirts around Silver Crag *(Glenridding comes into view across the lake)* then, after you have skirted round Silver Crag, follow the path straight on (Ullswater just down to your right). A stone-pitched path then rises up onto the small craggy 'rise' of land known as Devil's Chimney (crowned by Scots Pines) where you carry straight on to quickly join a wall on your right (NY 395 177). Follow the broad path straight on alongside this wall on your right, gently dropping down to the reach a ford across a stream set amongst woodland. After the stream, carry straight on along the stony track for a further 1.25 km alongside the wall on your right all the way (passing the campsite and then the head of Ullswater across to your right) to reach Side Farm. As you reach the farmhouse, turn right passing between the farmhouse and the barn (SP 'Glenridding') then re-trace your steps along the track back into Patterdale.

ROSTHWAITE

Borrowdale is arguably the most beautiful valley in the Lake District. The towering crags and mountains that hem in this valley are wild and dramatic, yet the lower slopes are thickly wooded, with an intricate pattern of drystone walls dividing up the flat valley pastures. There are just half a dozen attractive hamlets in the upper valley beyond Derwent Water, including Seathwaite that has the distinction of being the wettest inhabited place in England with around 3.5 metres of rainfall annually, thanks to the high mountains that surround it. Interestingly, at Keswick further down the valley they only get around 1.5 metres of rainfall a year. Between Rosthwaite and Grange the valley is virtually cut off at what is known as the Jaws of Borrowdale where Castle Crag and Grange Fell almost meet across the valley floor, through which the River Derwent has cut a narrow gorge, thickly wooded with ancient oaks. The flat valley pastures of the upper valley above the Jaws of Borrowdale were once filled by a lake after the last Ice Age, until the glacial meltwaters found a way through these crags; these pastures still flood after heavy rain. Castle Crag is a distinctive tower of rock, with the remains of an early British defensive fort on top; Borrowdale takes its name from the Old Norse 'Borgardalr' that means 'valley of the fort'. Rosthwaite lies in the heart of upper Borrowdale beyond the Jaws of Borrowdale near the confluence of the River Derwent and Stonethwaite Beck, which drains the dramatic side valley of Langstrath. Rosthwaite consists of a narrow lane lined by old cottages and farms that cluster around the slightly higher ground of The How, a hillock that lies near this river confluence. Indeed, the place-name of Rosthwaite is derived from Old Norse and means 'woodland clearing with the heap of stones', which probably refers to the boulders brought down by mountain streams.

THE VILLAGE

Rosthwaite offers two hotels, pub, several B&Bs, camping barn, Youth Hostel at nearby Longthwaite and a campsite between Rosthwaite and Stonethwaite. There is also a car park, general stores, tea rooms, toilets and bus service to Keswick.

ACCOMMODATION

Tourist Information Centre, Keswick   017687 72645

ROSTHWAITE PUB

Riverside Bar (Scafell Hotel)   017687 77208
An alleyway leads behind the Scafell Hotel to the Riverside Bar where you will find a boisterous mixture of walkers, climbers, tourists and locals. Warmed by an open fire during the winter months, this open-plan bar has a tiled floor and good range of Real Ales on offer. It is the home of the Borrowdale Fell Race with its gruelling course covering 17 miles and over 6,500-ft of ascent, the record is currently held by Billy Bland who completed the race in an amazing 2 hours and 34 minutes back in 1981.

PUBS ALONG THE WALKS

Langstrath Inn, Stonethwaite   017687 77239

Rosthwaite Walking Weekend
- Saturday Walk -

Rosthwaite, High Spy, Cat Bells, Derwent Water & the Jaws of Borrowdale

WALK INFORMATION

Highlights: Vertical slate steps, a wonderful ridge walk, the Tale of Mrs Tiggy Winkle, the Queen of the Lakes, a monastic farm and springtime tales about cuckoos.

Distance: 11.5 miles (18.5 km)   Time: Allow 6 - 7 hours

Map: OS Explorer map OL4 - *always take a map on your walk.*

Refreshments: Pub and cafe at Rosthwaite. Café at Grange.

Terrain: Steep climb up through Tongue Gill via Rigghead Quarries (slate) with stone steps in places to reach the boggy ground of Rigg Head. A rocky path then climbs up onto High Spy, with Eel Crags falling away to your left (west) into the Newlands Valley. A path heads northwards along this broad ridge before dropping down a rocky section to reach Hause Gate, from where it is a short climb onto the rocky crest of Cat Bells. The descent from Cat Bells is surprisingly steep in places with a number of rocky steps down along the ridge before a path winds down to the road at Hawes End. Woodland, lakeside, riverside and field paths return through Borrowdale to Rosthwaite.

Highest point: High Spy - 653 metres above sea level.

Total ascent: 700 metres

Escape Route: From Rigg Head, re-trace your steps back down through Rigghead Quarries. From Hause Gate (just before the path climbs onto Cat Bells) follow the path down to the right (east) to join the road where you turn right into Grange.

Caution: **Mountain Walk.** This is a strenuous walk to the summit of High Spy. The paths are generally well-trodden, although rough and rocky in places. The climb up through Rigghead Quarries and the descent from Cat Bells to Hawes End are steep and rocky in places. There are cliffs along the western edge of the broad ridge from High Spy to Cat Bells. OS map and compass essential. Do not attempt this walk in bad weather.

Rosthwaite

POINTS OF INTEREST

The High Spy range of mountains form a continuous ridge of high ground on the western side of Borrowdale from Honister Pass all the way to Derwent Water, separating Borrowdale from the Newlands Valley. After an initial steep climb through Rigghead Quarries, with its near-vertical slate steps and numerous shafts and levels, the flat col of Rigg Head is reached amidst wonderful mountain scenery with Dalehead Tarn set like a jewel beneath the towering slopes of Dale Head at the head of the Newlands Valley, whilst to your right rise the craggy slopes of High Spy. A rocky climb above sheer cliffs leads up to the summit of High Spy and a wonderful panorama across the northern Lakeland fells. The highlight of this walk is the magnificent ridge walk from High Spy to Hawes End via Narrow Moor, Maiden Moor and Cat Bells. For much of the ridge, the precipitous cliffs of Eel Crags fall some 400 metres (1,300-ft) sheer down into the Newlands Valley to your left, whilst there are also beautiful views across Derwent Water on the descent from Maiden Moor.

Derwent Water is perhaps the most beautiful of all of the lakes and is known as the 'Queen of the Lakes'. From just north of Grange to the outskirts of Keswick, Derwent Water stretches for over four kilometres through scenery that has inspired generations of artists and poets. Many famous viewpoints along its shoreline include Friar's Crag, which John Ruskin considered one of the finest in Europe. After the last Ice Age Derwent Water and Bassenthwaite Lake would have been joined together as one large lake; however, a build-up of silt deposited into the lake over thousands of years has created a wide alluvial plain that now separates the two lakes. The shallow waters have an average depth of just five metres and are home to the rare whitefish known as the vendace, a relic of the last Ice Age. Derwent Water is studded with four small islands, including St Herbert's Island where the Celtic saint had his hermitage in the 7th Century. St Herbert was a friend and disciple of St Cuthbert of Lindisfarne and one of the first Celtic missionaries to bring Christianity to Northern England. Lord's Island still has the remains of the manor house built by the Radclyffe family, Earls of Derwentwater. Derwent Isle originally belonged to the monks of Furness Abbey and was later occupied by the skilled German miners who were brought to the area during the 16th Century to develop the mines, but sought sanctuary on this small island due to hostility from locals. Still inhabited, the island is graced by a large Georgian house that is in the care of the National Trust. Along with the small Rampsholme Island there is also an occasional fifth island known as the Floating Island that appears every few years. Subject to much superstition, this 'island' is actually a mass of rotting vegetation brought to the surface by marsh gases. The Keswick Launch ferries passengers across the lake calling at several small landing stages dotted around its shoreline.

Grange was once an outpost of Furness Abbey who owned land in this area. This was where they had their monastic farm, known as a grange. The beautiful double-arched packhorse bridge was built in 1675 to provide access across the Derwent, and is built on rock that has been worn smooth and still has grooves scratched into it from the ice that moved down the valley during the last Ice Age. The path from Grange back to Rosthwaite was once the main route through Borrowdale before the present road was 'cut' through the Jaws of Borrowdale in 1842. This path is a delight to follow as it meanders through deciduous woodland and along the banks of the Derwent passing beneath the rocky ramparts of Castle Crag, which is scarred by disused quarries. This is ancient natural woodland with sessile oaks dominating, indeed the name of the River Derwent is derived from the Celtic words for 'river valley with oak trees'. This woodland is important as a diverse habitat for mosses, lichens, insects, flowers and birds. You may even hear a cuckoo in springtime. Tales of hapless attempts to capture a cuckoo are recounted through folktales throughout England and Borrowdale is no exception. As the sound of the first cuckoo heralds the onset of spring, the people of Borrowdale captured a cuckoo and built a high wall around the bird to prevent it from flying away, in the hope that they could capture spring forever. From then on anyone who did something silly was referred to as a Borrowdale Gowk, 'gowk' being the local dialect for cuckoo.

For more information about Cat Bells and the Newlands Valley,
see Walking Weekend 3

For more information about Friar's Crag and Derwent Water,
see Walking Weekend 9

ROSTHWAITE SATURDAY WALK

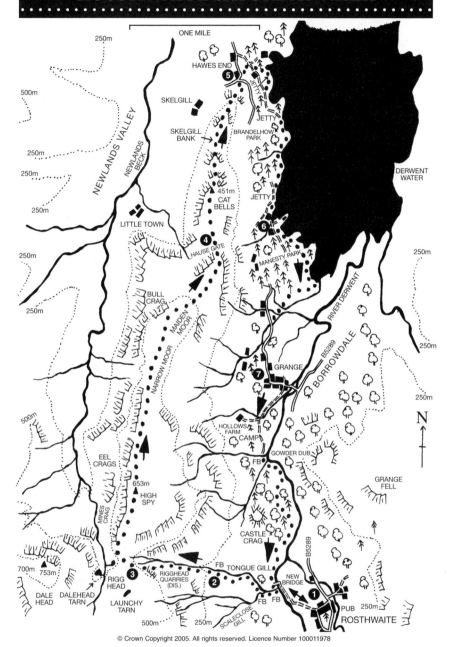

250m

ONE MILE

500m

HAWES END
⑤

SKELGILL

JETTY

JETTY

250m

SKELGILL
BANK

BRANDELHOW
PARK

NEWLANDS VALLEY

NEWLANDS BECK

250m

250m

451m
CAT
BELLS

JETTY

DERWENT
WATER

250m

LITTLE TOWN

④

HAUSE GATE

⑥

MANESTY PARK

250m

250m

BULL
CRAG

250m

NARROW MOOR

MAIDEN MOOR

RIVER DERWENT

BORROWDALE

B5289

250m

250m

500m

GRANGE
⑦

EEL
CRAGS

653m
HIGH
SPY

MINES CRAG

HOLLOWS
FARM

CAMP

GOWDER DUB

FB

N

GRANGE
FELL

CASTLE
CRAG

B5289

700m 753m

RIGG
HEAD
③

RIGGHEAD
QUARRIES
(DIS.)

②

FB TONGUE GILL

NEW
BRIDGE

①

DALE
HEAD

DALEHEAD
TARN

LAUNCHY
TARN

FB FB

PUB 250m

ROSTHWAITE

500m

250m

SCALECLOSE GILL

212

THE WALK

1. From the centre of Rosthwaite, take the lane opposite the village shop and follow this straight on passing the car park and village hall to reach Yew Tree Farm. Walk straight through the farmyard passing in front of the farmhouse, beyond which follow the enclosed track straight on leaving Rosthwaite behind to reach the River Derwent. Follow the track to the right along the riverbank to soon reach a stone bridge (New Bridge) across the river (NY 252 151). Cross the bridge and turn immediately left along the riverside path to quickly reach a small FB across Tongue Gill (side-stream). Cross this FB then turn immediately right over a stile - *do not cross the next FB*. After the stile, follow the path up alongside Tongue Gill on your right to reach a kissing-gate beside a gate across your path, after which follow the stream curving round to the right over another FB (across Scaleclose Gill) to reach a stile over a fence just beyond (Tongue Gill on your right). Cross the stile then head left along the wide grassy path heading up the hillside, with Tongue Gill just to your right, then winding steeply up through bracken to join a wall on your left. Ignore the ladder stile over this wall, but cross a small ford and continue along the grassy/stony track climbing straight up the hillside to reach a gate in a wall at the top of the field, with Tongue Gill just across to your right (NY 245 152).

2. Head through this gate and follow the path straight on climbing quite steeply up alongside Tongue Gill on your right *(heading up through the ravine of Tongue Gill)* to reach a stile over a fence at the bottom of the old slate workings of Rigghead Quarries (spoil heaps). Continue straight on along the pitched-stone path climbing up alongside Tongue Gill at first then bearing slightly left climbing steeply up through the old quarry workings (pitched slate path) passing old levels, spoil heaps and ruinous buildings to eventually reach the top of the old workings above which the path rises gently up across the grassy hillside to reach a fence at the head of the ravine of Tongue Gill (Rigg Head) - as you approach this fence the path forks, follow the left-hand path up to quickly reach a stile over the

fence, with the bulk of Dale Head rising up ahead (NY 234 154). *Ignore the stile just across to your right in the fence corner near the head of Tongue Gill.*

3. Cross the stile and head straight on across the flat boggy saddle of land *(compass bearing: 300 degrees)* bearing very slightly to the right (skirting around the boggy ground - no clear path) to pick up a narrow grassy path which you follow straight on across the boggy saddle of land (passing a small tarn just down to your left) to quickly reach a clear, stony path across your path above the dramatic ravine of the upper reaches of Newlands Beck, with Dale Head towering above. Turn right along this path and follow it climbing up across the rocky/grassy mountainside with the cliffs of Miners' Crag on your left *(caution- keep away)*. Follow this path climbing steadily up (cairns) across the left-hand side of the broad ridge for 1 km, with the cliffs/crags to your left, to reach the summit cairn of High Spy (NY 234 162). From the summit cairn, carry straight on along the path (cairns) along the left-hand side of the broad summit ridge (with Eel Crags to your left dropping sheer into the Newlands Valley) gradually losing height for 1.5 km to reach the appropriately named Narrow Moor *(caution - cliffs)*, after which follow the right-hand fork in the path across the middle of the broad, flat ridge of Maiden Moor to reach a rocky section where the ground steepens *(Cat Bells and Derwent Water come into view ahead)*. Follow the rocky path dropping steadily down along the ridge for 1 km, with a final rocky section that leads down onto the saddle of land between Maiden Moor and Cat Bells (Hause Gate) - NY 244 192.

4. At Hause Gate, carry straight on along the path climbing up across the broad ridge for 0.75 km to reach the rocky domed summit of Cat Bells (NY 244 198). From the top of Cat Bells, continue straight on across the summit to quickly reach the start of the long, steep and rocky descent that leads down from the summit (heading down along the crest of the ridge). Follow the path straight down this steep, rocky ridge to reach a small 'saddle' of land and a junction of paths at the bottom of the steep, rocky section. Continue

straight on along the crest of the fairly narrow, undulating ridge (Skelgill Bank) for 0.75 km to reach a 'short but steep' rocky section. Head down this rocky section *(memorial plaque to Thomas Arthur Leonard, 'father of the open air movement')* then follow the path straight on to soon reach the end of the ridge and an abrupt steep slope in front of you. Follow the clear path winding down the hillside then, as you approach the road at Hawes End and the path forks, follow the left-hand path down for 150 metres then turn right down a stone-pitched path to reach the road-turning towards 'Skelgill' by its junction with the hair-pin bend at Hawes End (NY 247 212).

5. Turn right to quickly reach the hair-pin bend where you carry straight on down along the road towards 'Portinscale, Keswick' and over a cattle grid. A short distance after this cattle grid, where the road bends sharp left, head straight on (to the right) along the footpath (SP 'Keswick, Brandelhow, Hawes End launch pier') and follow this down through woodland (wall on left) to soon reach a metalled lane at a junction. Turn right along the right-hand lane (SP 'The Lake, Manesty') then, where this lane curves to the right after 50 metres, branch off to the left along the path (SP 'Hawes End jetty') that leads down through woodland to reach the shore of Derwent Water beside Hawes End Jetty (NY 251 213). As you reach the lakeshore, follow the path bearing round to the right then straight on along the wooded lakeshore then, as you approach a metal fence, bear right to quickly reach a track and a gate in this fence. Head through the gate and follow the track straight on then curving left through a gateway set in woodland, after which continue along the track across a field to reach a gate in a wall to your right beside the lakeshore (Low Brandelhow jetty). Head through this gate and follow the lakeside path straight on through woodland (Brandelhow Park) passing the 'cupped hands' wooden sculpture, after which continue along the lakeshore path for 1 km to reach High Brandelhow jetty *(looking ahead across Brandelhow Bay towards the wooded promontory of Brandelhow Point with its white house)*. Just beyond this jetty the path heads through pine trees to

quickly reach a fork - take the left-hand path to join the lakeshore which you follow round into Brandelhow Bay to reach a bridlegate in a fence. Head through the gate to join a clear path which you follow to the left passing a house on your right (and a wooden garage on your left), just after which bear left to quickly reach a gate in a wall (start of a track) - NY 251 195.

6. Head through this gate and follow the track straight on for 75 metres to reach a fork where you turn right along the track through woodland to soon reach a stone-built bungalow on your right (start of a metalled lane). As you reach this bungalow, turn left along a gravel path (off the lane) through woodland and follow this to reach the lakeshore again (Abbot's Bay). Carry straight on along the path through woodland with the lake just to your left to reach a gate in a wall at the end of the dense woodland (NY 255 191). Head through the gate and follow the path straight on across boggy, sparsely wooded pastures (walk-boards in places) for 0.5 km then, as you reach the head of the lake on your left and the path bends distinctly round to the left around the head of the lake, turn right along a grassy path alongside an old wall/line of mature trees on your left (NY 256 187). Follow this path across rough pastures to reach a kissing-gate in a fence. Head through the gate and follow the wide path straight on to join a road. Turn left along the road into Grange.

7. Follow the road through the village passing the chapel on your left, immediately after which turn right along a lane (SP 'Rosthwaite, Seatoller') and follow this down out of the village then continue along this lane for 0.5 km then, where it bends round to the right up towards Hollows Farm, turn left along a stony track alongside a wall on your left to reach a gateway across the track. Head through the gateway *(campsite on your left)* and follow the track straight on alongside the wall on your left heading up through the valley for 400 metres to reach a fork in the path (where this wall bends round to the left and ends). Follow the path bearing round to the left (metal barrier) then alongside the River Derwent on your left, over two FBs in succession across side-streams (Gowder Dub), after which the

path forks - follow the left-hand path (SP 'Rosthwaite') up through woodland to quickly reach a gate in a fence (River Derwent down to your left). Head through the gate and follow the path straight on through woodland and down to river level then bending to the right away from the river (SP 'Rosthwaite') to join a wall on your left which you follow up to quickly reach a gap through this wall (NY 252 163). After the wall gap, follow the rocky path up through woodland to the top of the 'rise' just after which the path turns down to the left (SP) to reach a gap in a wall (old quarry spoil heaps). After the gap, follow the undulating path straight on through woodland (High Hows Wood) skirting around the foot of the steep wooded slopes of Castle Crag on your right for 0.75 km to reach a gate in a wall at the end of the woods. Head through the gate and follow the track straight on meandering across fields to reach New Bridge across the River Derwent again. Cross this bridge and turn right along the riverside track then left away from the river back to Rosthwaite.

Rosthwaite Walking Weekend
- Sunday Walk -
Rosthwaite, Stonethwaite, Dock Tarn
& Watendlath

WALK INFORMATION

Highlights: A monastic dispute, where eagles soared, a hidden tarn, a Viking's lakeside barn, Hugh Walpole's literary inspiration and an old packhorse route across the fells.

Distance: 5.75 miles (9.25 km) Time: Allow 3 hours

Map: OS Explorer map OL4 - *always take a map on your walk.*

Refreshments: Pubs at Rosthwaite and Stonethwaite. Cafés at Rosthwaite and Watendlath.

Terrain: From Rosthwaite, field paths and lanes lead to Stonethwaite, from where a pitched-stone path climbs steeply up through woodland. An undulating path then heads across rough, rocky moorland (boggy) passing Dock Tarn before dropping quite steeply down to Watendlath. A stony bridleway then climbs up across moorland before dropping back down to Rosthwaite.

Highest point: Dock Tarn - 430 metres above sea level.

Total ascent: 400 metres

Caution: The climb from Stonethwaite to Dock Tarn is steep. The terrain around Dock Tarn is rough and boggy underfoot and may be confusing in mist - map and compass essential. The descent from Dock Tarn and also Puddingstone Bank back to Rosthwaite is quite steep along rocky paths. There are a number of small fords to cross, which may be difficult after heavy rain.

POINTS OF INTEREST

Stonethwaite is situated amidst the spectacular mountainous landscape of the Langstrath Valley, near where it opens out into Borrowdale. This is one of the most picturesque villages in Lakeland, a cluster of old cottages and farms as well as a comfortable inn. The ownership of the Langstrath Valley was originally granted to the monks of Fountains Abbey in 1195; however, the rest of Borrowdale was sold to Furness Abbey in 1209. Both abbeys laid claim to the rich pastureland that surrounds Stonethwaite, and this soon developed into a land dispute to such a degree that in 1304 King Edward I intervened and confiscated the land. The monks of Fountains outwitted their Cumbrian rivals and bought it from the King for 40 shillings. St Andrew's Church marks the old boundary between their lands.

From Stonethwaite, a footpath climbs steeply up across the valley side, picking its way between moss-covered boulders and gnarled oak trees. The path emerges from the trees to reveal a wonderful view across the Langstrath Valley towards Eagle Crag. The path then twists and turns across moorland to reach the delightful Dock Tarn, cradled amongst the fells. This is a wonderful spot to rest awhile beside its reed-fringed waters. The path then meanders down to reach the hamlet of Watendlath (pronounced 'what-end-lath'). Originally a Viking farm (the name means 'water end barn' in Old Norse), this delightful hamlet provides a picture-postcard scene of whitewashed farms clustered around a small lake and surrounded by the fells of High Seat, High Tove and Ullscarf. To round off this idyllic scene, there is a small ford and narrow packhorse bridge as well as a tea room serving homemade cakes. Thankfully, this whole area is in the care of the National Trust. Hugh Walpole, a prolific and successful English novelist (1884 - 1941) once lived in a large house overlooking Derwent Water from where he gained inspiration from the landscape. One of his novels *Judith Paris* was set at Watendlath, which formed the second book in the popular Herries Chronicle series of four novels, a romantic story set in Cumberland about generations of the Herries family. The return to Rosthwaite via Puddingstone Bank follows the old packhorse route over to Borrowdale.

ROSTHWAITE SUNDAY WALK

ONE MILE

250m 250m 250m 250m 500m 500m

HIGH SEAT

RIVER DERWENT

BORROWDALE

GRANGE FELL

515m HIGH TOVE

N

FB 6 WATENDLATH

PUDDINGSTONE BANK

CASTLE CRAG

250m

BLEATARN GILL

WATENDLATH FELL

500m

5

ROSTHWAITE

PUB

1

500m

LONGTHWAITE Y.H.

PEAT HOWE

GREAT CRAG

DOCK TARN

WILLYGRASS GILL

250m

4

BLEA TARN

2 3

STONETHWAITE

PUB

STONETHWAITE BECK

700m

THE COMBE

250m

LANGSTRATH BECK

GREENUP GILL

726m

ULLSCARF

500m

EAGLE CRAG

ROSTHWAITE FELL

250m

500m 500m

THE WALK

1. From the centre of Rosthwaite, take the lane opposite the village shop and follow this straight on passing the car park and the Borrowdale Institute then follow the lane bending sharp left immediately before Yew Tree Farm. Carry on along the lane meandering through the village then take the track to the right just before Stone Croft (house) then almost immediately left through a gate out onto a field (SP 'Longthwaite YHA'). Head straight on alongside the wall (and houses) on your left to reach a wall-stile at the end of the field, after which turn right across the field through a gate in a wall then left to reach the whitewashed Peat Howe Farm. Head through the gate passing to the left-side of the house to join a road. Turn left along the road then, where it bends round to the left after 25 metres, take the narrow enclosed path to the right that quickly leads to a wall-stile on your left out onto a corner of a field. Head straight across the field keeping close to the low bank on your right, over a ladder stile then on to reach another stile in the field corner that leads onto the valley road (NY 255 140).

2. Turn right along the road for a short distance then, where it curves round to the left, take the path to the left through a gate (SP 'Stonethwaite Road'). Follow the grassy track straight on across the middle of the field to join a stony track in the far left corner. Follow this track to the left (with the wall on your right), through a gate and down along a walled track to emerge into a farmyard. Head across the farmyard and follow the metalled lane straight on passing St Andrews Church on your right down to soon reach a junction with the Stonethwaite Road on a slight bend. Turn right along this road into Stonethwaite.

3. As you reach the small 'square' in the centre of the village (phone box), turn left (SP 'Greenup Edge, Grasmere') and follow the enclosed track to reach a bridge across Stonethwaite Beck beyond which you come to a path junction just after a gate. Turn right (SP 'Grasmere via Greenup Edge') and follow the stony path straight on alongside a wall on your right heading up into the Langstrath Valley

for 300 metres then, just as the path gently curves down to the right away from the steep wooded hillside, bear left off the path passing to the left-hand side of a small circular stone-built sheepfold (NY 266 137). After the sheepfold, follow the grassy path straight on across the hillside for 50 metres (with the stony path just down to your right) then follow it as it very gradually slants up across the hillside (heading towards the woodland) to reach a wall-stile across your path that leads into woodland. Cross the stile and follow the stony path to the left slanting up across the wooded hillside to reach another stile set in a wall, with Willygrass Gill (stream) just to your right. Cross this stile and follow the stone-pitched path climbing steeply up across the wooded hillside, winding up to eventually emerge from the woodland just beyond which you reach the top of the climb beside a stone-built shelter (NY 269 139).

4. As you reach the top of the climb (beside the stone-built shelter) follow the path bearing up and gently round to the right up onto the top of the rough and rocky heather moorland (White Crag just across to your left). Follow this path straight on across the rough, rocky moorland (Willygrass Gill just down across to your right), meandering across undulating boggy terrain to reach a stile in a wall across your path. Cross the stile and follow the path rising up across the moorland then bearing to the right after a short distance to join Willygrass Gill on your right. Follow the path alongside this stream gently rising up for 300 metres (cairns) to reach Dock Tarn. Continue straight on along the path hugging the western (left-hand) shore of Dock Tarn beyond which the rocky path carries straight on across boggy moorland passing between low outcrops then along the foot of a low but quite steep bank/outcrops on your left *(heading through a 'pass' between the outcrops)*. After 250 metres, the path curves round to the right then continues straight on, still heading along the foot of the bank/outcrops (with the rocky ground of Great Crag rising up to your left), for a further 250 metres to reach the brow of a steep slope *(Watendlath comes into view ahead across to the right)*. From this brow, a pitched-stone path leads quite steeply down to reach a kissing-gate in a wall just beside a stream (NY 271 150).

5. Head through the gate and cross the stream then follow the path straight on alongside the stream at first then, after a short distance, the path heads away from the stream gradually bearing round to the right heading across the hillside following the foot of the steep bank/outcrops on your right (stone-pitched path in places). After 250 metres, the path leaves the outcrops behind and drops down to reach an area of boggy ground in a shallow 'dip' (hillside levels out) where you turn right (waymarker-post) along a stony/grassy path heading down towards the valley of Watendlath. Follow this path down to soon reach a wall across your path (and small sheep enclosure) where you head to the left alongside the wall on your right down to soon reach a gate/kissing-gate to your right in this wall (set in the wall corner). Head through the gate and follow the path down alongside a stream on your left. The path soon fords the stream, after which carry straight on along the path heading towards Watendlath in the distance. The path soon becomes a clearer track, which leads down over another ford and on to reach a gate at the start of an enclosed track. Follow this track straight on down to join the shores of Watendlath Tarn and on to reach a ford and stone-built packhorse bridge across the stream (issuing from the tarn) that lead into the hamlet of Watendlath (NY 275 164).

6. Leave Watendlath by re-crossing the stone-built packhorse bridge and re-tracing your steps along the stony track beside the tarn, however, where the stony track forks after a short distance (just after the gate beyond the ford), bear right climbing quite steeply up along the stony bridleway (SP 'Rosthwaite'). Follow this climbing quite steeply up for 400 metres then levels out and leads across the moorland of Puddingstone Bank to reach a gate in a wall (NY 268 159) just before the bridleway begins its descent into Borrowdale *(views of Borrowdale ahead)*. Head through the gate and follow the stony track heading steadily downhill to reach a ford over a small stream, after which follow the broad, rocky path (wooded stream on your left) heading quite steeply down to join a wall on your right *(ignore the bridlegate in this wall after a short distance)*. Head straight down along the stony path alongside this wall on your right, over a

bridge across this stream then round to the right to quickly reach a gate set in a wall (stream down to your right). Head through the gate and follow the stony path heading down across the hillside (heading towards Rosthwaite) to join a wall on your right at a junction of paths where you turn right through a gate in this wall (SP 'Rosthwaite'). After the gate, follow the stony path winding down across the sparsely wooded hillside to reach another gate that leads onto a walled path which you follow straight on to join a metalled lane beside a bridge across Stonethwaite Beck. Turn right over the bridge to reach the main valley road where you turn left back into Rosthwaite.

WASDALE HEAD

Wasdale Head consists of a scattering of farms, tiny church and an inn, but despite its size it is renowned throughout the country amongst walkers and climbers. Wasdale has four claims to fame: the deepest lake, the highest mountain, the smallest church and the biggest liar! It is true that Wast Water is England's deepest lake reaching a depth of 79 metres, and Scafell Pike is England's highest mountain at 978m. As for the smallest church, there are several contenders; however, St Olaf's Church hidden in a copse of yews certainly has a strong claim. This low stone-built church is at least 400 years old, although may date back to the 14th Century when it was possibly established as an outpost of St Bees Priory. The interior of the church is simple with a small window with the fitting inscription 'I will lift up mine eyes unto the hills from whence cometh my strength'. In the churchyard are graves and memorials to climbers killed on the surrounding mountains. Wasdale Head Inn has been the home of British mountaineering for over a century since Will Ritson converted his farmhouse into the 'Huntsman's Inn' in the 1850s. Towards the end of the 19th Century more and more people came to Wasdale to take part in the new sport of rock climbing and to meet the larger-than-life landlord of the inn. Will Ritson was well known for his humorous stories, which were delivered with a thick Cumbrian accent. He was also the biggest liar. A competition, started in the 19th Century, is still held in Wasdale every year to find the 'world's biggest liar'; Will Ritson won the title many times. One of his most famous stories concerns an eagle with a broken wing that was nursed back to health by a foxhound. The inevitable happened and soon winged foxhounds were to be seen swooping across the Screes.

THE VILLAGE

Wasdale Head offers two campsites, B&Bs, Wasdale Head Inn, self catering accommodation, a Youth Hostel (Wasdale Hall) as well as a car park. There is also an outdoor/climbing shop that sells limited provisions.

ACCOMMODATION

Tourist Information Centre, Egremont   01946 820693

WASDALE PUB

Wasdale Head Inn   **019467 26229**
This is perhaps the most famous walkers' pub in England. After a day on the fells, there is nowhere better to recuperate than the bar of the Wasdale Head Inn with its cosy alcoves, log burning stove and impressive range of beers brewed on site by the Great Gable Brewing Co. Old photographs of mountains and climbers line the walls, which add to the sense of adventure. The inn was the birthplace of British mountaineering and rock climbing in the 1880s.

Wasdale Head

Wasdale Head Walking Weekend
- Saturday Walk -
Wasdale Head, Burnmoor Tarn, Eskdale Moor, Miterdale & Illgill Head

WALK INFORMATION

Highlights: England's deepest lake, the haunted Corpse Road, a hidden tarn that defies nature, prehistoric stone circles, unfrequented Miterdale and sheer screes that plunge 2,000-feet.

Distance: 12.25 miles (19.5 km)   Time: Allow 6 - 7 hours

Map: OS Explorer map OL6 - *always take a map on your walk.*

Refreshments: Pub and shop at Wasdale Head. No facilities en route.

Terrain: Clear paths and tracks (Corpse Road) lead up over the pass towards Eskdale to reach Burnmoor Tarn, with boggy ground and several small streams to cross. A grassy path then heads across Eskdale Moor (Open Access) to reach several stone circles before dropping quite steeply down into Miterdale. Old paths and tracks lead through this valley before heading steeply up out of the valley (Open Access) to reach the top of the ridge above Greathall Gill. A path heads along the top of the broad ridge via Whin Rigg and Illgill Head, with sheer crags and gullies just to your left (Wast Water Screes). From Illgill Head, a grassy path heads quite steeply down to re-join the Corpse Road which leads back to Wasdale Head.

Highest point: Illgill Head - 609 metres above sea level.

Total ascent:	825 metres

Escape Route:	From the ridge above Greathall Gill (south-west of Whin Rigg), follow the path steeply down along the eastern side of Greathall Gill to reach the River Irt (near where it issues from Wast Water) from where it is a short walk to join the road through Wasdale. *There is no way down to the lake via any of the gullies between Whin Rigg and Illgill Head.*

Open Access:	The section from Burnmoor Lodge to the stone circles on Eskdale Moor and from Low Place (Miterdale) to Whin Rigg heads across Open Access land **www.openaccess.gov.uk**

Caution:	This is a fell walk across open moorland and a high, broad ridge, with a number of steep ascents and descents across grassy slopes. There are sheer cliffs and gullies along the northern edge of the ridge between Whin Rigg and Illgill Head, with a 530 metre drop straight down to Wast Water. This walk also crosses a number of streams. Navigation may be difficult across Eskdale Moor; map and compass essential.

POINTS OF INTEREST

The two mountain streams that drain the northern and western slopes of the Scafell massif are named after its near neighbour, Lingmell. From its source on the north side of Scafell Pike, Lingmell Beck plunges through the dramatic Piers Gill then rushes across the valley floor before emptying into Wast Water. This is a true mountain torrent river where flash flooding is commonplace and the course of the river changes regularly. Lingmell Gill also feeds Wast Water, its crystal-clear waters tumbling down from Lingmell Col on Scafell Pike's western side before draining into the lake. German POWs from the First World War re-routed the stream directly into the lake away from its natural course into Lingmell Beck, and they also constructed a concrete bridge across the stream. These streams emerge from Wast Water as the River Irt. Wast Water is England's deepest lake, the bed of which actually lies over 17 metres below sea level. On a still summer's evening the surface of the lake is as smooth as glass, but when westerly gales sweep up the valley it can resemble a wave-tossed ocean. Wast Water is extremely pure with so little nutrients that it supports minimal life except brown trout, char, a few rare crustacean and some plants. It is the least changed of all the lakes since the last Ice Age. The most famous feature of Wast Water are The Screes that plunge over 600 metres (2,000-feet) from Illgill Head to the bottom of the lake with millions of broken rock fragments varying in size from boulders to tiny stones.

Burnmoor Tarn is one of the largest of the 450 or so tarns that lie scattered across the Lakeland fells. It lies on the vast expanse of Eskdale Moor in the shadow of Scafell. The route across the moor from Wasdale Head was used for centuries by mourners on their way to the consecrated ground at Boot before a burial ground was made available at Wasdale Head in the early 20th Century. This is the Corpse Road. Imagine the scene on a windswept day with the sad procession heading across the moor with the coffin strapped to a pony. A story is told of one pony that took fright and galloped away. It was never caught, but often reappears as a ghostly coffin-bearing apparition to lone travellers on their way over to Eskdale. A maze of streams flow into Burnmoor Tarn separated by only a few metres of soggy ground before Whillan Beck flows out. Whillan Beck does not flow south-west to swell the waters of the River Mite as one would expect but flows south to join the River Esk; a quirk of nature. Eskdale Moor is littered with stone circles and clearance cairns dating back to the Bronze Age, including Maiden Castle ring cairn that lies just off the main path on the top of the pass. To the south-west of Burnmoor Tarn on Brat's Moss are an incredible collection of stone circles with five in close proximity, including two side-by-side. No-one is sure as to why they were built, although the most plausible theory is that they were built to interpret the passage of the sun and moon across the sky during the solstices.

Miterdale is a secluded valley that lies between Whin Rigg and Eskdale Moor, with only a handful of farms dotted along its narrow floor. The River Mite rises near, but not from, Burnmoor Tarn and has a short journey before emptying into the Irish Sea. The climb out of Miterdale is long and steep up onto the broad ridge of Whin Rigg, which you join at the head of the impressive gully of Greathall Gill. It is a fairly short walk up to the summit of Whin Rigg and the start of a memorable walk along the top of The Screes. On its southern side, grassy slopes fall away into Miterdale; however, on its northern side there are sheer crags and gullies that plunge almost 2,000-ft in a near-vertical drop. This is the top of the famous Wast Water Screes, a vast crest of crags and gullies that stretch along the entire length of the ridge from Whin Rigg to Illgill Head. The views down the forbidding gullies towards Wast Water far below are breathtaking, especially Great Gully just beyond Whin Rigg. The path between Whin Rigg and Illgill Head keeps away from the edge of these crags, passing several small tarns in the saddle between the two summits. The best view is saved until Illgill Head where, a few paces to the north of its cairn, the grassy slope abruptly ends giving way to cliffs falling sheer towards Wast Water. A little further on, just beyond Illgill Head's second but slightly higher summit, a perfect view unfolds of Wasdale Head.

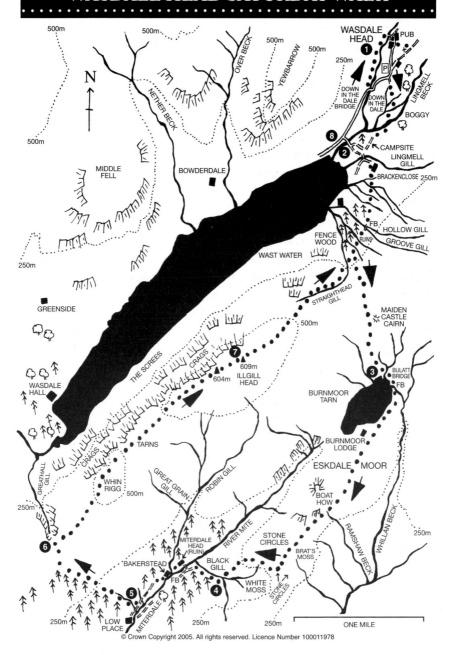

THE WALK

1. From the Wasdale Head Inn (with your back to the pub) turn left along the road then almost immediately take the path to the right (SP 'St Olaf's Church) and follow this across fields to join an enclosed track beside St Olaf's Church. Turn right along this track and follow it passing Lingmell House to emerge onto Wasdale Head Village Green (parking area), just beyond which you join the main valley road (NY 187 084). Turn left along this road and follow it for 150 metres then, where it bends right, head left off this bend through the right-hand of two gates (SP 'Eskdale/Miterdale, Campsite).* Follow the track straight on across fields (Down in the Dale) crossing a number of small streams and then through gorse bushes to reach the wide pebbly riverbed of Lingmell Beck *(usually dry, but floods after heavy rain)*. Bear slightly right across the riverbed to join a grassy path on the other bank, which you follow to the right (riverbed now on your right) for just over 100 metres then bear left away from the river and through a gate that leads into Wasdale campsite (National Trust). Follow the track straight on through the campsite then, where the track bends sharp right at the end of the campsite, head left through a kissing-gate in the fence corner (campsite boundary). After the kissing-gate turn immediately right to soon reach a stony track beside a cattle grid, with the bridge across Lingmell Gill just to your left (NY 183 074).

   * This path is liable to flooding. If impassable, follow the road for 1 km to reach the turning to the left that leads over the bridge across Lingmell Beck and follow this straight on to reach the next bridge across Lingmell Gill.

2. Turn left along this track over the bridge across Lingmell Gill. After this bridge, head left at the fork (SP 'Eskdale, Miterdale, Scafell Massif') and follow this track up alongside Lingmell Gill on your left for 100 metres then, where the track forks just before Brackenclose (Fell & Rock Climbing Club building), head to the right (SP 'Eskdale') along a path alongside the wall on your right (passing Brackenclose up to your left) to reach a gate in the wall corner. After the gate, follow the grassy/stony bridleway (Wasdale to

Eskdale 'corpse road') straight on climbing steadily up across the hillside alongside the wall on your right and crossing a number of small streams to reach Fence Wood on your right after 400 metres. Continue up along the bridleway with Fence Wood on your right, over a 'double' stone bridge across Hollow Gill and Groove Gill then, as you reach the end of Fence Wood (just after some ruinous buildings on your left), carry straight on along the bridleway (wall still on your right) for a further 150 metres then follow the path curving up to the left (away from the wall) to quickly reach a small stream. Immediately after the stream head left along a grassy path marked by cairns *(ignore path ahead that leads to Straighthead Gill)* gradually rising up for 0.75 km onto the top of the pass, with Scafell rising up to your left and Illgill Head to your right (NY 184 055). Where the path forks as you reach the top of the pass, carry straight on along the right-hand grassy path across the moor *(passing the prehistoric cairn of Maiden Castle just across to your left)* heading gradually down to reach the left-hand (north-eastern) side of Burnmoor Tarn (NY 186 048).

3. As you reach the tarn, carry straight on (tarn on your right) crossing the stream flowing into the tarn (boggy ground) and then, soon afterwards, Bulatt Bridge (FB) across the outflow stream (Whillan Beck), after which carry straight on for 100 metres then, at the fork in the path (just as you head up a slight rise of land), follow the grassy path bearing to the right skirting along the shore of the tarn (heading round towards Burnmoor Lodge). About 300 metres before you reach Burnmoor Lodge you reach a fork in the path - follow the left-hand path (wide, grassy path) straight on rising steadily up across the middle of the grassy hillside passing Burnmoor Lodge across to your right heading up onto Eskdale Moor *(small outcrop of Boat How comes into view ahead - do not head towards this)*. The path soon levels out and leads straight on across the hillside (Eskdale Moor) passing some distance to the left (south) of Boat How to reach the head of Ramshaw Beck (1 km after Burnmoor Lodge - NY 178 031). Cross this stream and carry straight on along the path, with the hillside sweeping away to your left into the valley of Whillan Beck, for 550 metres to reach a

shooting butt (small circular stone enclosure) beside the path on your right. Continue straight on along the path for another 150 metres to reach a fork in the path - head straight on (right-hand fork) to soon reach a Bronze Age stone circle (NY 173 024). As you reach this first stone circle, walk straight across the middle of it to quickly reach a second stone circle. Walk straight on across the middle of this second stone circle, just beyond which follow the grassy path curving to the right then gently dropping down into a slight dip in the grassy moorland where you cross a small stream/boggy ground (White Moss). After this stream, follow the clear grassy path bearing to the left then straight on across the moorland for 0.75 km to reach the top corner of a plantation overlooking Miterdale. As you approach the plantation, cross Black Gill (stream) and carry on to quickly reach the corner of the plantation and a wall on your right where you head through a gap in this wall and a bridlegate in a fence beyond it (NY 165 023).

4. After the bridlegate, head left and follow the path down into Miterdale alongside the plantation on your left (Black Gill across to your right) to reach a wall across your path almost at the bottom of the valley (plantation ends on your left) where you head left through a gate in the wall corner. After the bridlegate follow the path straight on for 25 metres then head down to the right and through a gap in the wall then follow the enclosed path to reach a bridge across the River Mite (NY 161 024). Cross the bridge and carry straight on to quickly reach the ruinous Miterdale Head Farm where you head straight on into the old farmyard (tumbledown walls and buildings) then bear left across the old yard, walking across the old buildings and out along an enclosed grassy track (heading down the valley). Follow this old track curving to the right after a short distance (forest on your right) then, just after you have curved right, head left through a gateway in the wall and follow the grassy path straight across two fields (River Mite across to your left) to reach Bakerstead Farm (outdoor centre). Just as you reach Bakerstead, cross the FB across the side-stream of Robin Gill (by its confluence with the River Mite) after which walk straight on passing Bakerstead on your right then bear slightly right across the middle

of the field to reach a gateway in a wall in the top right-hand corner of the field (forest on your right - NY 158 023). Head through the gateway and follow the path straight on alongside the forest on your right heading down the valley then, where the forest ends, continue along the path to soon reach a gate in a wall across your path. After this gate, carry straight on across the next field to reach another gate in a wall beside some stone-built sheep enclosures (with Low Place Farm just ahead). Head through this gate and turn immediately right *(do not follow the track to Low Place Farm)* and through a gate in the wall that leads out onto the bottom of the steep hillside of Whin Rigg (NY 155 020).

5. After this gate, head across to the left *(Open Access Land)* to join the wall on your left and follow this wall climbing steeply up the grassy hillside (out of Miterdale) with a coniferous plantation on your left. The climb is quite steep for the first 500 metres then the gradient eases as you head up across the grassy hillside (slopes of Whin Rigg) for a further 500 metres with the wall and plantation still on your left until you reach the end of the plantation on your left (NY 145 024). Where the plantation ends, follow the wall bending sharply to the right climbing up to soon reach the top of the broad grassy ridge. As you reach the top of the broad ridge, carry straight on alongside the wall on your left to soon reach a clear path running along the top of the ridge overlooking the head of Greathall Gill ravine (falling steeply away in front of you down into Wasdale) - NY 145 027.

6. Turn right along the grassy path skirting across the top of Greathall Gill then straight on rising steadily up across the left-hand side of the broad ridge for 1 km onto the low rocky outcrops of Whin Rigg (535 metres) to reach the left-hand of the 'twin peaks' on the summit, marked by a cairn/windbreak (NY 151 035). From the top of Whin Rigg, carry straight on along the path heading across the top (left-hand side) of the broad ridge *(cliffs and gullies above the Wast Water Screes just across to your left)* dropping down into the saddle of land between Whin Rigg and Illgill Head (with its small tarns) then gradually rising up onto the summit of Illgill Head

(2 km from Whin Rigg). Just before you reach the top of Illgill Head, the broad ridge levels out as the path passes more gullies to your left before gently rising up to reach the summit of Illgill Head (604 metres), marked by a cairn (NY 165 048). From Illgill Head, carry straight on across the top of the broad ridge for a further 450 metres onto the top of the next slight 'rise' of land (Illgill Head's 'second summit') marked by a windbreak shelter (609 metres).

7. From this windbreak on Illgill Head's 'second summit', carry straight on across the top of the broad ridge *(north-easterly direction)* for a further 350 metres to reach a small cairn that marks the end of the high-level ridge, with views of Wasdale Head ahead (NY 172 052). From this cairn, head straight on along the grassy path (cairns) bearing very slightly left down across the left-hand side of the broad hillside *(north-easterly direction)* heading towards Wasdale Head in the distance. After 750 metres you join a wall on your left beside the head of Straighthead Gill (small grassy gully). Cross over this wall and follow the grassy path quite steeply down alongside this wall on your right then, as you approach the bottom of the hillside/saddle of land, follow the path curving to the left (following the wall curving left) and drop down over this wall and across Straighthead Gill just beyond (NY 181 061). After the stream, head straight on to quickly re-join the Wasdale to Eskdale bridleway ('corpse road') which you walked up earlier. Re-trace your steps back down along this bridleway all the way to reach Brackenclose where you follow the track bending to the left down to reach the bridge across Lingmell Gill. Cross this bridge and follow the track passing the campsite on your right, over the bridge across Lingmell Beck to join the main valley road.

8. Turn right along the road and follow this for 0.75 km then, where the road bends right towards Down in the Dale Bridge (across Mosedale Beck) head straight on off this bend and through a kissing-gate (SP 'Wasdale Head'). Follow the path straight on across fields keeping close to Mosedale Beck on your right for 750 metres to reach the old packhorse bridge (across Mosedale Beck) at Wasdale Head. Cross this packhorse bridge and turn right back to the Wasdale Head Inn.

Wasdale Head Walking Weekend
- Sunday Walk -
Wasdale Head, Sty Head, Great Gable, Beck Head & Moses' Trod

WALK INFORMATION

Highlights: England's smallest church, a famous mountain pass, the birthplace of rock climbing, Lakeland's finest view, illegal whisky stills and following in the footsteps of Moses.

Distance: 5.5 miles (8.5 km)   Time: Allow 4 - 5 hours

Map: OS Explorer map OL6 - *always take a map on your walk.*

Refreshments: Pub and shop at Wasdale Head. Teas available at Burnthwaite Farm (seasonal). No other facilities en route.

Terrain: Rocky mountain paths virtually all the way, with steep ground and rough terrain in places. The path from Sty Head Pass to the summit of Great Gable (Breast Route) is long and steep (pitched-stone path most of the way). The summit can be confusing in mist due to numerous cairns and indistinct paths radiating in all directions across the rocky summit plateau. The descent to Beck Head is very steep in places, with boulders and scree. From Beck Head, a narrow path (Moses' Trod) heads down across a steep slope above Gable Beck ('airy' in places) back to Wasdale Head.

Highest point: Great Gable - 899 metres above sea level.

Total ascent: 810 metres

Escape Route: From the summit, re-trace your steps back down the pitched-stone path to Sty Head (Breast Route) and then down to Wasdale Head.

Warning: **Mountain Walk.** This is a strenuous walk to the summit of Great Gable with steep, mountainous terrain for most of the way. The descent from Great Gable to Beck Head is rocky and steep, whilst there are steep drops to the side of Moses' Trod. Navigation to the summit of Great Gable is straight-forward along clear paths, however, the summit can be confusing with numerous cairns; there are sheer crags on its northern and southern faces. Do not attempt this walk in bad weather. Map and compass essential.

POINTS OF INTEREST

The land that surrounds the hamlet of Wasdale Head is almost perfectly flat due to the scouring action of glaciers thousands of years ago. This alluvial plain is criss-crossed by drystone walls seemingly built at random, dividing the land into dozens of fields. Often several feet thick, these irregular walls also served as stone dumps when the pastures were cleared and may date back to medieval times. They are quite different from the straight walls of the Enclosure Acts of 1801. Wasdale Head lies at the end of the road, for only old packhorse routes head across the mountain passes to Ennerdale, Borrowdale, Great Langdale and Eskdale. The hamlet once provided shelter for packmen and drovers who came this way along the old routes across the fells. Until the beginning of the 19th Century slate from the Honister Quarries or graphite from Borrowdale passed through Wasdale Head en route to the port at Ravenglass. Our walk follows the old Wasdale Head to Borrowdale packhorse route via Sty Head Pass, an important crossroads of paths set in a huge 'basin' between Great Gable, Great End and Lingmell with Styhead Tarn cradled beneath Seathwaite Fell. This is the most famous mountain pass in Lakeland and a springboard to the peaks.

From Sty Head, a pitched-stone path climbs steeply up the south-eastern shoulder of Great Gable (the Breast Route) to its summit. Great Gable is perhaps Lakeland's most famous peak, which holds a special place in the hearts of fell-walkers and climbers. Although just short of the magical 3,000-feet mark, it is still a mighty mountain in terms of stature and appearance and it dominates the Lakeland skyline. When viewed from the south-west at Wasdale Head, it has a perfect profile, almost pyramidal, hence the name Great Gable. Its Norse name was Mykelgavel, which also translates as Great Gable! However, when viewed from the rest of Lakeland its distinctive summit appears as a mountainous dome rather than the classic pyramidal shape. On its steep slopes are sheer crags, scree slopes and challenging rock climbs, particularly on its southern flanks where there are numerous named climbs amongst the crags, pinnacles and gullies that make up the Great Napes and White Napes outcrops. These crags are separated by Little

Hell Gate and Great Hell Gate which are fearsome scree runs. A climbers' path known as the Traverse skirts precariously around these upper slopes allowing access to these famous rock climbs, thus providing a complete circuit of the mountain. Its summit is a domed plateau of broken rocks, with unrivalled views towards the Langdale Pikes, Scafell massif, Kirk Fell, Ennerdale and the High Stile range. Walk a short distance from the summit in a south-westerly direction (towards Wast Water) and you reach Westmorland Cairn set on the edge of a steep drop above Westmorland Crags with Wasdale sweeping away into the distance. The cairn was built in the 1876 by Thomas and Edward Westmorland to mark what they believed to be the finest view in the Lake District. The summit crags are also a war memorial to the men of the Fell and Rock Climbing Club (FRCC) who gave their lives during the First World War. The FRCC purchased 3,000 acres of high fells and mountains centred on Great Gable in memory of their fallen friends and gave it to the National Trust in 1923 *"for the use and enjoyment of the people of our land for all time"*. A brass memorial plaque was dedicated in the same year and a remembrance service is still held every November. The FRCC was founded in 1906, and their first president was the famous mountaineer and photographer Ashley Abraham.

From the summit, our route follows the north-western ridge down to Beck Head, with wonderful views of Ennerdale spread out far below. This ridge offers the best route down to Beck Head with the surest footing, as Great Gable's western slope is otherwise a steep scree run. There are a couple of tricky sections where large boulders need to be negotiated; however, the surrounding mountain scenery more than compensates for the demanding descent. The path leads down into the col between Great Gable and Kirk Fell known as Beck Head, with its two small tarns. This pass was once a busy route for packhorses taking slate from Honister to the coast, and was also a smugglers' route as the mountains provided perfect cover. This old route is known as Moses' Trod, named after a Honister quarryman who supplemented his income by smuggling and making illicit whisky in stills hidden amongst Great Gable's crags. This path traverses the steep south-western slope of Great Gable high above Gable Beck, which cuts a dramatic cleft between Great Gable and Kirk Fell.

WASDALE HEAD SUNDAY WALK

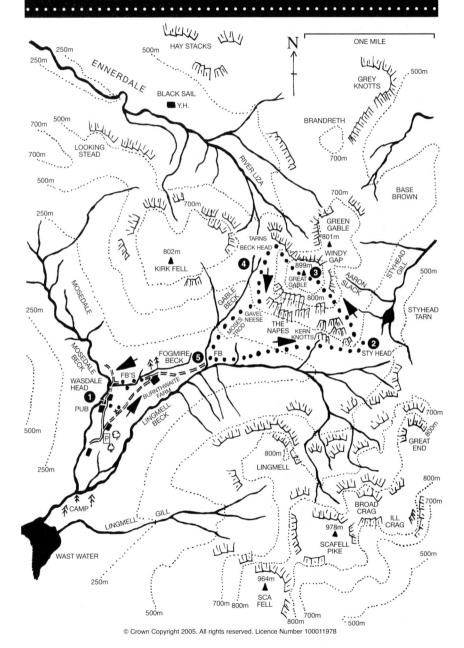

N

ONE MILE

HAY STACKS

250m
500m

250m

ENNERDALE

BLACK SAIL

■ Y.H.

GREY KNOTTS

500m

BRANDRETH

700m
500m

700m

LOOKING STEAD

700m

700m

RIVER LIZA

500m

700m

BASE BROWN

250m

802m

KIRK FELL

TARNS

BECK HEAD

GREEN GABLE
801m ▲

WINDY GAP

899m **3**

GREAT GABLE

4

MOSEDALE

GABLE BECK

800m

AARON SLACK

STYHEAD GILL

500m

STYHEAD TARN

250m

GAVEL NEESE

MOSES TROD

THE NAPES

KERN KNOTTS

2

STY HEAD

MOSEDALE BECK

FOGMIRE BECK **5**

FB

FB'S

WASDALE HEAD

1

PUB

BURNTHWAITE FARM

LINGMELL BECK

P

500m

250m

⋔ CAMP

LINGMELL GILL

LINGMELL

800m

700m

800m

GREAT END

800m

BROAD CRAG

ILL CRAG

700m

WAST WATER

978m ▲

SCAFELL PIKE

500m

250m

964m ▲

SCA FELL

700m 800m

700m

800m

500m

241

1. From the Wasdale Head Inn (with your back to the pub) turn left along the road then almost immediately take the path to the right (SP 'St Olaf's Church) and follow this across fields to join an enclosed track beside St Olaf's Church. Turn left along this track and follow it to reach Burnthwaite Farm (NY 193 091). As you enter the farmyard (with two barns in front of you) bear left passing between the two barns (sign on wall 'path') and then bear left through a gate just behind the farmhouse (and garden). After the gate, head right along the track passing behind the farmhouse and follow this wide stony track (Moses' Trod) straight on gently rising up into the dramatic valley of Lingmell Beck *(Great Gable rising steeply up ahead of you to the left)* for 0.75 km to reach a FB across Gable Beck just above its confluence with Lingmell Beck (NY 199 093). After the FB, carry straight on *(ignore path to left immediately after FB - this is Moses' Trod, our return route down from Great Gable)* along the stony path with Lingmell Beck on your right then, at the fork in the path after 400 metres, bear left and follow the path rising steadily up across the hillside to reach a gate in a wall across your path. Head through the gate and continue along the path rising more steeply up across the mountainside, with the valley of Lingmell Beck sweeping away to your right and the steep slopes of Great Gable rising up to your left. After 600 metres the path crosses a number of small streams beyond which you clamber up some low outcrops, above which the path levels out for a short distance before rising up again (upper reaches of Lingmell Beck down to your right) passing below the outcrops of Kern Knotts to reach the top of the pass *(steep ground on your left ends)* where you follow the path curving round to the left to soon reach the crossroads of paths at Sty Head beside the Mountain Rescue stretcher box (NY 219 095).

2. Turn left at this crossroads of paths (immediately after the stretcher box) to quickly pick up the start of a pitched stone path. Follow this

stone staircase (Breast Route) climbing steeply up for 1.25 km (with a height gain of 420 metres) onto the summit of Great Gable - the path is stone-pitched for most of the way, however, as you approach the summit the path becomes marked by cairns as it heads across rocks and boulders up to reach the summit of Great Gable (NY 211 103). *The actual summit is a small rocky outcrop on the domed summit plateau, with the Memorial plaque set on the north side of the summit outcrop - this plaque faces north.*

Caution: the route from the summit down to Beck Head and then along Moses' Trod is steep in places as well as rough and rocky underfoot with steep drops to the side of the path in places. Good navigation is required to locate this path from the summit in poor weather. If in doubt, re-trace your steps back down the Breast Route (pitched-stone path) to Sty Head and then back down to Wasdale Head.

3. As you reach the outcrops on the summit, carry straight on passing to the left side of the outcrops then head in a north-westerly direction towards the upper reaches of Ennerdale (with Crummock Water in the distance), following a line of fairly large cairns across the rocky summit plateau *(there are two paths leading north-west from the summit down to Beck Head - you want the right-hand of the two paths marked by larger cairns that leads down the rocky apex (north-west ridge) of the northern and western slopes).* The cairned path soon leads to the start of the steep descent down to the col of Beck Head (with its two small tarns). Initially, the path is very steep and heads down across boulders and rocks with some easy scrambling. This section is soon over and the path winds steeply down the north-western ridge of Great Gable (with Gable Crag just round to your right) heading down towards the col of Beck Head in between Great Gable and Kirk Fell *(ignore path that heads down to the right into the head of Ennerdale).* Just as you reach Beck Head (with the two small tarns just ahead - NY 208 107), follow the clear path down to the left *(south-westerly direction),* heading towards Wast Water in the distance, to reach the flat bottom of the col (with the two tarns now across to your right and the steep slopes of Kirk Fell rising up beyond). As you reach the flat ground of Beck Head, carry straight

on across the col towards Wast Water in the distance heading across boggy ground and springs (source of Gable Beck) to soon reach the southern edge of the col, with the steep valley of Gable Beck falling away in front of you down into Wasdale *(Wasdale Head comes into view)* - NY 207 105.

4. As you reach the southern edge of the col, you pick up a clear narrow path (Moses' Trod) on the left-hand side of the steep valley of Gable Beck (with the stream on your right). Follow this narrow path straight on heading steadily down across the steep mountainside *(take care)*, with the valley of Gable Beck falling steeply away to your right and the scree slopes of Great Gable rising up to your left. After 700 metres you reach the end of the scree slopes to your left and come to the top of the steep grassy ridge of Gavel Neese *(apex of southern and western slopes of Great Gable)* and the start of a pitched-stone path. Follow this pitched-stone path steeply down this grassy ridge - the path becomes grassy underfoot after a while and leads steeply down to eventually join a wall. Follow this wall down for a short distance to quickly reach a bridlegate to the left through this wall (where the wall ends and a fence begins) - NY 200 095. Head through this bridlegate and follow the path down to reach the FB across Gable Beck (near its confluence with Lingmell Beck) you crossed earlier.

5. Cross the FB and re-trace your steps back along the stony track to reach Burnthwaite Farm. As you reach the farm (buildings to your left) carry straight on along the track and through a gate in a wall across your path (just after the farm). After the gate, follow the enclosed track to soon reach a FB across Fogmire Beck (NY 192 091). Immediately after this FB turn left alongside the stream *(ignore gate ahead)* and follow this streamside path (enclosed by walls on either side) to reach a bridlegate in the wall corner across your path at the end of this narrow field. Head through this bridlegate and carry straight on along the streamside path, crossing and re-crossing the stream four times, to join a wide stony track alongside Mosedale Beck. Head left along this track, with Mosedale Beck on your right, back to the Wasdale Head Inn.

Top: Cat Bells

Middle: High Pike, Ambleside

Bottom: Hardknott Roman Fort

© Mark Reid

Top:
Brothers Water

Middle:
Dock Tarn Borrowdale

Bottom:
Mickleden

© Mark Reid

Top: *Wasdale Head*

Middle: *Old Dungeon Ghyll*

Bottom: *Crummock Water*

© *Mark Reid*

Top: Ullswater

Middle: The Band, Great Langdale

Bottom: Wasdale Head Inn

© Mark Reid